# GOLF in SCOTLAND & IRELAND

By the Editors of Golf World Magazine

Published in association with Golf World Magazine
A publication of The New York Times Magazine Group

SACKVILLE BOOKS

First published in 1987
by Sackville Books Ltd
Sackville House
78 Margaret Street, London W1N 7HB

© Sackville Design Group Ltd 1987

Designed and produced by Sackville Design Group Ltd
Typeset by Bookworm Typesetting Ltd, Manchester

Art director: Al Rockall
Editor: Heather Thomas

**British Library Cataloguing in Publication Data**

Guide to golf in Scotland and Ireland.
   1. Golf courses — Scotland 2. Golf
   courses — Ireland
   I. Golf world
   796.352′06′8411     GV984

ISBN 0-948615-15-X

Printed and bound in Italy by Sagdos s.p.a.

# Contents

*There are over 400 golf courses in Scotland making it probably the finest golfing venue in the world. Nowhere else can a player, whatever his ability, find so many courses with such a range of different challenges in settings that are as spectacular as they are beautiful. Many are fine links courses, created by nature on strips of sandy coastal land which were beneath the sea centuries ago. Today, this terrain is covered by fine, closely-knit turf, and the land's natural contours have been fashioned by some of the world's most famous, leading golf course architects into tees, fairways, greens and bunkers.*

*Scotland is the traditional home of golf and it offers the visiting golfer a unique atmosphere, whether you play on the matchless collection of coastal links, the great inland courses like Gleneagles and Blairgowrie, or on the beautiful offshore islands.*

*Everyone has heard and read about such great Championship courses as St Andrews, Muirfield, Turnberry, and Royal Troon but you might not be aware of*

*hundreds of less familiar names where you can enjoy a wonderful
test of golf, like Cruden Bay, Nairn and Royal Dornoch.
If you live in Scotland or are contemplating a golfing holiday in the land
of the heather and thistle, this Scottish section will prove invaluable as a reference
book, being the most comprehensive survey of Scottish golf courses ever
produced. If your preference is for links courses, then aim for those by the sea in
Ayrshire, Angus, Fife and East Lothian, and along the north-east coast from Aberdeen
to Dornoch. In the other coastal regions, with a few exceptions, most of the courses
are not links. However, if you venture inland into the
Highlands and the mountainous interior of northern
and central Scotland, you will discover magnificent
scenery, historic castles and fine courses resplendent
with bright yellow gorse and purple heather.*

*The lighthouse at Turnberry*

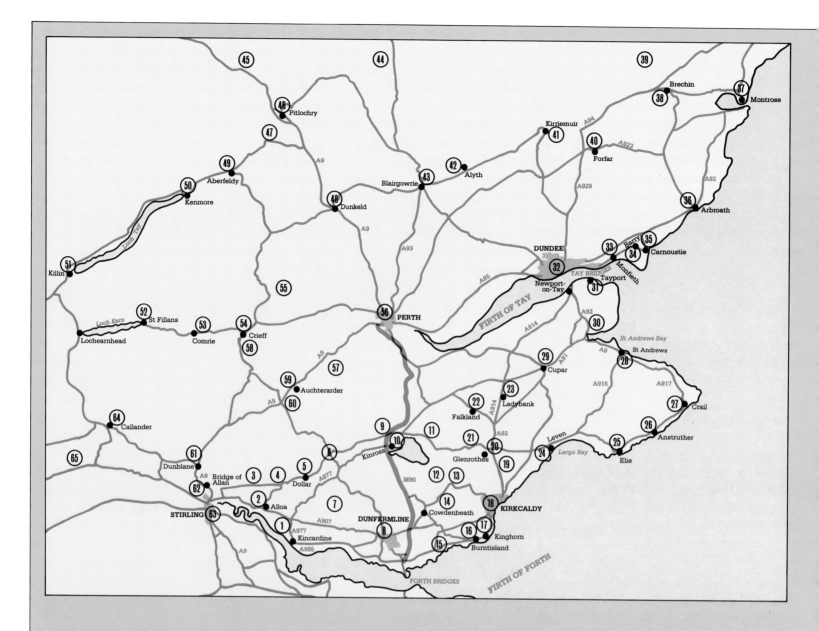

# Fife, Tayside and Perthshire

The entire area of Fife, Tayside and Perthshire is not very large (only about 70-80 miles from east to west, and 60-65 miles from north to south) yet some of the world's most famous golfing names lie in this corner of Scotland. St Andrews, Carnoustie and Gleneagles are but three of the big names among the many challenging courses awaiting your pleasure and a wider recognition. Wherever you are based, you can usually go and play a round on almost any course and return to your hotel on the same day.

It is easy to get around and visit new courses if you have a car. If you are on holiday, why not hire one? It will give you the freedom to discover the region at your own pace and discover less familiar courses as well as the historic celebrated championship courses which are every golfer's dream. Why not start your journey at the traditional home of golf – St Andrews.

**St Andrews,** the home of golf itself, is a magnet for golf addicts from all over the world who flock there to play on the Old Course. This course has played host in its time to many of golf's most memorable moments and you feel that you are surrounded by history and the ghosts of the past. In fact, it appears that a form of the game might have been played there as early as the mid-fifteenth century. The Royal and Ancient Golf Club itself evolved from the St Andrews Society of Golfers which was established in 1754.

St Andrews is easily reached by road via the M90 and A91 roads if you are travelling from the south. It is a relatively short journey from Edinburgh (about 60 miles), and can also be reached via the railway station at Leuchars from which it is only a short cab ride.

It is renowned as one of the world's greatest links courses, ranking alongside Birkdale and Ballybunion. With a reputation like this, it is not surprising that it is extremely busy during the summer months, especially with visiting golfers,

*St Andrews Clubhouse is probably the most famous in the world. It is the baronial home of the Royal and Ancient Golf Club*

so make sure that you book with the starter well in advance to avoid disappointment. Do not leave your booking to the last minute – allow three months or more if possible if your heart is set on playing there. You should be aware that there is no golf on Sundays on the Old Course (with the exception of the Open itself) and you will need a letter of introduction or a handicap certificate. The green fees on the Old Course are higher than those on the New, Eden and Jubilee Courses, and you must expect to pay more in summer than during the quieter winter months.

The course consists of huge double greens positioned along a relatively narrow course beside the sea. Most golfers cannot wait to play the most famous holes in golf – including the dramatically-named Elysian Fields, Hell's Bunker and the Valley of Sin at the 18th.

However, if you are spending a few days in the 'Auld Grey Toon', you may also wish to try one of its other fine courses. The Eden Course, designed by Harry S. Colt in 1913, has a layout that pays homage to its more illustrious neighbour. It has a double green, holes that cross over each other and a threatening, deep bunker at the 17th green that reminds you of another one not too far away!

As on the Old Course, it is the greens that add so much to its overall character, being large and weirdly sloping, fantastic creations, particularly on the par-3's. Unlike the other St Andrews courses, it is not basically an out-and-in course so you get a well-deserved break from the normal long battle with the wind to which you must accustom yourself when playing on the Old Course.

The New Course is older, being laid out by Tom Morris in 1894 on the undulating land to the east of the Old. The New has less of the subtleties of the Old and therefore is inevitably less exciting to play, but at over 6500 yards it is no pushover and should not be under-estimated. The best holes are out

at the turn, meandering through some of St Andrews' largest dunes.

Next to the New lies the Jubilee Course opened in 1897 to celebrate Queen Victoria's Diamond Jubilee. Over the years, it has changed gradually and almost imperceptibly, and has settled now as a par-69 of nearly 6300 yards. Again, like the New, the best holes are out at the far end among the dunes, from where you get an excellent view of all the courses spreading away towards the town. Unfortunately, in the height of summer on hot days, the Jubilee sometimes gets an overspill of beachcombers from the West Sands, either picnicking in the dunes or even building sandcastles assiduously in the bunkers!

## How to play the course

As befits any original work of such outstanding merit, the Old Course at St Andrews has been imitated in some respects but remains unique in many others. There would probably not be a golf course architect in the world today who would dare to present his client with a course featuring only two par-3's and two par-5's, although the pattern of the huge, rolling double greens of the Old Course has often been reproduced elsewhere. At St Andrews, those vast greens are there because nature dictated that was the only way a golf course could be laid out upon the land available. The 1st, 9th, 17th and 18th have regular single greens but the remainder are an echo of bygone days when golfers played a 22-hole round, journeying out towards the Eden estuary from the Royal & Ancient Clubhouse and returning using the same fairways and greens.

The wind has been a major influence on the game at St Andrews ever since 1552, the earliest date from which it is recorded that golf was played there. The R&A Golf Club was founded in 1754, and its officers later introduced 18 holes as the standard for a round of golf.

**Hole 1: 370 yards, par-4 (Burn)**
The tee for any major occasion at St Andrews is right in front of the main windows of the R&A Clubhouse. The widest fairway in the world beckons the drive, with no rough and no bunkers. The out-of-bounds over the white rails to the right is not usually a factor for the pros. The second shot is rather more demanding, for the green is set immediately beyond the Swilken Burn, which means that the golfer must ensure he has enough club to carry it. In 1970

Doug Sanders dumped his second shot of the Championship into the water and took six. The pin is usually set on the left side of the green.

**Hole 2: 411 yards, par-4 (Dyke)**
A classic St Andrews hole. A tee shot down the left side of the fairway, which itself has been narrowed with the rough being allowed to grow in, threatens little danger but leaves an impossible shot over the bunker directly to the pin. The only way in to the shelf on the left on

which the hole is invariably cut is with an approach from the right side of the fairway, and that means the drive must risk the perils of bunkers and gorse. Merely hitting the green with the second shot can quite easily involve a putt of more than 100 feet over the humps and hollows of St Andrews' double greens.

**Hole 3: 371 yards, par-4 (Cartgate-out)**
Again, the second shot is much easier from the right side of the fairway but

*This view of the Old Course at St Andrews is taken looking towards the 1st tee by the clubhouse on the left, and the 18th green with its infamous Valley of Sin on the right*

that requires a more daring tee shot. From the left, the Cartgate Bunker awaits the less-than-perfect iron towards the flag in the Championship position, but from the other side of the fairway the player is offered a clear line in so he can pitch comfortably to the hole or run the ball up.

## Hole 4: 463 yards, par-4 (Ginger Beer)

This is reckoned by many to be the hardest hole on the course. Few players risk driving into the gulley on the right side of the fairway. Instead the most sensible idea is to go left, away from the flag, and rather aim to find the plateau from which the approach shot can at least be played from a decent stance, although it is far from easy. The hole will probably be cut in the gulley on the left side of the green.

## Hole 5: 564 yards, par-5 (Hole o'Cross-out)

As at the previous hole, a drive towards the distant pin courts danger on the right, so most professionals probably aim to the left off the tee. Depending on the wind, the decision as to whether to go for the carry over the two bunkers some 60 yards from the green can be a tricky one. In the 1933 Open, the American Craig Wood drove into them with a strong tail-wind and rock hard ground. He eventually lost the title in a play-off to compatriot Denny Shute. The green, shared with the 13th, is the largest on the course. It takes a man three hours with a hand mower to cut it!

## Hole 6: 416 yards, par-4 (Heathery-out)

Once more the tee shot should be aimed away from the green to the left in order to be safe. A ridge in front of the green tends to deceive the player into imagining that the shot is shorter than it actually is, a state of confusion increased when the wind is especially strong.

## Hole 7: 372 yards, par-4 (High-out)

The 7th heralds the start of the Loop, a stretch of six holes averaging less than 300 yards each. It is often the scene of some spectacularly low scoring but to begin on the right note the drive should be played almost blind in the direction of the 12th tee. The hole doglegs to the right and so this angle of attack gives a fuller approach shot down the length of the green. A tee shot straight towards

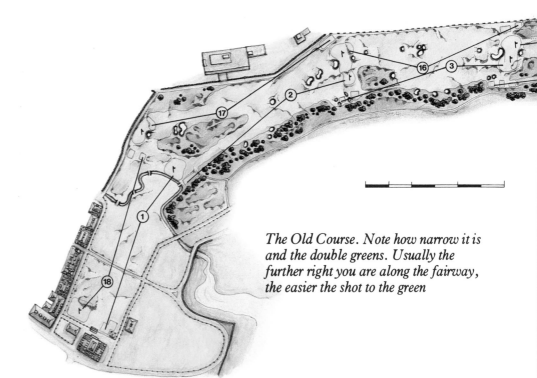

*The Old Course. Note how narrow it is and the double greens. Usually the further right you are along the fairway, the easier the shot to the green*

the green will leave a shorter shot but one that is practically impossible to get close.

## Hole 8: 178 yards, par-3 (Short)

If the wind is hard behind the golfer off the Eden estuary, to carry the bunker guarding the front of the green and then stay on is no easy matter.

## Hole 9: 356 yards, par-4 (End)

This is the easiest hole on the course on which to make a par. The only danger is if the drive, with a following wind, should finish in one of the bunkers some 70 yards before the green. Tony Jacklin made a two here in 1970 and reached the turn in 29 in that infamously aborted first round while defending his title. The flag position is generally left-centre of the green.

## Hole 10: 342 yards, par-4 (Bobby Jones)

There are no bunkers round this green but one on the right side of the fairway can catch a pushed tee shot. The flag will probably be on the left-front por-

tion of the green, on a little plateau. An inaccurate pitch or chip-and-run will cause the ball to fall away to the right. This was the last hole to be named, and fittingly St Andrews' favourite foreign son was the man to be honoured.

## Hole 11: 172 yards, par-3 (High-in)

Strath Bunker is the dominant factor here. It seems to eat into the very heart of the green, and if the wind is behind (i.e. in the opposite direction to the 8th) there seems to be almost no way to carry Strath and stop the ball short of the sands of the estuary behind the green. The venomous Hill Bunker awaits a pulled tee shot. The 11th at St Andrews is one of the greatest short holes in the world, often copied, albeit rarely successfully. This is the hole where Bobby Jones picked up in disgust in the 1921 Open having taken five shots and still not found the sanctuary of the cup. He vowed thenceforth to become a model·of sportsmanship, a promise to himself which he kept unfailingly.

## Card of the Course

| | | |
|---|---|---|
| **1** Burn | 370 yards | par 4 |
| **2** Dyke | 411 yards | par 4 |
| **3** Cartgate (out) | 371 yards | par 4 |
| **4** Ginger Beer | 463 yards | par 4 |
| **5** Hole o'Cross (out) | 564 yards | par 5 |
| **6** Heathery (out) | 416 yards | par 4 |
| **7** High (out) | 372 yards | par 4 |
| **8** Short | 178 yards | par 3 |
| **9** End | 356 yards | par 4 |
| Out 3501 yards par 36 | | |
| | | |
| **10** Bobby Jones | 342 yards | par 4 |
| **11** High (in) | 172 yards | par 3 |
| **12** Heathery (in) | 316 yards | par 4 |
| **13** Hole o'Cross (in) | 425 yards | par 4 |
| **14** Long | 567 yards | par 5 |
| **15** Cartgate (in) | 413 yards | par 4 |
| **16** Corner of the Dyke | 382 yards | par 4 |
| **17** Road | 461 yards | par 4 |
| **18** Tom Morris | 354 yards | par 4 |
| In 3432 yards par 36 | | |
| | | |
| Total 6933 yards par 72 | | |

## Hole 12: 316 yards, par-4 (Heathery-in)

A simple looking hole but its generous fairway is infested with evil bunkers, many facing the 'wrong way' from the times when the course was occasionally played the other way round, or left-handed. The last bunker on the course to be christened is on the 12th, just off the tee to the left. Named 'Admiral's Bunker', it rarely bothers the top professionals but it once caused an old seaman's pride to take a tumble. The story goes that he was so smitten by a striking young lady who had appeared on the course that he repeatedly turned round to stare at her and, having uttered some less than gentlemanly remark

about her sexuality, he fell into the sand because he was not looking where he was going. Up ahead on the green, with the flag at the front, the way in is via a run-up from the right or with a testing pitch over a bunker from the left.

## Hole 13: 425 yards, par-4 (Hole o'Cross-in)

The green here is on a plateau which starts some 100 yards out from the huge putting surface. The drive should be to the left by the 6th fairway, to give a clear line in and so that the player can see the flagstick. From the right, most of the pin is obscured.

## Hole 14: 567 yards, par-5 (Long)

This is a long par-5 which demands perfection with every shot. The drive requires a long carry if played into the wind. The fairway is known as the Elysian Fields, and to the left of this haven are the fearsome Beardies pot-bunkers, from which the only way out might be to play back towards the tee. To the right over the stone wall lies the Eden Course, which is out-of-bounds.

Even with a helping wind, the second shot over the cavernous Hell Bunker must be well struck, and failure to reach the green will mean a delicate chip to the pin on the right to make a four. The safe line with the second, to the left of Hell, leaves a more straightforward if longer pitch in search of a birdie.

## Hole 15: 413 yards, par-4 (Cartgate-in)

A relatively ordinary par-4 so long as the ubiquitous fairway bunkers are avoided. It was here that Simon Owen chipped in for a three in 1978 to take the lead over Jack Nicklaus in the final round of the Open. His advantage lasted for just one hole.

## Hole 16: 382 yards, par-4 (Corner of the Dyke)

This is yet another classic hole. The Principal's Nose bunker dominates the centre of the fairway. The safe line is to the left of it but that will leave a harder approach over Wig Bunker. However, to open up the green down the right requires finding the gap between the cluster of the Principal's Nose and the old railway line, which is now out-of-bounds.

### Hole 17: 461 yards, par-4 (Road)

This is arguably the most renowned hole in golf. The drive needs to be struck over the railway sheds (which have recently been re-introduced); the boundary wall of the Old Course Hotel signifies out-of-bounds in the hotel grounds to the right. The only way to get close to the hole with the second shot is to fire the drive down the right side of the fairway, the braver line, and draw an iron in along the green. From the left, the iron shot has to be played away from the bunker, and three putts then become very likely. Many golfers deliberately leave their second shots short of the green rather than flirt with the road, and then rely on a chip and a putt, but even then safety is not assured. Doug Sanders putted into the bunker with his third shot in the second round in 1970 and took six. He therefore played the first 36 holes of the Open with no bogeys but two doubles. In the last round, he played the most marvellous trap shot from the Road Bunker stiff to the pin and saved his par. Had he not three-putted the 18th 10 minutes later and fallen back into a tie with Jack Nicklaus, that would have been remembered as the stroke that won the Open. Fear of hitting from the sand onto the road was obviously in the mind of the Japanese player Tsuneyuki Nakajima, when he left his ball in the Road Bunker four times when well placed in the 1978 Open. However, he eventually holed out for a nine.

### Hole 18: 354 yards, par-4 (Tom Morris)

As open as the 1st – just do not hit a slice into the old town! The competitors at the Open will usually drive over Granny Clark's Wynd, the public road that cuts across the fairway. If they finish on it, there is no free drop – the approach has to be played from there. The most famous aspect of the 18th is the Valley of Sin, a deep swale which forms the front left side of the green and just beyond which the flag will doubtless be fluttering in the breeze. The pitch over the Valley must be perfectly judged – too short and it will roll back to the bottom of the green, too strong and three putts are likely from the back. That was the fate that befell the luckless Sanders in 1970. Purists feel that he should have run the ball up through the Valley, as he did in the play-off to earn a birdie. But by then it was too late: Nicklaus already had his three, having launched a massive drive over the back of the green. Even at perhaps the most innocuous finishing hole in championship golf, nothing can be taken for granted.

**Crail** Golfing Society, which plays over the Balcomie Links, is the seventh oldest in the world, dating from 1786. It is situated some 12 miles from St Andrews on the most easterly tip of Fife, and the course is essentially a vast, treeless meadow sloping down to the beach with a splendid view across the Firth of Forth to the Bass Rock and distant North Berwick. There are magnificent views across to the haunted Balcomie Castle and it is well worth a visit if you are staying in the area.

The greenstaff should be congratulated at Balcomie for always keeping the

*The infamous Hell Bunker at St Andrews' 14th hole is a trap for the unwary. You will need to strike an accurate second shot*

course and greens in wonderful condition. Although small, the greens are sloping and very fast. At 5720 yards with a par-69, it is a shortish layout but it is exposed to the elements and a prisoner of the wind which can make many of the card yardages virtually meaningless.

In the early days, golf at Crail was played on the Sauchope links nearer to the town, but moved on to the Balcomie site in 1859 when Richard Todd, a local farmer, laid out eight holes and maintained them for his golfing friends. After a period of decline, Tom Morris designed nine holes in 1894 and these were opened for play the following year. A great bazaar was organized in 1899 and the proceeds were donated to building a further nine holes. The links was bought from the town council by the Society as recently as 1973 and they proceeded to modernize the clubhouse. A practice ground has been built and a borehole sunk to supplement the water supply.

Among the Society's many annual tournaments there is one that stands out as being unique in golf in so far as it requires the finalists to play three rounds of foursomes golf in one day – the Ranken-Todd Bowl. After your game during which you will tackle holes with such strange and bizarre names as 'Hell's Hole' and 'Lang Wang', you can relax in the clubhouse which stands high over the course with views out across the North Sea. Enjoy the friendly atmosphere as well as the spectacular scenery. There is excellent, inexpensive food on offer, and visitors are welcome at any time other than competition Saturdays. It is still advisable to make an advance booking. Although it may not be the best golf course in the world, it is certainly one of the most hospitable and should not be missed on any golfing tour of Fife. Green fees are reasonable, and if you are thinking of staying a few days you might consider buying a special short Temporary Membership deal which is very economical. Telephone or write to the Secretary for further details (see the addresses section at the back of the book).

**Elie** lies only 10 miles west of Balcomie along the bank of the Firth of Forth. At 6241 yards, the links are splendid and maintained in top condition. There are no par-5's on the course and only two

*The 6th hole (in the foreground) and the 4th at the well-maintained Balcomie Golf Course at Crail with its treeless links*

par-3's, but generally all the other holes have their own charm and character. The land is open and windswept, almost devoid of bushes and trees and completely natural. Not one of the green sites was actually built; instead the fine terrain was utilized sensibly to great effect.

The fairway on the 5th hole is particularly memorable owing to its severe 'bumps' which were once coal workings. Drive into them and from the inevitable tricky stance you have an exceedingly awkward pitch to an out-of-sight sunken green. At the next, when you reach the rise of the fairway you are confronted by the full magnificent sweep of the West Bay right round to Kincraig Point. The peculiar-looking rock formation there is called 'Daniel preaching to the lion'.

The short par-4 7th hole is called 'Peggy's' and is named after an old lady who used to live nearby and bleached her clothes in the sun by spreading them out on the green, much to the consternation of the Golf House Commit-

tee. The 11th is a fine short hole beside the rocks, whereas the 466 yards 12th is a good dogleg left around some 'bents' or ridges beside the beach.

Next comes the 13th which is not over-long at 380 yards but looks further. The drive should be to the right to avoid a grassy hollow but the essence of the hole is the approach itself. The elevated green is set at an angle to the fairway and is very long and narrow. Anything short is dead but you can be too bold and bounce back from a hill. James Braid who learned the game at Elie and caddied there too, once described it as "the finest hole in all the country" during one passionate golfing discussion.

These are but a few of the holes at Elie of which every one has a name and a story. Like many other Scottish

*This view shows the 13th hole at historic Elie. This is not a long hole at 380 yards but you need a good approach*

courses, it goes back a long way, and golf was first played on the 'Ferry Links' as long ago as 1750. However, some claim that its history started around 1450. The first official layout was around 1770, and Elie became, along with Crail, one of the first courses to use iron bands for the holes in 1874. Until then, golf holes were ragged, and this led ultimately to the standardization of hole size in 1897 and the introduction of the 'cup'.

The present Golf House Club was formed in 1875 when some extra land was made available for expansion. Previously there had been an Earlsferry and Elie Club but this was disbanded in

1912. More land was leased and this permitted the layout of the course in 1895 virtually as we find it today. Much of the credit goes to Colonel T. Craigie for recognizing the need to expand and bringing in Old Tom Morris to lay out the full 18-hole course. James Braid was also called in on two occasions, in 1926 and 1948, to advise on the design although not all of his suggestions were subsequently implemented.

Make sure that you visit Elie but do remember that it is a popular holiday resort and therefore booking in advance is a sensible move to be sure of a game. Green fees are moderate and well within the touring golfer's reach. You can also sample the gentlemanly atmosphere of the Golf House Club – an attractive white and green building where a jacket and tie are required of members and guests alike.

Not to be missed is the peculiar construction perched alongside the first tee on top of the starter's box. On close inspection, you will discover that this is no less than a giant periscope from a submarine. You will notice that the view from the first tee is completely blocked by a massive ridge some 150 yards in front. Thus the starter uses the periscope to give the all clear. Before its installation in 1966 a mirror was attached at the proper angle to one of the chimney breasts on the clubhouse. In earlier days still, a local boy was sent up on to the ridge with a flag.

**Lundin Links** and **Leven Links** lie eight miles further along the coast on Largo Bay between the towns of Lundin and Leven. The Leven Golfing Society was formed in 1820 and played over the long strip of links. As demand grew, the land was divided and new holes were added inland to produce the two 18-hole courses as we know them today. Lundin Golf Club was established later in 1869.

Lundin Links is a first class course with truly excellent greens, a lasting testimonial to George Suttie who has lovingly tended them for nearly 40 years. There are many memorable holes, and the layout demands high quality approach play and a fine short game to overcome the devious contouring of the greens and their surrounds.

Two holes in particular, among the many gems, stand out – the 1st and the 14th. The former is a 424 yarder played from high to a valley sheltered from the bay by a high ridge to the left. From there it climbs to a green situated up on the ridge between low, tussocky dunes

*From the 175-yard 14th hole at Lundin Links you can look out over Largo Bay. This hole, nicknamed 'Perfection', is considered to be one of the finest holes*

not too far from the beach. The green itself is a veritable roller-coaster. Even after an excellent drive followed by a well-struck 8-iron you can find yourself only just through the back. You can hit what appears to be the perfect chip and it hits a contour a few feet short of the flag and rolls swiftly to the right coming to rest some 25 feet from the hole!

You get a slight breather on the next two holes, but the long 4th is ferocious at 452 yards with a burn just short of the green. By the time you stand on the high 14th tee you are in love with the course and indeed this short hole of only 175 yards is called 'Perfection'. The green is way below, surrounded by bunkers and an out-of-bounds wall not more than a few feet to the back right. This is a great hole with a magnificent view out across Largo Bay.

There used to be a railway line running through the middle of the course and to this day that narrow strip

is still out-of-bounds and can come into play on six holes. When the great Jack Nicklaus watched his son fail to qualify for the 1984 Open Championship at Lundin, he just shook his head in disbelief. But the railway line has been there for years so why change the strategic qualities of the course?

The green fees are very affordable at Lundin and higher at weekends than on weekdays. Parties are welcome from Tuesdays to Fridays but you should still check with the Secretary and book in advance as with other courses. It will be a decision that you will not regret.

**Leven Links** is another fine test for the golfer but Lundin probably has the better land. The holes on Leven are not as memorable nor is the condition up to the high standards of its neighbour. However, it does have a superb last hole – a par-4 of 457 yards. A wide burn meanders around the front of the green, beautifully sited below the Leven Golfing Society clubhouse. Downwind it is a mere wedge for the second shot but into the wind you may have to lay up or risk all with a wood or long iron. The green fees are marginally cheaper than Lundin, but it tends to be busier as it is played over by two clubs – Leven Golfing Society and Leven Thistle.

**Ladybank** Golf Club lies several miles inland to the north of Largo Bay. To get there you bypass the two courses at Glenrothes, less than 20 years old but among Scotland's finest inland courses. The green fees are very low indeed here making it well worth a visit.

Ladybank was formed in 1879, and Tom Morris assisted in the original design which amounted to six holes outwards, these being played in reverse on the inward half. However, the course has been gradually extended over the years and is now one of the great inland courses. It was suitably rewarded in 1978 and 1984 when it was chosen as a Final Qualifying Course for the Opens. Situated in the heart of Fife, it is a beautiful heathland course with a profu-

sion of heather, wiry broom and pine trees which all add up to a picturesque but demanding test of golf.

Possibly the best hole on the course is the 397 yards 16th, especially from the medal tee. The narrow fairway doglegs sharply to the left between the closely planted trees. Cut the corner too finely and you will encounter all manner of difficulties, but play on too safe a line and you also run out of fairway. Get your drive away and you are confronted by a fairly demanding second shot. The ground around the green slopes from left to right and the trees and rough encroach well in from the left.

The course measures 6617 yards from the back, and with four par-5's and four par-3's it has a par of 72. Score well here and you will deserve a drink in the friendly clubhouse bar afterwards. The excellent meals and snacks are reasonably priced, and the green fees are

*The 18th hole at Leven is located right in front of the impressive clubhouse. This is the most memorable hole on the course*

affordable, too. Weekdays should not be too busy unlike weekends, especially in the morning.

**Cupar** lies a few miles north-east of Ladybank in a valley. The course, however, is built on the side of a large hill and is an excellent lesson in shot-making from awkward lies as, apart from the greens, you never get a level stance. Two limping lines add up to 5182 yards, some very economically priced green fees and an unusual game of golf. If you yearn for something different and out of the ordinary and have one leg longer than the other, then this may be the course for you!

**Scotscraig** Golf Club is only 10 miles from St Andrews at the most northerly tip of Fife near the picturesque town of Tayport on the Tay estuary. The thirteenth oldest club in the world, it was founded in 1817, and the course was redesigned by James Braid in 1904. Although it is highly regarded in the region by local golf buffs, it is relatively

unknown further afield despite the fact that it was used as an Open qualifying course in 1978 and 1984.

Although the site is about half a mile from the nearest beach, the course has true links turf except for one lower lying corner where the grass is more lush. There is a proliferation of heather, whin and gorse bushes, and the many fir trees give the impression that it is a heathland course. Some people think that it has lost too much of its essential links character over the years, but nevertheless the fairways are typically links and are normally very hard with many punishing bumps and hollows ready to deflect your ball into trouble.

The first hole is called 'Admiral' after the famous past captain Admiral Maitland-Dougall who held the office in 1887. He was a fine golfer, winning some 16 Spring and Autumn medals of the Royal and Ancient Golf Club at St Andrews. In fact, one of his greatest golfing feats was to win the 1860 Autumn Medal after pulling the stroke-oar of the St Andrews lifeboat for five hours in a gale force wind. His portrait graces the Scotscraig clubhouse.

Two of the best holes on the course – the 4th and the 7th – are both par-4's. Although the 4th is only some 355 yards, the second shot must hold a tiny island green sited some 12 feet above the fairway with out-of-bounds just over the back. The drive too must be placed accurately between bunkers to the left and a jungle of bushes to the right. Neither should it go too far or it will end up on a heathery downslope that cuts across the fairway.

The longer 400 yards 7th offers a choice from the tee: you can either hit a long iron onto a plateau which is clearly visible from the tee and then run the risk of having to use the longest club in your bag into a headwind to reach the distant, low-flying green, as many of 1984's Open pre-qualifiers failed to do much to their chagrin and disbelief. Otherwise you can elect to hit the driver over the plateau only to end up in a

*These Open pre-qualifiers are putting on the 400-yards 7th hole at Tayport's Scotscraig Golf Club.*

series of severe ridges with the odd steep bank of rough providing only a slim hope of being left with a decent lie but nonetheless a much shorter second shot.

However, despite all this, to play to your handicap on your first visit to Scotscraig you must be on top form. If you are passing through Tayport it is well worth a visit.

**Caird Park** and **Camperdown** are two good public courses in Dundee which is situated on the north bank of the River Tay estuary. To get there from Scotscraig you drive over the Tay Road Bridge from Newport out of Fife. You can play on these two courses at any time of the week.

**Downfield** Golf Club is undoubtedly the best course in Dundee. Opened in 1933, it was designed originally as a nine-hole layout by David Millar, the professional at Rosemount. However, so great was the local demand for golf that James Braid was called in almost immediately to extend it to 18 holes, and the course was completed in 1934.

In 1956 the then Dundee Corporation offered an exchange of ground for the convenience of siting a housing estate, and 82 acres were handed over with 126

acres of new land gained on the opposite side. The 82 acres accommodated 11 of the holes so the Corporation donated £12,500 towards the construction of 15 new greens, 14 tees and 12 fairways.

Architect C.K. Cotton was hired as a consultant but the original ideas for the new layout were conceived by the club's Green Committee. The excellent new course was opened in 1964 at some 6899 yards from the medal tees. Downfield has hosted many amateur and professional tournaments. In the 1972 Sunbeam Electric Scottish Open John Garner, Roberto Bernardini and Peter Oosterhuis shot five-under-par 68's which still stand as the professional record. Neil Coles won the event after a sudden death play-off with Brian Huggett. Five times Open Champion Peter Thomson was in the field and he commented: "Downfield is one of the finest inland courses I've played anywhere in the world. It's tough, demanding and is amidst some of the most picturesque scenery – you have to be very long and straight to succeed here!"

Visitors are welcome only on weekdays and must play away before 4pm; you can only play at weekends if introduced by a member. Green fees are more expensive than those charged by the public courses.

**Monifieth** lies on the long stretch of coastline between Dundee and Carnoustie to the east. In fact, this is the home of six 18-hole links courses – three at Carnoustie itself, one at Barry and two at Monifieth.

The Monifieth Links were first used for golf in 1845 when Allan Robertson and Alexander Pirie of St Andrews designed a nine-hole layout and this was extended to 18 holes by 1880.

Nowadays there are two fine courses at Monifieth – the Medal course and the shorter Ashludie. The Medal at 6657 yards is not the prettiest links course in the world but it is an excellent test of golf even though the greens are not as good as they used to be in the 1960s. In 1986, the Scottish Amateur Championship was held here.

The first six holes follow the Dundee to Aberdeen railway line and it is, naturally, out-of-bounds. The 7th turns back in the opposite direction and is one of the best holes on the course. The drive at this 419 yarder has to avoid a looping burn to the left and two bunkers to the right. This is not too daunting with a following wind but is another story altogether into a stiff breeze or a howling gale. Negotiate the drive and the approach has to find a long, narrow, well-contoured green which is guarded by two bunkers and an unseen shallow gulley in front.

The soil is typical, hard links with a sprinkling of gorse and many pine trees. There are not too many bunkers, the layout relying rather on the natural undulations for hazards.

The shorter Ashludie course at 5123 yards is also most enjoyable with some very fine golf holes. It is used by many of the locals, especially the less experienced golfers and beginners.

The courses are jointly managed by the elected representatives of the four affiliated clubs. You should direct any enquiries to the Links Secretary (see the list at the back of this book). You will find that the club members are friendly and welcoming, and it would be difficult to meet a keener bunch of golfers.

**Panmure** Golf Club lies only a couple of miles away from Monifieth in the small village of Barry. Like Monifieth it is an excellent links course. Formed in 1845, its members played originally on the Monifieth Links until 1899 when they became too crowded for comfort. They moved along the coast to Barry and set up their own private course. In fact, its far reaches met up with the perimeter of Monifieth's Medal Course.

The real meat of the course begins at the 4th hole, which although not long at 350 yards requires a delicate second shot to the well-guarded plateau green. The 5th is a good par-3 and then comes the sensational 6th.

The 366 yards 6th is undoubtedly the best hole on the course. It calls for an accurate drive over a stretch of gorse and some rough strewn humps and hollows ending with a bunker. Then, from a very undulating fairway, the second shot is uphill between the dunes to a high plateau green with out-of-bounds just through the back – a very intimidating shot indeed!

In 1953 Ben Hogan played a few practice rounds at Barry in preparation to winning the Open Championship at Carnoustie. He fell in love with the hole and even suggested the addition of a greenside bunker which was duly added afterwards.

From here the course meanders through the lowish dunes and over the Buddon Burn which guards the approach to the beautifully sited plateau green of the 12th hole. The last two holes, like the first few, are flattish but into a wind they take two well struck blows to get home, even although they are just 401 and 404 yards respectively.

The clubhouse of this very traditional club is extremely distinguished with splendidly old fashioned rooms which evoke the atmosphere of the club's

*Carnoustie is one of the most famous golf courses in the world. The game has been played here for over 300 years and it is every golfer's dream to play this tough links course*

history. Green fees are relatively low on Panmure (higher at weekends than on weekdays), and visitors are not allowed to play on Saturdays.

**Carnoustie,** host of five Open championships, is no distance at all down the coastal road. It is a matter of some dissent among golfers as to which course is the best in Britain, but many devotees of the game believe Carnoustie to be the gem in the British golfing crown. It is certainly one of the most challenging courses, providing even the star players with one of their toughest tests of golf. In fact, only some of the greatest names in golfing history have won the Opens staged at Carnoustie – Tommy Armour, Henry Cotton, Ben Hogan, Gary Player and finally Tom Watson in 1975 when he pipped the unfortunate Jack Newton in a play-off.

Carnoustie has a long history like Scotland's other fine courses. Although

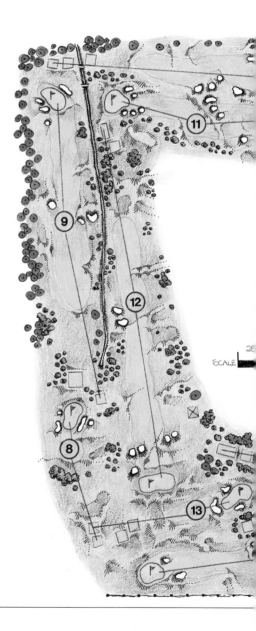

the first club was founded in 1842, it is thought that golf was played on the links three centuries earlier. Laid out initially as 10 holes by Allan Robertson, it was extended to 18 by Old Tom Morris and later improved on by James Braid in the 1920s. The wild and bleak landscape of Carnoustie is without doubt one of the oldest and greatest links courses in the world so play there if you get the opportunity. You will discover that every hole has character, and there are never more than two holes that follow the same direction. Difficult at the best of times, when the wind gets up, Carnoustie has to be one of the toughest tests in the world.

The first hole is tough, needing a long second shot to find the hidden green. The 2nd is a classic long par-4 of 432 yards with a well placed bunker in the middle of the fairway to threaten the drive.

The 3rd is just a drive and a pitch, but to a sloping green just over 'Jockie's Burn'. And so it goes on. The 6th is a tremendous par-5, probably one of the best in the world. At 529 yards there is

*Gigantic bunkers such as these are some of the many hazards that lie in wait for the unwary at Carnoustie. The course is widely acknowledged as one of Scotland's best*

out-of-bounds all the way up the left and two bunkers dead centre at driving distance. The second shot must thread between the out-of-bounds and a burn short right of the green. Avoid all that and you can pitch up to the flag. Ben Hogan made two birdies on the last day of the 1953 Open on his way to victory.

The last four holes must be among the most ferocious finishes in the game. The 460 yards 15th swings around a rolling ridge. The 248 yards 16th has a shelf green well protected by bunkers and the 432 yards 17th crosses the Barry Burn twice (if you play it correctly – otherwise it could be more). The last has the burn just short of the green, as well as coming into play from the tee.

**Many people say** that Carnoustie is in poor condition. It is normally very hard but links are meant to be like that. Granted the bunkers could do with some fresh sand, but the greens are

usually very true and fast.

The other two courses are the shorter **Burnside** and the recent Peter Alliss and Dave Thomas designed **Buddon Links** which tends to be disappointing and not very memorable. Although opened in 1981 it is debatable whether Carnoustie needed another course and it is often virtually deserted when the Championship course is packed. The need in the area lies in or nearer to Dundee.

Green fees over the Medal Course at Carnoustie are slightly higher than normal but you can buy a weekly ticket if you intend to stay a few days. The Burnside and Buddon courses are cheaper. Six clubs play at Carnoustie and the Medal Course is frequently busy, so you must book in advance with the Carnoustie Golf Links Management Committee. If wished, you can even hire a caddie's services.

*Unusually for a Scottish links, there are trees at Carnoustie. The plan shows that this is no typical out-and-back layout. The burns come very much into play on the 17th and 18th, where some championship hopes have been destroyed*

## Card of the Course

| | | | | |
|---|---|---|---|---|
| **1** Cup | 395 yards par 4 | **10** South America | 426 yards par 4 |
| **2** Gulley | 432 yards par 4 | **11** Dyke | 370 yards par 4 |
| **3** Jockie's Burn | 345 yards par 4 | **12** Southward Ho! | 476 yards par 5 |
| **4** Hillocks | 381 yards par 4 | **13** Whins | 161 yards par 3 |
| **5** Brae | 376 yards par 4 | **14** Spectacles | 482 yards par 5 |
| **6** Long | 529 yards par 5 | **15** Luckyslap | 460 yards par 4 |
| **7** Plantation | 384 yards par 4 | **16** Barry Burn | 248 yards par 3 |
| **8** Short | 169 yards par 3 | **17** Island | 432 yards par 4 |
| **9** Railway | 425 yards par 4 | **18** Home | 440 yards par 4 |
| Out 3436 yards par 36 | | In 3495 yards par 36 | |

Total 6931 yards par 72

**Montrose,** the fourth oldest golf course in the world, lies 20 miles away from Carnoustie. Golf has been played on its gorse spattered links since 1628 making it one of the east coast's most famous courses.

There were originally only 17 holes on the Medal Course but it was extended to 18 in 1863. It is still basically the same course today. As it lies roughly between Dundee and Aberdeen it has been neglected too often by the touring golfer based in either city. Do not make that mistake as a round on the Medal Course is well worth anyone's time.

The Earl of Dalhousie owned the land and he and Queen Victoria's husband, Prince Albert, were close friends. It is thought that Albert played over the course on more than one occasion with the Earl. The Medal is an excellent golf course of 6451 yards over true, hard links. There are many fine holes, with the 2nd having one of the humpiest

*This is the 4th hole on Montrose's famous Medal Course. Although it measures only 363 yards, it is still a very tough par 4*

fairways you will ever encounter. When you climb to the elevated 6th tee you are confronted with a marvellous view of the eight miles long, virtually deserted Montrose beach.

On most holes the driving zones are generous but on the three short holes you have to be very precise with your shot-making. All Montrose's greenside bunkers are devilish but the sand is as beautiful as you could ever wish and the greens are fast and true.

The course evolved gradually with no known architect and the shorter, flattish Broomfield 18 (4815 yards) was added just before the turn of the century.

The courses are run by the Montrose Links Trust which was established in 1980 to take over the administration from Angus District Council, and they

are played by five different clubs: The Royal Albert, Caledonia Golf Club, The Mercantile Golf Club, The Victoria Golf Club and North Links Ladies. Despite this, visitors are welcome at any time other than Saturday mornings. Green fees are very reasonably priced and you can purchase a special weekly ticket if wished, whereas a party ticket entitles you to two Medal rounds, coffee, bar lunch and high tea. Furthermore, the Links Trust has an arrangement with the nearby Park Hotel which offers an all-inclusive package of accommodation, meals and four Medal rounds – perfect for a short golfing break. For further details contact the Secretary by letter or telephone.

**Edzell** lies 10 miles inland from Montrose, with splendid views of the Grampian mountains. The golf club was founded in 1896 and the course was designed by Bob Simpson of Carnoustie. In its first year, the entry fee was one guinea with an annual subscription of another guinea.

'Residents within the water drainage area' were entitled to play for five shillings a year with no rights of access to the clubhouse if they did not want to pay full membership. The Edzell record books are full of such interesting details.

The 6299 yard course is parkland but many holes have fine heathland turf. Most of the holes are interesting, with the 184 yards 17th being a favourite, calling for a well-struck long iron to a small sloping green perched above a shallow valley. It is by no means a championship course and indeed has no pretensions to such. However, it is a *good* golf course and excellent as a holiday venue as it does not necessitate too much length of the tee to cope with the modest yardage.

**Letham Grange**, near Arbroath, is a new 18-hole course – an attractive mixture of rolling terrain, woodland and water. It was the dream and realisation of a lifetime's ambition for Ken Smith who took over the farming operation of the Letham Grange estate in 1976. Already, many experts are predicting that Letham Grange may become one of Scotland's finest inland courses when it matures, even capable of holding Championship events.

The course falls naturally into three distinct types of landscape. The first six holes are situated in relatively flat meadowland, the next six in a wooded area and the last six holes on rolling open land crossed by a meandering burn. It is well worth a visit if you are in the Tayside region for its natural beauty and the challenging nature of the course.

**Forfar** is to be found down the A94 road to the north of Dundee. It offers a fine if less challenging course set in a wooded landscape.

Nobody knows exactly when golf was first played at Forfar but some locals claim it dates back to before 1651 when, unfortunately, the borough's records were destroyed by Monk's dragoons. It was in 1871 that the present site was donated by a Colonel Dempster to 'those favourable to the formation of a golf club in Forfar'. The first secretary was James Brodie, a mathematics master at Forfar Academy, who served the community and the golf club for 20 years, and it was he who brought in Old Tom Morris to lay out the course. In

*The 12th hole at Letham Grange is set in woodland. Although quite a new course, it is already being hailed as a great one*

those days the course measured only 5079 yards, so James Braid altered the design in 1926 to measure 5598 yards. It is still basically Braid's layout that is played today, with a few amendments and added yardage, making it a par 69 of 6257 yards. Although still relatively short it is no pushover and demands golf of the highest calibre to score well.

The main feature of the course is the undulations of regular folds in most of the fairways, generally at right angles to the line. In fact, it reminds you of enlarged corrugated iron roofing and means that it is very rare indeed to get a level stance or lie and makes the shot-making that much more difficult and interesting. Varied theories are advanced for their existence, the most

popular being that it is a remnant of flax cultivation. Over the years conifer trees have been added and have now grown tall enough to enclose more of the fairways, enhancing the visual aspect of the course. Despite the trees, however, the wind can play a big part at Forfar, often changing direction and strength during the course of a round – a condition normally only encountered on seaside courses.

There are very few weak holes on the course, as they wind through the tightly packed trees and deep, heathery rough. Many have unusually sited plateau

*This somewhat daunting view from the 1st tee at Pitlochry shows the bunkers, trees, out-of-bounds and a burn to be avoided*

greens often set at varying angles to the fairway with deviously placed deep bunkers waiting to suck in the errant shot. The turf is perfect for golf, reminding you of Walton Heath or Sunningdale. The course is an excellent testimony to the architectural skills of both Morris and Braid.

Visitors are welcome at any time except Saturdays but it is advisable to phone ahead to book a tee time. If you are in the vicinity, do not drive past Forfar, or you will live to regret it. It truly is a little gem.

**Kirriemuir** lies some 15 miles to the north of Dundee and although at 5591 yards it is not in the Championship class, it is enjoyable to play and provides

Rosemount Course which was ranked by Britain's *Golf World* Magazine in the top 50 British courses.

The first nine holes of this classic inland course were laid out in 1889 on the Marquis of Lansdowne's densely wooded Meikleour estate. It was extended later to a full 18 holes under the watchful eye of Dr Alister McKenzie in 1927. Then James Braid designed eight new holes, further altering the layout, in 1934.

At 6581 yards, it is not over-long and the course meanders through silver birch and pine trees, broom and heather over some outstanding golfing terrain. More heavily wooded than most Scottish courses, it is reminiscent of Sunningdale and the great Berkshire courses in the south of England.

Over the years, Rosemount has hosted many amateur and professional tournaments including the British Boys Championship and the Martini International won by Greg Norman in 1977. Both the back and front nine have two par-3's, five par-4's and two par-5's, with a course record of 66. The second 18 holes on the Lansdowne course are nearly as impressive as those of the Rosemount. Some 300 yards longer, it is judged by some golfers to be even tougher.

You can relax afterwards in the restaurant or two bars, and there are many good, reasonably priced hotels nearby. Green fees are not unreasonable but you must book starting times in advance through the Club's Professional. Visitors can play on Mondays, Tuesdays, Thursdays and some Fridays but must provide proof of handicap.

**Pitlochry** is right on the edge of the beautiful Scottish Highlands some 25 miles up the A9 north of Perth. The town of Pitlochry is famous for its Festival Theatre and it is an ideal holiday centre for fishing, sailing, pony trekking, mountaineering and skiing, and visiting the Highland Games.

the golfer with some pleasurable holes. The front nine are disappointing, being ordinary parkland, but the back nine are a definite improvement. The terrain is more contoured with heathland-type turf which lends itself to some fine holes. And there are plenty of whin bushes just off the fairways to ensnare the errant drive, as well as some cunningly placed greens.

There is a well-designed welcoming clubhouse, a pleasant professional's

*It is worth discovering Letham Grange. The 7th hole pictured here is the first of six holes in a beautiful stretch of woodland*

shop and low green fees to tempt you further. Please note, however, that you need to be accompanied by a member at weekends.

**Blairgowrie,** only 15 miles from Perth, has two 18-hole courses and a nine-holer. The most famous of these is the

At 5811 yards, the par-69 Pitlochry Golf Course will not humble the top stars in golf, but nevertheless it has many fine attributes, especially its magnificent setting. It lies above the town and offers some exhilarating views of the surrounding hills and valleys.

The present site was first used in 1909 when Willie Fernie of Troon laid out 18 holes. During World War I, no golf was played and the course deteriorated rapidly. However, in 1919 the course was purchased by Colonel C.A.J. Butler and redesigned by Major Cecil Key Hutchinson. It has remained basically the same ever since that date.

The layout makes excellent use of the awkward hilly landscape and no two holes are even remotely alike, which makes for interesting golf. There are no par-5's at all and only three par 3's, but the course is kept in top condition and provides the holidaying golfer with a most enjoyable day's play. Fees are reasonable and there are good meals in the clubhouse.

**Taymouth Castle** Golf Club lies next to beautiful Loch Tay. This shortish course of just over 6000 yards was designed in the mid-1920s by James Braid and is situated in a mountain conservation area of great natural beauty. The holes themselves are fairly flat, but they meander between ancient trees and a couple of water hazards. Behind the pro shop looms the old Taymouth

*The 17th hole on Blairgowrie's Rosemount course is known as the 'Plateau'*

Castle – once the seat of the Campbells of Breadalbane.

If you intend visiting this course, you may enjoy staying in Scotland's oldest inn – the Kenmore Hotel which dates back to 1572. During the busy summer months of July and August, this historical hotel offers video golf clinics in addition to its usual comforts. And it is a perfect centre for exploring the southern Highlands, with sailing, water-skiing, fishing, riding and shooting all available nearby.

## You and your tartan

Here the British golfer Brian Barnes is pictured in unusual golfing attire – a kilt. In Scotland most families or clans have their own distinctive tartans which probably date from the mid-seventeenth century. The Highland regiments and the British Royal Family have popularized the wearing of tartans and they are now very popular and fashionable. If you have Scottish ancestry and wish to find out more about your own traditional clan tartan you can visit The Scotch House in London, where you will receive advice about your tartan and can have it made up into a kilt. There is an exceptionally wide range of colours and tartans to choose from if you are not of Scottish descent but would like a kilt all the same.

*This view is taken from behind the green at the tree-lined 388 yards 7th hole at the undulating Murrayshall golf club course*

**Crieff** is to be found to the west of Perth. It offers the 18-hole Ferntower course and a smaller 9-holer. The Ferntower is a fine rolling parkland course with some enjoyable holes but overall it lacks distinction. Visitors are welcome but should book in advance, while juniors must be accompanied by an adult.

**Craigie Hill, King James VI Golf Club, North Inch Course** and the **Murrayshall Golf and Country Club** are all located either in or around Perth. The slightly hilly parkland course of the Murrayshall was opened in the spring of 1981 in the grounds of the Murrayshall Hotel. It was designed by Hamilton Stutt and plays to 6416 yards, mainly over undulating tree-lined fairways, although there are a couple of unmemorable holes that stretch beyond the trees and run adjacent to some fields.

There are two ponds to be avoided – one at the short 4th hole and the other at the 315-yards 10th. The architect made good use of the existing trees, and from many of the tees you have to make sure of a well-placed drive to avoid being partially blocked out for the ensuing approach shot.

There is a well-stocked professional's shop and electric golf carts for hire for people who dislike walking. The hotel itself is excellent and is situated close to the historic village of Scone, where all the Kings of Scotland were crowned. It has well-furnished rooms, a restaurant offering a varied menu which is open both to residents and non-residents, and has a comprehensive wine list.

**Gleneagles** has four courses –the King's, Queen's, Prince's and Glendevon – all set in the foothills of the heather-clad Grampian Mountains. Not only is there superb golf, but there are also spectacular views of the distant mountains. The moorland terrain is dotted with silver birch, rowan and purple heather and you may even catch a fleeting glimpse of a deer.

The most celebrated courses, the King's and Queen's, were laid out by James Braid in a beautifully tranquil landscape. They opened in 1919 to universal praise. The Prince's and Glen-

devon courses are much newer, having been laid out in 1974 and 1980.

Gleneagles can be reached by road or rail – a bus service links the course with Gleneagles Railway Station. King's Course at 6452 yards with a par of 71 is the longest of the four courses, the Queen's being slightly shorter at 5964 yards with a par of 69. The holes on all four courses have their own special names and they promise you a glorious day's golf. If you can afford it, there is

*You can see the heather-covered Grampian Mountains in the distance from the 18th hole on Gleneagles' celebrated Queen's course, set on a moorland plateau*

no better place to stay than the luxurious Gleneagles Hotel – surely, one of the best-known golfing hotels in the world. With 252 bedrooms, there are many holiday packages on offer and it is worth enquiring about availability and cost. The hotel manages the four courses, and special arrangements exist for hotel guests and members when it comes to teeing times. Green fees are high but arguably worth it for the privilege of playing on such a legendary course. Because of its popularity, you must book ahead.

There is also a Gleneagles Dormy House with a bar and restaurant offering a wide choice of food and drink from snacks and buffet meals to a full à la carte menu. It is a good place to relax and go over the day's play.

*Gleneagles is more than just a golf course – it is also a beautiful, luxurious place to stay where you can get away from it all and enjoy a golfing break. The course itself is challenging and dotted with bunkers*

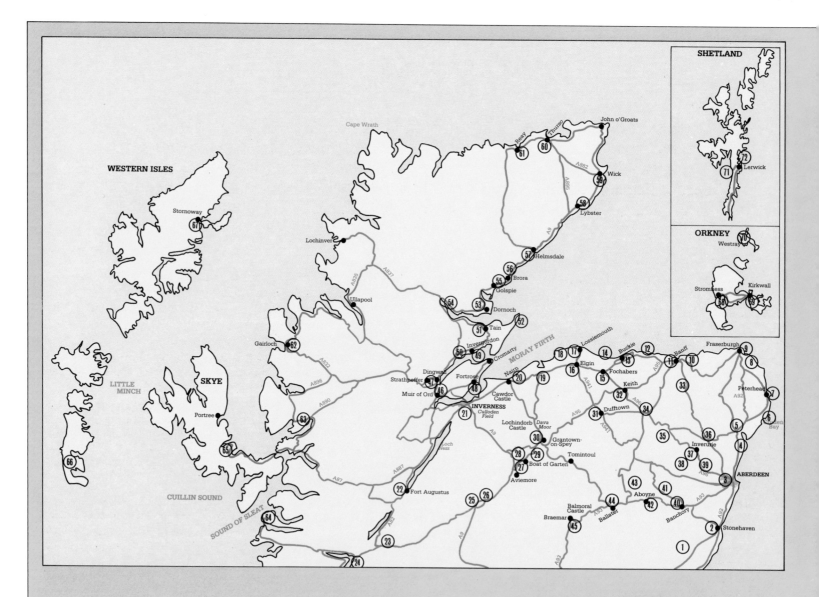

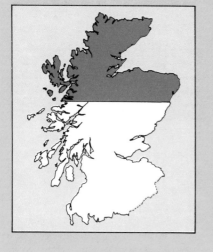

**Key to map**

1 Auchinblae (9)
2 Stonehaven (18)
3 Auchmill (9)
   Balnagask (18)
   Deeside (18)
   Hazlehead (45)
   King's Links (18)
   Murcar (27)
   Royal Aberdeen (36)
   Westhill (18)
4 Newburgh-on-Ythan (9)
5 McDonald (18)
6 Cruden Bay (27)
7 Peterhead (27)
8 Inverallochy (18)
9 Fraserburgh (18)
10 Royal Tarlair (18)
11 Duff House Royal (18)
12 Cullen (18)
13 Buckpool (18)

   Strathlene (18)
14 Spey Bay (18)
15 Garmouth & Kingston (18)
16 Elgin (18)
17 Moray (36)
18 Hopeman (9)
19 Forres (18)
20 Nairn (27)
   Nairn Dunbar (18)
21 Inverness (18)
   Torvean (18)
22 Fort Augustus (9)
23 Spean Bridge (9)
24 Fort William (18)
25 Newtonmore (18)
26 Kingussie (18)
27 Boat of Garten (18)
28 Carrbridge (9)
29 Abernethy (9)
30 Grantown-on-Spey (18)
31 Dufftown (9)

32 Keith (18)
33 Turriff (18)
34 Huntly (18)
35 Insch (9)
36 Oldmeldrum (9)
37 Inverurie (18)
38 Kemnay (9)
39 Kintore (9)
40 Banchory (18)
41 Torphins (9)
42 Aboyne (18)
43 Tarland (9)
44 Ballater (18)
45 Braemar (18)
46 Muir-of-Ord (9)
47 Strathpeffer Spa (18)
48 Fortrose and Rosemarkie
   (18)
49 Invergordon (9)
50 Alness (9)
51 Tain (18)

52 Tarbat (9)
53 Royal Dornoch (27)
54 Bonar Bridge & Ardgay (9)
55 Golspie (18)
56 Brora (18)
57 Helmsdale (9)
58 Lybster (9)
59 Wick (18)
60 Thurso (18)
61 Reay (18)
62 Gairloch (9)
63 Lochcarron (9)
64 Traigh (9)
65 Sconser (9)
66 Askernish (18)
67 Stornoway (18)
68 Stromness (18)
69 Orkney (18)
70 Westray (9)
71 Scalloway (9)
72 Shetland (18)

# The Highlands

People have been discovering the Highlands ever since 1848 when Queen
Victoria established the royal precedent of taking summer holidays at Balmoral,
and the trend is growing. There are many reasons for the golfer to visit this
beautiful area of Scotland apart from the superb golf on offer – for example, the
salmon and trout fishing (arguably the best in the world), the mountain climbing,
the walking, the urge to 'get away from it all' or even to spot the Loch Ness Monster.

Following the east coast northwards from Aberdeen takes the golfer to some of the finest links courses in Britain and also a few of the great *undiscovered* golfing destinations of the world. Royal Aberdeen and Murcar, side by side to the north of the old granite city of Aberdeen, Cruden Bay and Nairn have all been ranked among the top 50 courses in the British Isles by the UK's *Golf World* Magazine. So too is Royal Dornoch, that almost legendary golfing gem north of Inverness which, like the fabled monster of Loch Ness, possesses a reputation in golfing circles the world over but which few golfers have actually visited and played.

These famous five are the most celebrated of the courses in the Highlands region of Scotland but they are just the tip of the iceberg, for there are many other challenging and beautiful courses just waiting to be discovered by the visiting golfer. As with all Highland pursuits they are best appreciated in the late spring or early autumn when the weather is at its kindest – warm with only a little rainfall. In the early summer months of May and June the landscape is bright with the golden flowers of the gorse (or 'whin' as the Scots sometimes refer to it) and redolent with its sweet fragrance, whereas in September and October the moorland is ablaze with purple heather. This is not to say that the courses are not crowded in July and August, too – the peak summer months. However, it is sometimes difficult in the high holiday season to enjoy the brisk pace of play to which you are accustomed.

Although the Scots are renowned for haring round a golf course as if some demon is back at the bar consuming all the malt whisky, they are sometimes too quick for their own good, or so the locals say. However, when it comes to serious competition nobody is going to concede the five-footers that are treated regularly as 'gimmes' north of the border, and their ethnic delight of a leisurely round on the links means that 36 holes a day, either side of a clubhouse lunch, are a cinch! And you can even continue playing after an excellent Highland tea late into the evening until dusk in the summer months. The further north you travel the lighter it stays, and on Midsummer's Day around Dornoch, it hardly seems to go dark at all!

Even a winter golfing break in the Highlands is possible due to the benign influence of the Gulf Stream which helps keep snow and severe frost to a minimum along the coast. This permits the possibility of a December round at Royal Dornoch even though the town is on the same latitude as Juneau in Alaska! The Moray Firth which runs out to the North Sea from Inverness is particularly blessed in this respect, making Nairn worth a visit even in February.

The greatest concentration of courses is to be found in the east, especially along the coast, with its matchless collection of links. Of course, the Highlands has its fair share of inland courses too, but it is for the quality of its links that it is best known and loved. Although we have started our golfing journey at Aberdeen which is strictly in the Grampian Region rather than the Highlands, we shall include it here for the purposes of convenience, especially as it is a good starting point for any golfer setting out on a voyage of discovery through the Highlands.

Aberdeen is called rather dourly the 'Granite City' and although it is predominantly grey, many of its buildings are imposing and majestic and, thanks to the boom in North Sea oil, it is the thriving and prosperous city of the region. You can either fly there or go by train or car.

**Royal Aberdeen** is a superb links course which celebrated its bicentenary in 1980. Founded by a handful of gentlemen in 1780 as the Society of Golfers at Aberdeen, its membership applications were subjected to the notorious 'black ball' system. The original ballot box used to decide the fate of these eighteenth century candidates is now one of the club's most treasured possessions. Although the Society was abandoned, the Aberdeen Golf Club was founded in 1815 playing originally over seven holes on the neighbouring King's Links and later moving to its existing location at Balgownie across the River Don in 1866. It was granted Royal patronage in 1903.

Although the Aberdeen Ladies' use the same course albeit with a different clubhouse, the club is a male bastion and women guests are still not allowed in the bar although they may, in the priceless words of the club's handbook, be introduced 'to the large lounge, dining room and toilet at the north entrance'.

Royal Aberdeen opens with a comfortable but not easy downhill par-4 of 409 yards, straight out towards the North Sea. The course then veers left and, the short eighth apart, heads north. The first nine often play into the wind, and as holes two to four measure 530, 223 and 423 yards respectively, there are initially no easy pickings.

In terms of length, the subsequent four holes are less testing but you cannot afford to stray from the fairway. After the 9th, a tough two shotter of 453 yards, the golfer turns and heads for home. Or, at least, he should do. A story, perhaps apocryphal, is told of four Americans who wandered from the 9th at Royal Aberdeen to the 4th tee at adjacent Murcar, which is not only on

Aberdeen's land (at a rent of a penny per year) but is, unlike the correct 10th tee, readily visible from the 9th green.

The two layouts are separated merely by a few small white stakes and the tale goes that the Americans proceeded to complete their match at Murcar. No doubt perplexed at having to traipse round 24 holes before returning to an unfamiliar clubhouse, the visitors were totally flummoxed when they were unable to find their vehicle in the car park.

However, assuming that the intrepid golfer has discovered the right tee, there are still nine holes of Royal Aberdeen to enjoy. The back nine is usually played

*The 3rd hole at Royal Aberdeen is a tough par-3 of 223 yards which requires all your skill to hit the ball against the wind*

into the wind, making it a very stiff par of 34. It has plenty of subtle hazards, like the gentle plateau on which the 12th green is set and the grass dyke that protects the entrance to the 14th, and an heroic finishing hole of 434 yards. However, with a favourable breeze and under fast-running summer conditions, at precisely 3000 yards the homeward half is a little on the short side.

Royal Aberdeen would be described colloquially as an out-and-back design because the 9th is at the furthest part of the course. In as much as it implies lack of imagination, this description is false and as misleading as it would be to make the same point about Sunningdale or Wentworth. Even though the outward nine generally head in one direction and the inward go the opposite way, the

*The 5th hole at Murcar – the spectacular links course that offers testing golf and tremendous views of Aberdeen itself*

potential tedium inherent in such a routing has been avoided cleverly in several ways – by setting the tees and greens at different angles to the fairways; the use of doglegs, however slight; and most effectively by designing the holes so they tack to and fro across 180 degrees while generally moving in the same direction. This is a trait of many fine courses in the Highlands. Dornoch, Cruden Bay and Murcar are three other examples of the same ingenuity.

The architect responsible for Royal Aberdeen was Robert Simpson, a revered surname in those parts. His namesake Andrew, the greenkeeper at Aberdeen in the late nineteenth century, built Nairn, Archie Simpson designed Murcar, while the great Tom Simpson collaborated with his colleague Herbert Fowler on the construction of Cruden Bay golf course.

To alleviate the traffic over Aberdeen's championship course and to provide a pleasant and relaxing interlude for the members, the club opened an 18-hole short course in 1983.

Green fees are lower in the week than at weekends, and societies are generally welcome with sufficient notice as are visitors, barring Saturday mornings which are the most popular time for club fixtures. However, as usual, it is best to check with the Club Secretary in advance.

**Murcar** is another tremendous course and, like Royal Aberdeen, its outward holes tend to hug the coastline. Although the terrain is intrinsically the same as at Aberdeen, the elevations are more spectacular.

Murcar opens with a par-4 of 322 yards, which can be driven with some assistance from the wind. After this mundane beginning, the course reveals its true character with the 3rd. The fairway plunges down from the tee and large sandhills reminiscent of Royal Birkdale protect the green. The 6th is a dogleg left of 440 yards which makes optimum use of the rolling and undulating land. The 7th is a classic.

The elevated tee commands a wonderful outlook of the North Sea breakers to the right. The drive has to carry some 180 yards to reach the fairway beyond two loops of a burn created by a small, peacefully meandering stream. (The hole is appositely called 'Serpentine'.) The fairway is accommodating enough not to be intimidating, although a large grassy hillock to the left warns against a hook. From the tee, the flag is visible some 420 yards away. Only from the fairway is it apparent that the green is raised and, beware, however much club you think you need, take at least one more. You will need a couple of extra if the hole is cut at the back. The 8th and 9th, getting progressively shorter, are fine holes too. The humps and hollows have been utilized perfectly to offer a challenging, fair and intriguing test.

The back nine is not quite so splendid, although most courses in Britain would be grateful to own a stretch of the quality in evidence on holes 14-17. The view from the 15th tee takes in Aberdeen itself, and while the fairway is invitingly spread out below for the

drive, the green is dauntingly perched on a high bank above a shallow stream at the other end of it.

Green fees are similar to those at Aberdeen and again it is sensible to check with the Secretary as in all private clubs throughout the region. It is worth adding that Murcar has a small nine-hole course as well which, although not of the same calibre, makes a useful practice ground before venturing out to tackle the big one.

**Hazlehead** public courses, two 18's and one nine, are a mere five minutes' drive from the heart of Aberdeen. The original No. 1 course, opened in 1928, is set well away from the sea among attractive trees and bushes. No. 2 was inaugurated less than 10 years ago by merging an existing nine-hole design, and nine further holes were constructed by the golfers Neil Coles and Brian Huggett. The green fees are lower priced than at Royal Aberdeen and Murcar and more in line with the normal tariff in Scotland. Visitors are welcome at any time but it may be necessary to reserve a tee-off time on course No. 1. This can be done on the same day that you wish to play, although it is better done in advance for weekend games.

**Cruden Bay** Golf and Country Club lies 24 miles up the coast from Aberdeen – a mere 30 minutes' easy motoring. The golf course is an unspoilt par-70 links *par excellence*, and a secluded sanctuary in the true Scottish tradition. Its remoteness only adds to its natural beauty and charm although it was not always so quiet. In March 1899, the Great North of Scotland Railway opened its magnificent and luxurious hotel there, built of pink Peterhead granite. It signalled the beginning of an opulent era for the little village. The wealthy used to travel up the new

*From the smooth green at the 260-yards 8th hole at Cruden Bay, you can see the North Sea and the mountainous sand dunes*

railway line from Aberdeen and play on the course which was inaugurated the same year with a tournament attended by the likes of Harry Vardon, James Braid and Ben Sayers. Thus Cruden Bay soon became the playground of the rich and famous.

But these halcyon days were brought firmly to a halt by the outbreak of World War II, and in 1947 the hotel, the 'palace in the sandhills' as it was known, was sold for demolition. The future of the golf club was finally secured in 1951 when a syndicate of local businessmen and golf enthusiasts bought the course from the British Transport Commission on behalf of the club.

The view from the simple clubhouse is stunning: most of the holes are visible from this high vantage point, winding in and out of formidable dunes along the spectacular coastline, while between the course and the sparkling blue sea are the famous sands of Cruden Bay itself, which are allegedly as 'smooth and firm as the floor of a cathedral'.

The course has all the requirements needed to assume cult status. Some holes are, granted, a little on the tricky side. The par-5 13th demands a blind pitch for the third shot, the 14th measures 372 yards and presents almost no view of the fairway from the tee and absolutely no sight of the green from the fairway, and the 15th – horror of horrors – is a blind par-3. The 8th is little more than a 260 yards fill-in, and the 9th, set high upon the cliffs, is no architectural masterpiece.

Why, then, all the fuss – simply because Cruden Bay possesses that intangible aura of bygone days. The links not only exudes the impression that it has been almost untouched by human hand (which is false since relatively recent changes have been made to some holes) but even when other people are out playing one hardly sees them as they disappear behind a sand-hill or round a curve in the course. The isolation is splendid indeed.

Some of the holes would never be designed today. The huge plateau green on the 2nd terrifies the golfer into

pushing his approach down the steep bank to the right. The 3rd, a mere 286 yards, is a tantalizing dogleg with a punch bowl green set beyond a severe mound: if the tee shot is not ideally placed, a bogey five is tough enough to achieve.

The awesome view atop the 5th tee of the hole ahead, which runs between some of the highest dunes, is one of the most stimulating on the course, as is the hole itself. The par-5 6th calls for a pitch to a slippery contoured green protected by a devilish bunker in front, and the 392 yards 7th requires a long iron approach uphill through a narrow alley to a green nestling among the sandhills.

So it goes on. Although some of the holes may be regarded as a little quirky, they beautifully epitomize the old-fashioned style of links golf. And however you score, you will never forget panoramas like that from the 10th tee, with half the back nine down at beach level, laid out far beneath you. Once these holes were threatened by the construction of the Forties Field pipeline but thankfully commonsense prevailed and the crude was kept off Cruden Bay.

*The punchbowl green and mound of the 3rd hole of 286 yards at Cruden Bay. Although it is not over-long, this is still one of the toughest holes on the course. Play here to enjoy old-fashioned links-style golf*

Green fees are very reasonable (more at weekends than weekdays) and cheaper still over the nine-hole St Olaf course. The club professional is a famous name, too – Harry Bannerman who represented Great Britain and Ireland in the 1971 Ryder Cup.

**Royal Tarlair** and **Duff House Royal** are two little-known Royal courses in nearby Macduff and Banff. The latter is the only club in the world to boast its regal status as a suffix rather than a prefix. Both are meadowland courses although Royal Tarlair is built upon the rocky cliffs along the shore. Its best hole is the short 13th, only 152 yards but nevertheless a poser which demands a precise iron shot. Played from an elevated tee, the prospect of the green perched, seemingly precariously, on the very edge of the ocean is enough to induce a fatal tightening of the grip.

Duff House Royal began life as the nine-hole Banff Golf Club in 1871. The

*Called 'Clivet', the treacherous short 13th hole at Royal Tarlair – the green clings to the side of the cliff-face*

present course was laid out in 1909 and the club received its Royal patronage in 1923. It was then redesigned by the Mackenzie golf architect brothers. Indeed, it was Dr Alister Mackenzie's last assignment in the United Kingdom before emigrating to the United States where he went on to create the celebrated courses of Augusta National and Cypress Point. However, unfortunately Duff House Royal is not in that league.

The revised course was opened officially by an exhibition match between Ted Ray and Sandy Herd (they tied with 71's). Visitors from all over the world now enjoy its gentle wooded terrain. Green fees are moderately priced although, as usual, they cost more at weekends.

**Moray** and **Forres** are two clubs in Morayshire which operate under a scheme administered by the Moray District Council along with eight other clubs (**Buckpool, Cullen, Garmouth and Kingston, Keith, Spey Bay, Strathlene** and the 9-hole **Dufftown and Hopeman**) This scheme enables you to purchase a five-day, low-priced ticket permitting play on eleven courses between April and October, the only restriction being that a maximum of 36 holes is allowable on any one. And for younger golfers under 18 years old, the price is even lower.

**Old Moray** was designed by Tom Morris and it is justly renowned for its finishing hole of 423 yards, played to a raised green invitingly set below the old stone clubhouse. **New Moray,** the work of Henry Cotton, was opened in 1979 and it is fortunate that his initial inten-

tion to alter the 18th on the Old to accommodate the New was opposed.

Both Morays run the narrow gauntlet of land between Lossiemouth beach and a large Royal Air Force base. Thus the only disadvantage of these courses is that there may be considerable aircraft noise and aerial activity on some days. Inland and to the west at **Forres** there are no such problems, however. Like so many old British golf clubs, Forres no longer occupies its original site. Founded in 1889, the first course was designed by the then R & A professional Andrew Kirkaldy. But in 1903 the members moved to the present Muiryshade course which was extended to 18 holes in 1912.

Since then the course has undergone substantial development but nevertheless it has lost none of its varied scenic attractions. Whereas some holes are fairly flat, others are gently undulating.

Several holes bring trees into play while others are quite open. From some holes, you can see right across to the distant Moray Firth.

**Elgin Golf Club** lies 12 miles away down the A96 highway. The circuitous route through Dallas via the B9010 may be a tempting diversion but you will search in vain for Ewing Oil in this quiet backwater of the Highlands! Formed in 1906, at Hardhillock just outside Elgin, the county town of Morayshire, the course presents the golfer with a stringent test of 6402 yards and a par of 69. However, the plantations of pine and silver birch, the purple heather and bright yellow gorse, and the fine moorland turf make Elgin a beautiful place for a game of golf even if it is hard to match your handicap.

There are many memorable holes at Elgin, and certainly few tougher than the couple that first greet the golfer on his arrival. At 459 and 483 yards respectively, the 1st and 2nd holes are awesome par-5s if you are playing into the wind rather than the par-4s indicated on the card. The 440-yards 18th is an ideal finishing hole, the green being in the lee of the neat white clubhouse.

A round at Elgin is very reasonably priced indeed, even in the busy months from April to September when the cost is marginally higher than during the rest of the year.

The locals will tell you that Elgin is in an especially favoured position, surrounded by hills which protect the course from the worst excesses of the weather but not too influential to prevent it benefiting from the proximity of the Moray Firth which usually brings clement weather conditions to this beautiful part of Scotland.

**Nairn** stands on the southern shores of the Firth with fine beaches and kind weather. This has earned it the name of the 'Brighton of the North' (intended as a compliment), and it is certainly a popular holiday resort for golfers and non-golfers alike. It has had some illustrious visitors in the past. For example, Charlie Chaplin used to spend about one month every summer there in 'the Garden of Scotland', and former British Prime Minister Harold Macmillan was another regular visitor.

*The 4th hole at Elgin lies at the end of the beautiful tree-lined fairway. Unusually, the best holes are the 1st and 2nd*

Although there are two courses in Nairn, only one was rated in the British *Golf World* Magazine's top 40 courses in the British Isles. Nairn Golf Club has long been famous for the excellent quality of its true, fast greens, but if that is to suggest that the putting surfaces are Nairn's sole virtue, the impression is misleading.

Nairn does not instantly attract the golfer's attention in the same striking fashion of Royal Aberdeen, Murcar and Cruden Bay. The land is essentially 'flat, even featureless, and there are no dramatic sandhills or spectacular views.

Only on the 430 yards 13th, which requires an uphill approach to a two-tiered green, and the downhill 210 yards par-3 14th, are there any appreciable changes in the landscape. Nevertheless, despite these potential shortcomings, Nairn is a tremendous golf course and an eminently fair one.

Tom Morris and James Braid independently improved upon Andrew Simpson's original work and now Nairn is no stranger to important tournament occasions. It has hosted many Scottish titles and in 1979 it staged the Ladies' British Amateur Championship. In 1987, the club celebrates its centenary.

The first seven holes run alongside the pebbled beach, and if the tide is high you might almost find the sea lapping against the edge of the tee on some holes. The par-3's are particularly

*The white clubhouse can be seen in the distance on Nairn's old-fashioned links with its famous fast and accurate greens*

challenging. The 4th heads back towards the clubhouse, in the opposite direction to the first three, and, as befits a hole of only 145 yards, the green is very narrow. The 6th green is fiendishly contoured, tending to throw off the tee shot which will have to be struck with at least a 5-iron, even if assisted by a favourable breeze.

Inevitably the wind poses the main problem at Nairn – the difficulty of hitting a straight shot far enough if playing into it, selecting the correct club if going downwind, and maybe even of simply standing up if it is at its strongest. And for the errant shot, there is no shortage of gorse – in late spring so seductively pretty and yellow, but all year round so evil and fearsome when it comes to playing a golf ball out of it.

Daily green fees at Nairn are at the higher end of the Scottish range but still very affordable. Adjoining Nairn proper is the nine-hole Newton course, a pleasant diversion for those who do not feel up to the main test.

**Nairn Dunbar** is located at the other end of the town. Opened at the turn of the century, it is perhaps a more exacting examination than its more illustrious neighbour, although lacking the same intrinsic charm. Green fees are much cheaper, but in May each year, the two clubs combine to run Nairn Golf Week, the original of many such occasions held at various Highland golf courses throughout the high summer months. The area has other attractions, too, besides golf. Nairn is only 16 miles, a short drive, from Inverness, the 'unofficial Capital of the Highlands' where you can shop or eat out.

*The 2nd hole at the Boat of Garten course is a par-4 of 347 yards, which beckons you into some exhilarating golfing country*

**Boat of Garten** lies 35 miles due south of Nairn in the heart of a major tourist area. It is only six miles from the famous Aviemore Centre, which is so popular with skiers in the winter. The Strathspey Railway, a delight for steam train afficionados, links Boat of Garten with Aviemore and is well worth a ride if you enjoy the romance of steam.

There are three other golf courses in the immediate vicinity – **Grantown on Spey,** a pleasant yet undemanding layout; and the 9-hole courses of **Carrbridge** and **Abernethy.** But it is Boat of Garten that is the gem in this quartet. There is little indication of its quality from the first tee – only the appealing sight of the snow-capped peaks of the

Cairngorm mountains on the horizon. The hole is called 'John's View' in memory of one John Grant who was the club professional for many years. However, it is rather a mundane par-3 of 186 yards – comfortably the least distinguished hole of the course. From the 2nd, a gentle dogleg uphill right of 347 yards, things start to get distinctly better for the golfer.

The Boat is probably among the finest 'short' golf courses you will ever play. It measures 5672 yards with a par-69. Only four holes are over 400 yards and one of these is the solitary par-5. It would be demeaning to describe it as a 'holiday course' because there is a great deal more to the Boat than is inherent in such a label. Although the powerful player can score exceptionally well, he will have to keep out of the pines and possess the ability to both fade and draw the ball. James Braid was responsible for the course as it is today and he utilized the tumbling terrain marvellously well.

At the low green fees charged by the club, the Boat is tremendous value for money. And even if you are spraying the ball all over the place, you cannot fail to appreciate the majestic beauty of the ever-present mountains. You may even catch a fleeting glimpse of a deer bounding over the hillside, or spot an osprey plucking fish out of the nearby River Spey. For sheer scenery and Highland atmosphere, the Boat must not be missed.

Another worthwhile aspect of the trip from Nairn to Boat is the journey itself. A short distance out from Nairn, you will see the alarming signpost that points to Cawdor Castle. This is the Cawdor of **Macbeth,** and although Shakespeare was exercising his artistic licence in using the castle as the setting for King Duncan's murder, it has been the ancestral home of the Thanes of Cawdor since the thirteenth century. The A939 then runs over Dava Moor,

an awesomely bleak and forbidding stretch of desolate Highlands which has an eerily dark brooding atmosphere. A brief detour to Lochindorb Castle will help to enhance your mood. Built on a tiny island in the middle of a secluded lake, this now ruined fortress was once occupied by the English king Edward III and later served as the almost impenetrable lair of the infamous Wolf of Badenoch – the outlawed son of King Robert II of Scotland, who used this remote retreat as a base to terrorize the local communities.

**Inverness** lies up the A9 from Boat passing by the historic site of Culloden Field where the Scots and English once fought a bloody battle in the eighteenth century. In 1746, the English troops of King George dashed Bonny Prince Charlie's and the Jacobites' hopes of seizing the English throne. Bounded by the waters of the Moray Firth to the

*An elevated tee with few hazards and some marvellous views make the 9th hole at Grantown-on-Spey a golfer's dream*

east, Inverness stands at the entrance of the Caledonian Canal and thence to the secrets of Loch Ness to the west, as well as being the gateway to the north of Scotland. It is a friendly, attractive town with its own airport and an ideal point of entry and exit for any golfer wishing to explore the Highlands.

Inverness has two golf courses – the private **Inverness Club,** the home of Scotland's leading lady amateur, Gillian Stewart, and the municipal **Torvean.**

Heading northwards into Easter Ross (which refers to a geographical region of Ross-shire rather than the religious festival) one finds a comprehensive package, not unlike 'Moray for Golf', assembled by the Ross & Cromarty Tourist Board. From April to June, a small financial outlay secures a special deal of five nights' half board at one of 11 hotels and four days' golf with eight different courses to choose from. Four of these – **Alness, Invergordon** and **Tarbat,** plus **Gairloch** on the west coast – are only nine-holes, and Gairloch is closed on Sundays.

**Fortrose and Rosemarkie, Muir-of-Ord, Strathpeffer Spa** and **Tain** all have 18 holes, and of these Tain is surely the best.

Tain was laid out by Tom Morris in 1890 and the course is immensely enjoyable. It is an intriguing mixture of links and inland golf. In some respects, Tain suffers because of the reputation of its exalted neighbour which lies only four miles away across the Dornoch Firth. Nevertheless, its Golf Week in early August always proves enormously popular, and many visitors eager to sample another course apart from Dornoch make the journey to Tain and return home proudly boasting of having 'discovered' another great Scottish treasure. It is a wonderfully cheap find, too.

One day, someone will build a bridge to span the Dornoch Firth, but until they do the route to Dornoch from Tain will remain 28 miles by road rather than four miles as the crow flies.

# In praise of Scotch Whisky

If there is one thing for which Scotland is more famous than for being the home and the cradle of golf, it is for being the birthplace and manufacturing centre for whisky – even to the extent that when a tot is requested almost anywhere in the world, it is referred to as 'Scotch'. However, every whisky has its own uniquely special flavour, and a true whisky drinker will always ask for his Scotch by name.

Distilling has been practised in Scotland for hundreds of years. Whisky – which draws its name from the Gaelic 'Uisge Beatha', meaning 'water of life' – has been produced from at least the fifteenth century. Basically, there are two types of Scotch – malted whisky and grain whisky. The malts are made by distilling malted barley, and the grains from distilling maize and unmalted barley. The most famous whiskies – Johnny Walker, J and B Rare, Grant's Famous Grouse, White Horse, Haig, Whyte and Mackay, Teachers, Bell's and others are blended whiskies made from a blend of several individual malt and grain whiskies. Some of these blends can have as many as 50 different malts in the mixture.

Everyone in the world knows of these famous blends but far fewer people know that in Scotland there are over 100 separate distilleries, each producing its own malt whisky. Some of these malts never see the counters of bars, being made purely for local or private consumption. Others are too heavily flavoured to be sold separately and are made purely for blending.

All alcohol is produced by the action of yeast upon sugar. In barley, which is used solely in the making of malt whisky, the sugar is potentially there in the dry kernel but is not easily accessible. To release it, the barley is immersed in spring water for two or three days and the soaked grain then spread on an open malting floor to a depth of about one foot. After a few days, the temperature rises and the germination process begins whereby the starch in the barley is prepared for conversion into sugar. At the appropriate moment, germination is halted by drying the malted barley in a kiln.

The dried malt is then ground and the grist mixed with water so that the soluble starch mash is converted into a sugary liquid. This liquid is attacked by living yeast and turned into a crude alcohol which is then heated in large copper stills to a temperature at which the alcohol vaporizes. The vapour rises up the still and is cooled through copper tubing where it is condensed into a liquid state. This first distillation separates the alcohol from the fermented liquid, and during a second distillation the spirit reaches an acceptable level.

After distillation, the new spirit is stored in oak casks which, being permeable, allow air to enter and evaporation to take place. By this means, the harsher constituents in the new spirit are removed and it becomes, in due course, a mellow whisky. The period of maturation varies but whisky is never bottled until it has matured in the casks for at least three years. Some malts mature for up to 15 years and even longer. When it enters the cask, the spirit is a colourless liquid. It gets its warm, whisky colouring from the wood of the cask and from the maturation process.

Each individual distillery produces a malt whisky with a different and unique flavour, which is determined mainly by the spring water used to mash the malted barley, but also by the shape of the pot stills, the aromatic smoke from the peat used to heat the barley and the subtle chemical reactions within the spirit and the oak of the cask during the years of maturation. The unique Scottish air, temperature and weather also play a part, as does the skill of the distiller whose experience tells him when the new spirit running from the still has the quality for which he is looking.

*Top: a Scotch whisky distillery.*
*Above: some large copper stills.*

## Malt whiskies

These can be divided into four separate groups:

**1 Lowland malts** made south of an imaginary line drawn across Scotland from Dundee to Greenock.

**2 Highland malts** made north of that line, including the River Spey valley.

**3 Islay malts** from the Isle of Islay.

**4 Campbeltown malts** from Campbeltown and the Mull of Kintyre.

Each group has its own clearly defined characteristics and it is a matter of taste and experience for the discerning drinker.

Malt whisky is sold as either a single malt or a vatted malt. A single malt is the product of one distillery and is bottled under the distillery name. If the whisky is given a name or label which is not that of the operating distillery, then it is not a true malt but a vatted malt – a mixture of malts.

**Dornoch** is the third oldest course in the world after St Andrews and Leith. Golf was first played there as early as 1616. Its remoteness (even on the increasingly improved roads, it is a good two hours' drive north of Inverness) has added unquestionably to its charisma and mystery, and the 1985 Amateur Championship was the first major golf championship to be held at Dornoch.

The Dornoch Golf Club was formally created in 1877, King Edward VII conferring its Royal status in 1906. Tom Morris laid out the first nine holes for the new club, and the club secretary and leading light for over half a century, John Sutherland, completed the 18. Sutherland strengthened the course shortly after the turn of the century and by the time of World War II, Dornoch had two 18-hole courses.

The Royal Air Force soon took care

of that, and several holes were requisitioned to make way for an airstrip. George Duncan was called in after the war and he built six new holes, the 6th to the 11th. What is now the 18th was formerly the 12th and play used to continue on six of the holes which today constitute the little Struie course, a nine-holer of 2485 yards. Among the consequences of these enforced changes was a considerable stiffening of Dornoch's hitherto weak finish. The course is demonstrably the better for no longer concluding with two ordinary par-3's.

The golf architect Donald Ross was a Dornoch man, and the influence of home is to be found in much of his work in America. Ross emigrated in 1898,

*In spring, the 6th hole at Royal Dornoch nestles among the flowering, golden gorse and is widely known as 'Whinny Brae'*

and Seminole, Oakland Hills and Pinehurst are just three of the great creations that fortified his reputation as one of that country's foremost designers. Pinehurst No.2 is acknowledged as the most searching examination of chipping in the United States, and the manner in which he built those greens is reminiscent of Dornoch.

The standard pitch-and-run, the Scottish shot, is often totally redundant at Dornoch. The greens sit on small, and sometimes not so small, rises, with steepish banks and contoured run-offs which not only tend to throw off a less than perfect approach but make the execution of a recovery shot an extremely delicate affair.

As one would expect of a course spared the incessant pounding inflicted upon the more accessible Old Course at St Andrews, Dornoch is always in fine

The 336-yard par-4, 1st hole at Royal Dornoch is a relaxing introduction to a course that gets progressively tougher

fettle. The course has always been ranked among the best 10 in the British Isles and this fact alone testifies to its quality.

Like most great courses, Dornoch opens with a comfortable par-4. At 336 yards, it gets you safely out into the country, while the 179 yards 2nd gives an early indication of the troubles that lie in store when it comes to negotiating Dornoch's humps and mounds.

The 3rd to the 6th is as stimulating a sequence of holes as you will come across anywhere. The first three of these are par-4's, not intimidatingly long given that they are played from elevated tees, but the greens are so hard to hit and hold.

The 3rd measures 414 yards with a cluster of bunkers in the driving zone to the right of the fairway, while a hook will find the huge bank of gorse which covers the hill protecting this stretch of the course. The 4th is of similar design and length, the correct line for the drive

being the huge statue of the Duke of Sutherland on a distant hill above Golspie. ("It's the most expensive marker post in the world" says Willie Skinner, the dry-humoured Dornoch professional.)

A favourite hole with many golfers is the 5th. The ideal drive will find the valley way below the tee, from where the iron shot has to carry a battery of bunkers protecting the elevated green. The short 6th is the first of Duncan's holes but so perfectly does it fit into the pattern that you imagine that it must have always been there, its green nestling attractively in the shelter of the whin-strewn hill.

There are no poor holes at Dornoch; it is simply that some are great and others merely good. One of the more prosaic is the 7th, a terror of a par-4 at

465 yards which runs atop the highest part of the course but is of no outstanding architectural or scenic virtue.

The best of the rest is surely the 14th. Like most holes on the old Scottish courses, it has been given a name, and 'Foxy' is a very apt one. It is 448 yards from tee to green, and about 230 yards out the fairway curves to the left. If a draw is the shot to seek with the driver, the next should have a touch of fade to take it towards the flag set beyond a dune which runs down the right side of the fairway.

This ingenious double-dogleg is a classic example of an architect making optimum use of the land. It has no sand bunkers because there was no need to insert any. Instead the green is sited on a raised plateau four feet above the fairway. Only an excellent second shot will find the putting surface and only an exquisite chip or pitch will salvage a four should the green be missed.

Unlike many great British links, Dornoch presents few blind shots – unless, of course you are hopelessly off line – but it demands a series of good ones if a pleasing score is to be returned. At 6577 yards, par-70, Dornoch is not long. It is not even expensive. And at how many other of the world's great courses could you just turn up at the weekend and be optimistic of getting a game within minutes? It is always wiser to be safe than sorry, however, and to check beforehand with the secretary, but there are no undue formalities. Dornoch epitomizes Highland golf at its best.

Dornoch is almost the end of the Highland golfing trail, but not quite. There are understandably popular 18-hole courses at **Golspie, Brora** and **Wick,** and nine-hole layouts at **Helmsdale** and **Lybster,** before one reaches the very northern tip of golfing Britain at **Reay** and **Thurso.**

**Reay,** close to Dounreay nuclear power station, is the most northerly British links. There are no bunkers on its 5876 yards, despite several holes running close to the beach, but it does have a few fine holes, notably the 6th and 7th. Whereas Reay dates from 1893, **Thurso** was built in the 1960s by local volunteers anxious to have somewhere to play the old game 70 miles north of Dornoch. John O'Groats is 20 miles from Thurso, the 876 miles separating it from Land's End representing the greatest distance between two points on the British mainland.

In a short stay you cannot hope to visit *all* the golf courses to be found in the Highlands of Scotland and we have just focused on some of the more interesting and easily accessible ones. However, there are other beautiful and challenging courses in the region including **Ballater** and **Deeside** near Aberdeen; **Fort William** set among the foothills of majestic Ben Nevis (the highest mountain in the British Isles); and **Newtonmore,** the club that claims to be the Mecca for left-handed golfers.

# The secret of Loch Ness

Although golfers will come to Scotland in the hope of shooting at least a few birdies, most of them will also want to indulge in a spot of monster hunting.

Nessie, the mysterious and elusive inhabitant of Loch Ness, was first allegedly sighted as long ago as 600 A.D. That means that either he/she is endowed with phenomenal longevity, or that there have been several generations of Nessies, or that all the filmed and scientific evidence is faked and the monster-spotters for nearly 1400 years are either liars or have been imbibing too much good local whisky.

The official Loch Ness Monster Exhibition at the delightfully named Drumnadrochit, on the loch's northern shore, was established in 1980 with the aim of throwing some light on the subject – no easy task when the world's most famous lake is 720 feet deep and its waters are so peat-ridden that even the technical expertise of the British Royal Air Force could not spot a galvanized dustbin lid when it was lowered just seven feet below the surface of the dark and murky loch.

Just a mile away is Urquhart Castle. It was once one of Scotland's largest castles but since the Jacobite Rising of 1689 it has had to be content with being an impressive ruin. The Loch Ness Monster has been seen from its crumbling walls on more than one occasion – or has it? Drumnadrochit is only 14 miles from Inverness, so take time out for a little private investigation of your own.

Nearly half its members play the game the wrong way round, a piece of genetic trivia attributed to the town's historical prowess at the traditional Highland game of shinty.

If you are expecting to see such traditional Highland spectacles as kilted men playing bagpipes and tossing cabers or dancing over crossed swords, you are likely to be disappointed unless you make a detour to the Highland Games. However, you will almost certainly be offered porridge for breakfast (but with salt, not sugar!) and maybe the odd haggis (surprizingly good), and will enjoy a glass of fine old Scotch whisky after a day outside on the golf course. And you will have the pleasure of playing some of the world's most marvellous courses where the quality is excellent and the golf is still relatively cheap. Visitors are always welcome and made to feel at home in this hospitable part of the world, although it is both courteous and sensible to check in advance with the Secretary before visiting a new club (see the list at the back of this book).

There is an abundance of hotels ranging from the comfortable to the luxurious, guest houses and friendly intimate bed-and-breakfast establishments offering pleasant accommodation at reasonable prices and you should consult the local tourist centre for advice on where to stay. There is also a list of the larger hotels at the end of this book. If you are considering a golfing break in the Highlands, you might do well to consider one of the many special packages assembled by the Highlands and Islands Development Board. The courses may not always be the finest in the world but the prospect of a rare game at Orkney or Shetland, at **Sconser** on Skye or **Stornoway** on Lewis may prove irresistible to you and have a unique attraction. This all goes to prove that golf in the Highlands is very much within your reach. It is accessible, affordable and infinitely enjoyable. You should try it and see for yourself.

# Baronial, bonnie and beautiful

The Highlands is an area of outstanding beauty and interest, both natural and man-made, and not all these assets are golf courses. There are plenty of historic castles, including Kilravock, Rait and Cawdor near Nairn. The latter is particularly worth a visit. It is the family home of the Earl and Lady Cawdor – and only just a little larger than most detached residences. The notes explaining the historical importance or otherwise of various exhibits, penned by his lordship, include remarks like "the incredibly boring bit of rock on the right of this pile of rubble", thereby setting a light tone to the tour. The grounds of the Royal Family's summer home, Balmoral Castle, are open for part of the year, and the fairy-tale splendour of Dunrobin Castle, near Golspie in Sutherland, deserves a detour.

The Highlands is full of reminders of Bonnie Prince Charlie – from Glenfinnan where he raised his standard to Loch Nan Uamh from where he departed from Scotland for ever, his Highlanders having been crushed by the Duke of Cumberland's troops on Culloden Moor in 1746.

In the western Highlands stands Ben Nevis, Britain's highest peak, and off Scotland's west coast lie most of its enchanting islands – North and South Uist, Lewis, Harris (as in tweed), Skye, Canna, and that wonderful trio, Rhum, Eigg and Muck. What a cocktail! North of John O'Groats are Orkney and, further northwards still, Shetland.

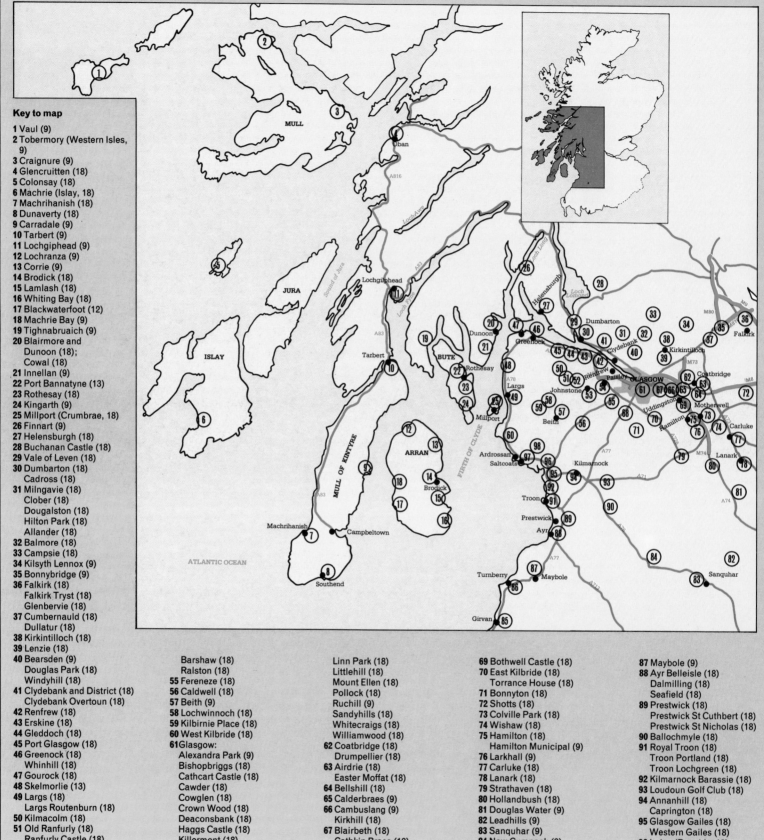

**Key to map**

1 Vaul (9)
2 Tobermory (Western Isles, 9)
3 Craignure (9)
4 Glencruitten (18)
5 Colonsay (18)
6 Machrie (Islay, 18)
7 Machrihanish (18)
8 Dunaverty (18)
9 Carradale (9)
10 Tarbert (9)
11 Lochgiphead (9)
12 Lochranza (9)
13 Corrie (9)
14 Brodick (18)
15 Lamlash (18)
16 Whiting Bay (18)
17 Blackwaterfoot (12)
18 Machrie Bay (9)
19 Tighnabruaich (9)
20 Blairmore and
    Dunoon (18);
    Cowal (18)
21 Innellan (9)
22 Port Bannatyne (13)
23 Rothesay (18)
24 Kingarth (9)
25 Millport (Crumbrae, 18)
26 Finnart (9)
27 Helensburgh (18)
28 Buchanan Castle (18)
29 Vale of Leven (18)
30 Dumbarton (18)
    Cadross (18)
31 Milngavie (18)
    Clober (18)
    Dougalston (18)
    Hilton Park (18)
    Allander (18)
32 Balmore (18)
33 Campsie (18)
34 Kilsyth Lennox (9)
35 Bonnybridge (9)
36 Falkirk (18)
    Falkirk Tryst (18)
    Glenbervie (18)
37 Cumbernauld (18)
    Dullatur (18)
38 Kirkintilloch (18)
39 Lenzie (18)
40 Bearsden (9)
    Douglas Park (18)
    Windyhill (18)
41 Clydebank and District (18)
    Clydebank Overtoun (18)
42 Renfrew (18)
43 Erskine (18)
44 Gleddoch (18)
45 Port Glasgow (18)
46 Greenock (18)
    Whinhill (18)
47 Gourock (18)
48 Skelmorlie (13)
49 Largs (18)
    Largs Routenburn (18)
50 Kilmacolm (18)
51 Old Ranfurly (18)
    Ranfurly Castle (18)
52 Cochrane Castle (18)
53 Elderslie (18)
54 Paisley (18)

Barshaw (18)
Ralston (18)
55 Fereneze (18)
56 Caldwell (18)
57 Beith (9)
58 Lochwinnoch (18)
59 Kilbirnie Place (18)
60 West Kilbride (18)
61 Glasgow:
    Alexandra Park (9)
    Bishopbriggs (18)
    Cathcart Castle (18)
    Cawder (18)
    Cowglen (18)
    Crown Wood (18)
    Deaconsbank (18)
    Haggs Castle (18)
    Killermont (18)
    King's Park (9)
    Knightswood (9)
    Lethamhill (18)

Linn Park (18)
Littlehill (18)
Mount Ellen (18)
Pollock (18)
Ruchill (9)
Sandyhills (18)
Whitecraigs (18)
Williamwood (18)
62 Coatbridge (18)
    Drumpellier (18)
63 Airdrie (18)
    Easter Moffat (18)
64 Bellshill (18)
65 Calderbraes (9)
66 Cambuslang (9)
    Kirkhill (18)
67 Blairbeth (18)
    Cathkin Braes (18)
68 Newton Mearns:
    East Renfrewshire (18)
    Eastwood (18)

69 Bothwell Castle (18)
70 East Kilbride (18)
    Torrance House (18)
71 Bonnyton (18)
72 Shotts (18)
73 Colville Park (18)
74 Wishaw (18)
75 Hamilton (18)
    Hamilton Municipal (9)
76 Larkhall (9)
77 Carluke (18)
78 Lanark (18)
79 Strathaven (18)
80 Hollandbush (18)
81 Douglas Water (9)
82 Leadhills (9)
83 Sanquhar (9)
84 New Cumnock (9)
85 Girvan (18)
86 Turnberry: Ailsa (18)
    Turnberry: Arran (18)

87 Maybole (9)
88 Ayr Belleisle (18)
    Dalmilling (18)
    Seafield (18)
89 Prestwick (18)
    Prestwick St Cuthbert (18)
    Prestwick St Nicholas (18)
90 Ballochmyle (18)
91 Royal Troon (18)
    Troon Portland (18)
    Troon Lochgreen (18)
92 Kilmarnock Barassie (18)
93 Loudoun Golf Club (18)
94 Annanhill (18)
    Caprington (18)
95 Glasgow Gailes (18)
    Western Gailes (18)
96 Irvine (Bogside, 18)
    Irvine Ravensport (18)
97 Auchenharvie (9)
98 Ardeer (18)

# Glasgow and the West

Glasgow is the ideal starting place for golfers who want to discover
the beautiful Western Isles and the West Coast of Scotland. The challenging links
courses, many of them renowned throughout the world, magnificent
scenery and rugged landscape, secluded beaches and excellent trout
and salmon fishing make this area a golfing holiday paradise. Even the weather
is kind due to the influence of the Gulf Stream which brings many hours
of warm sunshine in the late spring, summer and autumn.

**Turnberry** is the course at which most golfers visiting the West Coast of Scotland around Glasgow either start or finish their stay. It is still a legend in golfing circles, and the courses, the scenery, the views and the hotel facilities are all impressive and well worth a visit if you have the time.

You can see the luxurious hotel – a splendid white building with a red roof – from almost anywhere on the course. It stands out like a welcoming beacon. From the early 1920s until the outbreak of World War II, the rich and famous used to arrive at the local railway station and then travel to the hotel by an interlinking tunnel. The train, meanwhile, puffed on, empty, a few miles further down the track to Girvan to return the following day at 8.30am loaded with caddies. Now, Turnberry is only a short journey by road from Glasgow or Prestwick on the A77.

Bob Jamieson has been the professional for the famous Ailsa and gentler Arran courses for 24 years. Although he was not there in pre-war times when the trains used to come, he can still regale you with stories of those halcyon days.

On one or other of its beautiful courses, Turnberry has hosted every major golf championship except the Ryder Cup. It is on the British Open Championship rota and is particularly memorable for the famous Nicklaus-Watson shoot-out in the 1977 Open – the first to be held there.

Even though the weather can be unpredictable and the surrounding roads blocked with snow in winter, Bob

*A panoramic view of Turnberry showing some of the spectacular holes which run along the shore line above the sea*

Jamieson can remember only 12 days when snow made play impossible. Even during the really bleak winter of 1962/63, the Arran course stayed open and playable throughout, and catered for 120 golfers every day.

The views across the water to the Isle of Arran and Mull of Kintyre are breathtaking, and on a clear day you can

sometimes see all the way to Ireland. However, the magnificent backcloth to Turnberry is Ailsa Craig, a 1208ft high hunk of rock. Now a bird sanctuary, it was once the happy hunting ground for the special form of granite used to make curling stones (a traditional Scottish game played on ice).

The two courses have fortunately withstood their unlikely conversion to an airfield, complete with concrete runways, in both World Wars. Parts of these runways remain as does a memo-

*Turnberry was the venue for perhaps the greatest major championship ever staged, the 1977 British Open. Watson won by a single stroke after a head-to-head with Nicklaus to become the world number one*

rial tower to those who died attached to the wartime gunnery on the course. It is remarkable that so much land was successfully reclaimed and that such fine courses survived.

There are remains too of earlier strife – the ruins of Robert the Bruce's castle stronghold stand next to the gleaming white lighthouse. And, as you leave the 10th green, take a closer look at the rocks as you gaze out to sea. There, in stark relief, naturally formed on the rockface is a profile of Bruce himself, complete with beard and helmet!

As for the courses themselves, the Ailsa was ranked justifiably in the top 10 of the best 50 golf courses in the British Isles by Britain's *Golf World* magazine. Green fees differ significantly depending on the time of day and which course you play, the Ailsa being more expensive than the Arran. The Golf Club Manager can arrange for you to play on either Championship course. While the Ailsa course is a par-70, 6408 yards from its medal tee, the Arran is 6276 yards, par-69.

Bob Jamieson's shop is always busy. With his seven assistants, including his son Gregor, he offers an on-the-spot club repair service, guaranteeing completion within 24 hours. There are 30 sets of clubs available for hire at any time. And there is a practice ground 400 yards long and 120 yards wide with a green and a bunker. There is also an excellent clubhouse with its own bar and restaurant.

Part of the pleasure of playing at Turnberry is staying at the hotel. Terms vary but all rooms have private bathroom, telephone and colour television and come inclusive of a full Scottish breakfast. As a hotel resident, you benefit from specially reduced green fees. If you can afford such luxury, there is no better place to stay.

# Turnberry under scrutiny

Open Championships, apart from bringing immortality to the winners, are all about history, tradition and permanence. Turnberry has hosted two Opens (in 1977 and 1985) and this has helped establish it as one of the most prestigious British courses, and earned its place in the fields of golfing history, permanence and tradition.

The course has come of age and proved itself on these two occasions, as it faced up to the challenge of one of the biggest events in international golf and emerged with flying colours.

The first thing to realise about Turnberry is that it was laid out to be played in the prevailing wind which comes from the west. During the Open in 1977, for some reason, throughout the four days of the championship the wind was from the north-east. Consequently, some of the holes were made easier and some far more difficult.

It is the wind, as much as anything, that helps to make Turnberry a true links course. The sand dunes may not be as high as those at Royal Birkdale, for instance, but it is nevertheless a true links course.

Between the Opens of 1977 and 1985, several changes and adjustments were made to the Ailsa course. It now plays to a length of 6957 yards – 82 more than in 1977. However, only three holes were changed in length – the 1st was shortened by five yards, the 5th increased by 30 yards, and the 12th lengthened by 57 yards. But there were other changes, too.

The 5th was lengthened to bring the two pot-bunkers on the fairway into play. The distance was achieved by bringing the tee back to be level with the front edge of the 4th green.

The 6th green was also altered, mostly for cosmetic reasons. Spectators and players could not see the sea from this green because of a large sandhill. Bulldozers moved this hill towards the sea to allow for better spectator movement around the green and for the creation of

two new tees for the 7th. One existing tee was also flattened and now the hole affords uninterrupted, spectacular views right up the Mull of Kintyre and of Ailsa Craig. One of the new tees did actually extend the hole by some 15 yards but the R and A, in their wisdom, decided to use the other new tee which gives the same length as the old one.

At the 4th, the spur at the front right-hand side of the green was removed and the back of the green was extended by some 10 feet, although the undulations were preserved. It was felt that the green was really too small to hold a downwind shot from the tee 167 yards away.

During the winter also, a piece of land on the right-hand side of the 9th green prevented approaching players from seeing the surface of the green. The land was lowered some eight feet so that players could clearly see the green. Incidentally, this is the only hole on the course – and one of the very few in championship golf – not to have a single bunker.

Also, the tees for the 9th were rebuilt completely using concrete dug up from the now disused runway as support. Young naturalists from Culzean, aged 12 to 16, under supervision of senior wardens, planted thrift and other wild flowers into the peat between the slabs to bloom in the warm summer months.

At the 11th, the late Russell Brown masterminded the building of a wall linking the forward and back tees. He and his staff built it with concrete lifted from the runway next to the 8th hole, all in big slabs. The wall was completed by the greenkeeping staff after his death, with no trapped fingers nor other injury – a remarkable achievement considering that the wall is 30 yards long and 17 feet high.

Turnberry also bought the quarry to the left of the 11th green and filled in

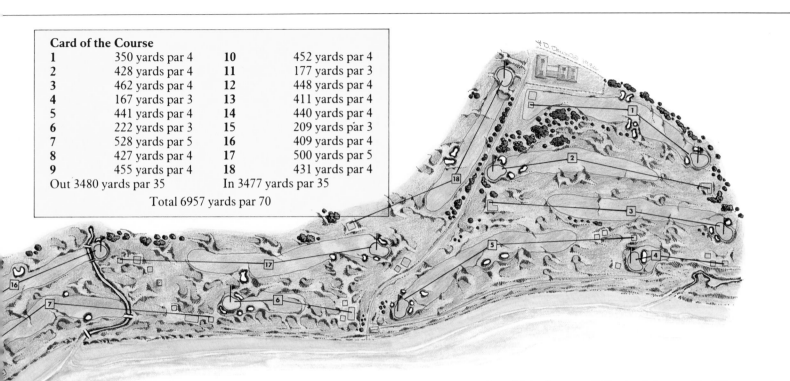

## Card of the Course

| | | | | |
|---|---|---|---|---|
| 1 | 350 yards par 4 | 10 | 452 yards par 4 |
| 2 | 428 yards par 4 | 11 | 177 yards par 3 |
| 3 | 462 yards par 4 | 12 | 448 yards par 4 |
| 4 | 167 yards par 3 | 13 | 411 yards par 4 |
| 5 | 441 yards par 4 | 14 | 440 yards par 4 |
| 6 | 222 yards par 3 | 15 | 209 yards par 3 |
| 7 | 528 yards par 5 | 16 | 409 yards par 4 |
| 8 | 427 yards par 4 | 17 | 500 yards par 5 |
| 9 | 455 yards par 4 | 18 | 431 yards par 4 |
| Out 3480 yards par 35 | | In 3477 yards par 35 | |

Total 6957 yards par 70

25yds 50yds 100yds    200yds

*This rocky feature, Bruce's Head, is so called because in profile it resembles King Robert the Bruce*

*The 15th is the most difficult of the par-3's. The green is hard to hold with a long iron or wood. Watson holed out from well off the green in 1977 to catch Nicklaus*

the bunker at the back of the green, but leaving the undulations. Two new tees were built in the quarry, adding 57 yards to the 12th. This has the effect of bringing the bunkers on the 12th very much into play.

On the 13th, the fairway bunkers on the right were filled in – they seldom caught the tee shots. They were replaced by a second bunker on the left, just on the slight bend, some 20 yards behind the already existing bunker.

Similarly, a bunker on the right was removed along with another bunker, short right of the green on the 18th.

On a general basis, every bunker on the course except the 10th – the island bunker – was revetted. Turf comprising a most beautiful fescue grass was cut and brought down from a nearby moor owned by the Marquis of Ailsa. The man who supervised and arranged the re-examination was the greenkeeper, George Brown.

## How to play the course

*After a quiet start, the 4th, a par-3, brings you alongside the sea for several spectacular holes. For good players, the broad burn should be in play only on the 16th*

**Hole 1: 350 yards, par-4**
Assuming that there is a prevailing wind from the west, many top-class players open up with a 3-wood and play safe to the centre left side of the fairway to open up the green for their 6- or 7-iron second shots. The stronger players often lead off with their driver with the intention of a 9-iron second. It is not the easiest of holes – it is a soft one for an Open but not for the club golfer.

**Hole 2: 428 yards, par-4**
This hole is normally played downwind. The pros drive down the right-hand side of the fairway using an 8-iron, or even a 9-, for their shots to the green.

**Hole 3: 462 yards, par-4**
In the wind, this hole is a totally different animal – it is a driver, then probably a 4-iron at least. There are two bunkers guarding the green but none to guard the tee shots. However, against this the fairway is very narrow, and it is not potentially a birdie hole.

**Hole 4: 167 yards, par-3**
This hole is the first of the par-3's, and is a relatively easy 8-iron to the green in a prevailing wind.

**Hole 5: 441 yards, par-4**
Two fairway bunkers on the left are brought into play at the 5th, and the longer hitters then go with a 7-iron to a very closely guarded green. Most pros are happy to walk off with a four.

**Hole 6: 222 yards, par-3**
The 6th calls for a very good shot off the high championship tee because the wind is not quite behind you. The hole almost appears to go round the bay, and anyone who gets a three at this difficult hole should be well satisfied.

**Hole 7: 528 yards, par-5**
You are already a third of the way round the course and no birdies, but this is where many top players look for one.

**Hole 8: 427 yards, par-4**
For the calibre of the Open player, this is a driver followed by an 8-iron. It is a deceptive hole at which many amateurs are likely to over-club. The two-tier green gives the impression that it is further away than it actually is, which is the complete reverse of most holes.

**Hole 9: 455 yards, par-4**
From the spectacular tee, this is a drive and a 5-iron job. It is a particularly difficult hole as the fairway is almost saddle-backed. Although the club wanted to raise the level on both sides, it was found to be impractical.

**Hole 10: 452 yards, par-4**
A real potential birdie hole, this is a drive and maybe an 8-iron for strong players, made easier if they can drive down the left-hand side of the fairway to what is known as the plateau.

**Hole 11: 177 yards, par-3**
Another hole that requires a really good shot to a green which is guarded front and right with bunkers, especially if there is a strong cross-wind blowing.

**Hole 12: 448 yards, par-4**
The tee on the 12th brings the bunkers into play. You are playing mainly against the prevailing wind coming slightly from the left. The second shot is a 3-iron or possibly a 4.

**Hole 13: 411 yards, par-4**
In the last Open to be held at Turnberry in 1986, the ladies' tee on the 9th was used for the 13th. With the extra bunker, the players had to make cautious approaches. You may decide to play a 3-wood into the neck leaving a 5-iron to the green, but big hitters try to go past the corner with a drive to leave themselves a 7-iron. This hole has the slowest green on the course, and requires a totally different pace.

**Hole 14: 440 yards, par-4**
The prevailing wind comes into action at this hole, slightly across and against you, provoking a 3-iron or 4-wood shot into the green for the second shot.

**Hole 15: 209 yards, par-3**
The same club again is probably needed for the tee shot at this hole.

**Hole 16: 409 yards, par-4**
This is where some players come unstuck as you have to hit a drive past some bunkers. In the 1963 Walker Cup, several players hit 6-irons from just level with the bunkers and finished in the brook. They should have used at least

5-irons or maybe even 4-irons.

### Hole 17: 500 yards, par-5

This hole is never reachable in two when the prevailing wind is blowing. Short of the green lies a little ditch and it is probably a drive and a 3-wood to get up there.

### Hole 18: 431 yards, par-4

At this hole, you drive straight into the wind and your second shot is from right to left. It is usually a drive and a 6-iron. In 1977, Watson drove it to the bunker with a 3-wood and then hit a 7-iron. He commented afterwards: "I hit a 7-iron exactly 172 yards."

**Girvan**, only a few miles down the road at the most southerly part of this area of Scotland, has a good municipal course owned by the Kyle and Carrick District Council. This is an enlightened local authority with a difference – it recognises the value of its sporting facilities and does its best to help people enjoy them. The Council operates a system of green fees on a group basis – the groups representing the standard of courses.

Thus Girvan is in Group 2, paired with **Ayr Dalmalling**. In the slightly superior Group 1 are the courses at **Ayr Belleisle**, **Troon Lochgreen** and **Troon Darley** where green fees are marginally higher. They are less at the Group 3 courses of **Ayr Seafield** and **Troon Fullarton**, and even smaller at the 9-hole Group 4 course, **Maybole**.

Although the Girvan course is not usually included on the touring golfer's itinerary, it is worth a visit. The first eight holes are semi-links beside the sea, whereas the remaining 10 lie further inland on the other side of a minor road. The River Girvan also crosses the course and provides a real challenge at the 15th where a carry of 170 yards is needed off the tee. And the strong prevailing winds frequently put the greens out of reach at the longer par-3 holes for all but the longest hitters. The 223-yards 17th has a steep bank 50 yards in front of the green, some 20 feet above the level of the tee. Most people seem to play their second shots blind from the bottom of this hill.

The difference in the two halves of the course is noticeable with the grass on the inland 10 holes being far lusher than the coastal holes. Another notable feature of this course is the clubhouse itself, which is run as a public house independently of the club yet still has changing rooms and meals at the most inconvenient times!

**Ayr Belleisle** is one of the best of the other courses within the groups run by Kyle and Carrick Council. At 6540 yards, par-71, it is considered by many to be the finest inland course in Scotland. Laid out by James Braid in 1921, it has hosted several tournaments including the British Ladies' and the Coca-Cola Championship. In fact, in 1979, it was a qualifying course for the

*Some of the bunkers at Prestwick are shored up by rail sleepers, although not at this hole. The original course may be gone, but Prestwick is golf old-style*

European Open. As with many other Scottish courses, a burn runs through part of the course, adding to the challenge for tee shots on the 16th and 17th. Set in the heart of Burns country, this typically parkland course has much to commend it. And the 3-star Belleisle House Hotel makes a comfortable base. If you are seeking less of a challenge, you can always sample the easier adjoining **Seafield** course.

**Old Prestwick**, further along the coast, is the original home of the Open Championship and a Mecca to many golfers

the world over. American Generals Lee and Jackson were preparing for the imminent Civil War when the first Open was played at Prestwick in 1860. A stone cairn close to the gateway entrance marks the spot where the first tee used to be. It is mind-boggling just to stand on that spot and imagine how Young Tom Morris, in one of his Championship victories, managed to get a three over its 578 yards, holing out on what is now the 16th green.

Every challenge you could wish to meet is here at Prestwick alongside the ghosts of the past. But when you play, beware the out-of-bounds railway line, abutting the fairway all along the right of the first hole; and the Cardinal bunker on the immaculately conceived 3rd; and the blind tee shot at the long, short Himalayas. And if you cannot

*The Postage Stamp, where a German competitor in the 1950s took 15. He went from bunker to bunker. Arnold Palmer, in 1973, escaped with a 7!*

avoid these hazards, then enjoy them for what they are as you take your place in their history.

Frank Rennie is the professional and the genial Mr J. A. Reid, Club Secretary, is extremely helpful to visitors. If you want to test your skills over these historic links, then ideally you will need a letter of introduction and plenty of notice. Ladies are welcome but will find little in the way of facilities – no changing rooms and no ladies' tees.

**Prestwick St Cuthbert** and **Prestwick St Nicholas** lie close by. The latter is another fine, challenging links course

used as a qualifier for the 1982 Open at Royal Troon. Many great golfers have come unstuck here. Visitors are welcome on weekdays by prior arrangement or invitation. Prestwick St Cuthbert is a more modestly priced flat (not links) course of 6470 yards with a par of 71. Again, visitors are welcome on weekdays.

**Royal Troon**, in the top 20 courses in the British Isles listed by *Golf World* (UK), is no distance at all from Prestwick. Golf was first played there over a reputed five holes in 1878. In 1923, it won its place on the rota of Open Championship courses when the winner was the young Arthur Havers. It is the proud possessor of the longest (554 yards, par-5 6th) and the shortest (123 yards, par-3 8th, the famous Post-

*Royal Troon's most famous holes are the 8th, the Postage Stamp, and the 11th. The railway runs close to the green on the right and is more threatening the nearer you get to the green*

age Stamp) holes on any Open Championship course, and is a really tough test for any golfer. It was in 1973 that the ageing Gene Sarazen came to the Postage Stamp and holed his 5-iron tee shot to the delight of millions of television viewers in the Open won by Tom Weiskopf.

Royal Troon welcomes visitors on weekdays (excepting the second Wednesday of each month). Ladies can play on the Old Course on Mondays, Wednesdays and Fridays but there are some antiquated rules regarding which entrances they can use to enter the clubhouse! Not surprisingly, green fees are higher on the Old Course than on the easier Portland Course where visiting times and regulations are less strict.

## How to play Royal Troon

Brian Anderson, the professional at Royal Troon for many years, probably knows the course better than anyone – the bumps and hollows of the undulating links, and how the wind and weather can change its essential nature and character. Before turning professional in 1964 he played for Scotland. Here, he gives his own hole-by-hole analysis of the Championship Course.

*The 18th green with clubhouse beyond. Nick Price needed a birdie here in 1982 to tie Tom Watson, who won his fourth Open Championship*

## Card of the Course

| | | | | | |
|---|---|---|---|---|---|
| **1** | Seal | 362 yards par 4 | **10** | Sandhills | 437 yards par 4 |
| **2** | Black Rock | 391 yards par 4 | **11** | The Railway | 481 yards par 5 |
| **3** | Gyaws | 381 yards par 4 | **12** | The Fox | 432 yards par 4 |
| **4** | Dunure | 556 yards par 5 | **13** | Burmah | 468 yards par 4 |
| **5** | Greenan | 210 yards par 3 | **14** | Alton | 180 yards par 3 |
| **6** | Turnberry | 577 yards par 5 | **15** | Crosbie | 457 yards par 4 |
| **7** | Tel-el-Kebir | 400 yards par 4 | **16** | Well | 542 yards par 5 |
| **8** | Postage Stamp | 126 yards par 3 | **17** | Rabbit | 223 yards par 3 |
| **9** | The Monk | 419 yards par 4 | **18** | Craigend | 425 yards par 4 |
| | Out 3422 yards par 36 | | | In 3645 yards par 36 | |

Total 7067 yards par 72

## Hole 1: 362 yards, par-4

A comparatively easy, opening hole which can lull the unsuspecting into a state of false security. To tighten it up a little, a new bunker has been created on the left, just a few yards behind the original one, to catch a long, slightly off-line, drive. The modestly elevated green is protected by bunkers left and right but these should not come into play very much as the second shot is usually with a lofted iron. If the wind is right, the likes of Seve Ballesteros and Tom Weiskopf could reach the green with their drives.

## Hole 2: 391 yards, par-4

A really good drive is essential here as the fairway is well trapped with cross bunkers. On the left there are additional bunkers to catch the pulled or hooked shots. The ball must really land on the right side of the fairway otherwise one or other of the traps will gather the ball. The second shot will be with a mid-iron to a well-guarded green where addition-al bunkers are waiting for anything that falls short. This is not a difficult hole providing the drive is sufficiently long and straight.

## Hole 3: 381 yards, par-4

A long drive here will find trouble in a burn which cuts diagonally across the fairway. A 2-iron or a 3-wood is the ideal tee shot but there is a bunker in the middle left of the fairway, short of the burn and ready for the unsuspecting. It is about 250 yards to the burn for the straight hitter. After that it is a simple enough shot to the green which slopes away slightly from the player so, ideally, it should be a high shot with plenty of bite.

## Hole 4: 556 yards, par-5

The first of the par-5s and a slight dog-leg right. The tee shot is slightly away from the Firth of Clyde. There is a deep bunker right in the neck of the dog-leg to prevent corner-cutting, and anyone going in is almost bound to lose a shot. It is really a simple enough hole if played as a par-5. There are bunkers on the right and left just short of the green leaving only a very narrow entrance for the long hitters who try to get up in two. The pin is likely to be placed well on the right or on the left so, ideally, the second shots, if the green is not in range, should be aimed slightly away from the pin.

## Hole 5: 210 yards, par-3

This is the hole closest to the Firth of Clyde where the prevailing wind blows in from the sea, from right to left, and on the left are three bunkers, in line, waiting to gobble up the ball. It requires a long iron shot to clear all the trouble and fly to the heart of the green. Although there are not too many problems, it is a hole where there are not likely to be too many birdies.

## Hole 6: 577 yards, par-5
This is the longest hole in British Championship golf. There is a bunker on the right which should not really come into play from the tee, but two on the left, the second of which encroaches into the fairway, are a real danger as the ground tends to throw the ball towards them. The tee shot should really be on the right half of the fairway. The second shot should be a fairway wood aimed slightly left to avoid a bunker on the right, ready for a soft pitch-in to an elongated narrow green, framed on three sides by large sand dunes. Beware the rough on the right of this hole – it is tiger country.

## Hole 7: 400 yards, par-4
Probably the best hole at Troon and one of the best at any Championship venue, it is a sharp dog-leg right with a huge sandhill in the corner. From the elevated tee it was possible for the long hitters to get over this hill and that is why a new tee has been built, some 30 yards to the left, to prevent this happening. There are bunkers on the left to catch anything slightly off line. Most of the pros still go a little left to give a clear view for a lofted iron shot to send the ball over a slight gully to a well-bunkered green nestling between two more sandhills.

## Hole 8: 126 yards, par-3
Not only does Troon have the longest hole in British Championship golf but also the shortest. And this is it, the famous Postage Stamp – the most difficult stamp in the world to lick. Gene Sarazen had a hole-in-one here during the 1973 Open but hundreds of others have come to grief and had their chances ruined. The tee is high up and there is a

gully full of trouble on the way to a very narrow green with a huge sandhill on the left and a crater bunker on the right approach. There is no safe way to play the hole. The ball must be flighted and find the green from the tee. Getting into any of the deep bunkers on either side could easily lead in going from one to the other. Mostly, this hole is a problem of the mind – what else with a green only 25 feet across at its widest point?

## Hole 9: 419 yards, par-4
The big problem on this hole occurs on the tee where the player has to make up his mind whether to try to carry the fairway bunkers at 240 yards or lay up short. There is heavy rough on both sides of an undulating fairway. The green used to be in a hollow almost straight down the fairway but has now been moved to slightly higher ground, well to the right, making the hole more of a dog-leg. It is essential that anyone laying up short with his drive is on the left of the fairway for a sight of part of the green. It is still a good 3-iron or 4-iron from there. In front of the green is a huge mound which shields most of the green from sight.

## Hole 10: 437 yards, par-4
Not the longest but probably the most difficult par-4 on the course. The tee is set low and the drive, of paramount importance, has to be long and straight up and over a range of sandhills in which a small depression has been cut. Any slight mistake from the tee is bound to end in trouble in impenetrable rough. Over the sandhills is the fairway. If the drive is correct to the iron it is no more that a 6-iron to the green. If it is ever so slightly wrong it is a 3-wood – a long raking shot to a plateau green which eats into a rise on the left and falls sharply to the right. This is the hole to un-nerve anyone building up a good score. A par here is good and many professionals will be glad to get away with a bogey.

## Hole 11: 481 yards, par-5
Fairly short as par-5's go but in the prevailing winds it plays every inch and is generally reckoned to be the toughest hole on the course. It must be played as a five. When Jack Nicklaus first played it he was lucky to escape with an 11. That was in 1962 and it still has not got any easier. A slightly off-line drive will find thick gorse on the left or the railway line, which runs the whole length of the hole, on the right. From there the fairway narrows to almost Indian file proportions and with the gorse and the railway line coming ever nearer as you

approach the little green, almost anything can happen. This has to be one of the toughest holes in Championship golf today.

## Hole 12: 432 yards, par-4
Back to comparative sanity and a conventional hole with plenty of scrub and rough on either side of a fairway that is at its narrowest where most drives will land. From a straight drive there are no real problems in the second shot to a guarded green which falls off left, down a bank, with a fairly deep bunker on the right. This is one hole where players

usually look for possible birdies to make up for the dropped shots on holes 10 and 11. The prevailing winds will cut the distance down and many pros take no more than a 7-iron for second shots.

## Hole 13: 468 yards, par-4
On this hole the drive has to be big and straight to give a chance of getting up in two. The ball is going to land on an undulating fairway and in dry weather, the bounce is in the lap of the gods. The main feature of the hole is the second shot played to an elevated green. There is an optical illusion which makes the

*Bobby Clampett was running away with the 1982 British Open at Troon after the first and second rounds until he reached this hole, the 6th, a 577 yards par-5, in his third round. He staggered off the green with an 8!*

green appear much closer than it actually is. Take one more club than you think for your approach. There are no traps but the ground falls away. This is the first of a straight run of six holes leading back towards the clubhouse and home, generally all against the prevailing winds.

**Hole 14: 180 yards, par-3**

Another devilish short hole with a narrow entrance, little more than two feet wide closely guarded by bunkers on both sides. It requires a well-struck and flighted shot to land in the centre of the green, clear of the trouble. Pin placement, as on many holes at Troon, can be all-important. There are two bunkers on the right and, really, players would be well-advised to go for the centre of the green and hope to sink a longish putt for their birdie rather than go for the pin.

**Hole 15: 457 yards, par-4**

This needs to be played as a long par-4. The drive has to be big and accurate. Before, it was possible to carry the solitary bunker on the left, the correct line into the green, but now there is a new bunker behind it. Now the player needs to go straight up the middle and, even then, after a good one, he is still faced with an accurate 3-iron or so to reach the green.

**Hole 16: 542 yards, par-5**

Care must be taken here not to drive too far into the burn, some 290 yards from the tee but anyone with pretensions of getting up in two has to be very close to it. The usual winds will make it impossible to reach the burn but when the wind turns round, it is definitely on. There is no trouble with the second shot when playing the hole as a par-5 but the green is very well protected by bunkers, five of them, with an additional one 30 yards short of the green on the right to catch anything short.

**Hole 17: 223 yards, par-3**

A real pressure hole which, in normal conditions will take as much as the player has in his bag. None of the short holes at Troon are easy and anyone walking off having completed all four in 12 strokes should be well-satisfied. The green here is like a hog's back, falling away on both sides from the centre, to sand traps on the left and right.

**Hole 18: 425 yards, par-4**

Sand traps just to the left and right of the fairway are designed to catch anything other than a deadly accurate straight drive. But once you leave the tee, having hit a good straight drive, the second shot is not difficult and any problem is all in the mind. There are bunkers short of the green to collect the mis-hits and there are bunkers to both sides of the green which lies immediately in front of the clubhouse. The advice here is to be bold and go for the heart of the green.

**Kilmarnock Barassie**, or the Barassie Course, is also at Troon, or very nearby. It started life in 1887 as the Kilmarnock Golf Club even though it is eight miles from the town of that name. It is sufficiently tough to be used as a qualifying course when the Open is held at Troon or Turnberry. But although some of the holes look deceptively easy, they are challenging nevertheless and Barassie is an ideal stop if you have difficulty getting a round at Troon, Turnberry or Prestwick. It has many devotees who return each year.

A relatively small club, Barassie is informal with a simple charm and plenty of atmosphere. Green fees are lower than those at its more illustrious neighbours, and visitors are welcome on Tuesdays and Thursdays, and after 10.30am on Mondays and Fridays (not at weekends or on Wednesdays).

**Western Gailes** is the adjoining course to Barassie – a fine links course measuring 6763 yards off the back tees. It was used as a qualifying course for the Open Championships of 1973, 1977 and 1982. But like all Scottish links courses, the weather plays an important part in a round of golf. When the wind blows from the south-west, the long stretch between the 6th and 13th holes is not only a trial of skill and strength but also something of an endurance test. A

*The 18th green and clubhouse at the splendid Western Gailes course – one of the best courses in the region*

well-balanced par-71 course, it has two par-5's, both over 500 yards, one in each half, and three par-3's.

Visiting golfers are welcome on weekdays, although they have to play with a member on Thursdays, but it is still preferable to write or telephone before you visit to avoid disappointment. However, there are no lady members and no ladies' tees although they can enter the clubhouse on certain specified days (but not on Tuesdays, Thursdays or Saturdays).

This is a club for golfers, not hackers. One of its most distinguished members, Lord Brabazon, once said: "If you have the time, play just three courses – Western Gailes, Prestwick and Turnberry".

If you are contemplating playing any of these local courses, there are many small and large hotels in the area that would serve as a comfortable base (see the Hotel Guide at the back of this book). There is a wide choice of

*Surprisingly, Brodick Golf Course on the beautiful Isle of Arran is not a links course although it follows the shoreline*

courses, all within easy driving distance of Prestwick Airport, and you will enjoy discovering them.

**Brodick, Blackwaterfoot** and **Lamlash** are all fine courses on the beautiful Isle of Arran in the shadow of the often snow-capped Goat Fell. You can reach Arran on the Hebridean and Clyde Ferries. You can take your car on this hour-long journey between Ardrossan on the mainland and Arran's picturesque port of Brodick. On board there are snack meals, a bar and hot drinks to while away the time. You can even complete the round-trip in a day and still enjoy a game of golf on Arran. The green fees at all seven clubs on the island are ridiculously cheap and make it well worth the visit apart from the natural beauty of the place.

Golf has been played at **Lamlash** since 1891 on this hilly 4681-yards, par-64 course. You will enjoy spectacular views of the coastline and Holy Island in front, and of the majestic mountains and Goat Fell behind. Dress and practice are more informal than at most clubs, and thus it is not surprising to see bare-chested male golfers, or visitors casually organising their own games, competitions and sweeps. They even do their own handicapping! So win a holiday medal and then play to your new handicap when you return home if you can! There are also a small bar and a public tea room in which you can relax after your game.

Nearby is the lovely coastal golf course of **Brodick**, just half a mile from the ferry terminal. The holes of the course follow the shoreline, but it is not a links course, the grass being of a different texture. One of the problems suffered by Brodick is the 6,000 tons of sand that are taken away each year from the adjoining beach, thus causing erosion of the land and ultimately threatening the 11th, 12th and 13th holes. You will be amazed to learn that this sand is being exported to the Middle East of all places!

However, you can still enjoy a great game of golf in superb surroundings on the 18-hole, par-62 course of 4404 yards. There a friendly clubhouse and bar, too.

The other courses on Arran are the 9-hole **Lochranza** course (flat, 1700 yards and par-29); **Machrie** (9 holes, flat, 2082 yards, par-32); **Corrie** (9 holes, 1948 yards, par-31 and picturesquely set in the mountains); **Whiting Bay** (18 holes, very hilly with tiny greens, 4405 yards and par-63); and, lastly, **Blackwaterfoot** – a beautiful 12-hole links course, over 3000 yards long and par-41.

**Greenock**, **Gourock**, **Largs** and **Largs Routenburn** and **Skelmorlie** are back on the mainland in the region around Largs. They are all welcoming and worthy of a visit. At **Skelmorlie**, just half a mile off the main road at Wemyss Bay, golf has been played since 1897. A hilly moorland-type course with a total yardage of 5056 and a Standard Scratch Score of 65, Skelmorlie has just 13 holes. However, you will need every club in your bag to play it. To get a full round in, you must play the first five holes twice. This sounds strange but works well in practice as the 5th green is at the side of the clubhouse. The 10th, 5th and 18th greens all have double pin placements, and Skelmorlie is probably unique in that it is the only course in the world where players have to tee up out of bounds on the short par-3 third hole.

Visitors are made very welcome indeed and are encouraged to join in the club's social events, including barbecues and discos. Green fees are higher at weekends than on weekdays but are still very reasonable. And there are fine views of the Argyllshire hills and over the Firth of Clyde to Arran.

*The 8th at Rothesay is just over 200 yards, all downhill. This makes the hole play shorter but increases club selection problems*

**Rothesay Golf Club** is just across the water on the Isle of Bute. You can get there by taking the ferry from the Wemyss Bay Ferry Terminal. The sea trip takes only 30 minutes and once there you can play on Rothesay's hilly course, a cross between moorland and heathland with plenty of trees and heather. This is a course to savour and enjoy, and the only trouble for players lurks at the back of the greens. The 5370-yard course, par-69, was opened in 1892 and is owned by Argyll and Bute District Council. Probably the best hole is the 8th 'Ardbranan', a 204-yard, par-3 hole, all downhill with spectacular views of the sea and the other islands beyond.

Rothesay is one of 10 clubs that compete annually for the Firth of Clyde Cup, the oldest amateur team trophy in the world, which was first played for in 1899. In the spacious clubhouse is a magnificent display of trophies including a silver submarine and the mounted Dunlop 4 golf ball with which HRH Edward, Prince of Wales, played the course on 17th June 1933. Nearby are several reasonably priced hotels to use as a base on Bute.

**Kingarth** and **Port Bannatyne** are the other two courses on the island, and again green fees are well below average. It is worth spending two or three days there to enjoy playing all the courses. While Port Bannatyne is a 13-hole course similar in style to Rothesay, the private 9-hole links course of Kingarth is often invaded by cattle!

**West Kilbride** is back on the mainland – a links course which is sandwiched between the main A78 road and the sea just south of Largs. Unlike many other links courses in the area, it is very flat and there are no huge dunes. However, it does have deceptively subtle undulations and the ever-present Westerly wind blowing inland off the sea in varying strengths creates other tests for the golfer. There are also 160 bunkers to contend with, although, strangely, no pot bunkers.

Accurate driving is essential, but if you are going to be wayward, be very wayward. This may sound like 'double Dutch' but a ball struck slightly off line is almost certainly going to end always in trouble. However, one well off line will probably end up more favourably positioned.

There are spectacular views of Arran and Goat Fell across the sea, and also to Cumbrae and even the Paps of Jura over the Mull of Kintyre. Green fees are reasonable and visitors are welcome during the week. At weekends, they can play only by invitation of a member.

**Largs Golf Club** is just up the road from West Kilbride. Although it is another course by the sea, it is more parkland than links. Accurate shots from the tee are essential on this type of course, and there are plenty of trees and a large number of dog-leg holes. Whereas the course is fairly flat, with slight undulations, there are hilly sections on the first and 17th holes. It measures 6257 yards off the back tees with a par and SSS of 70. There are three par-3s and one par-5 on the front nine and one of each on the back nine. Although the longest hole is only 496 yards, do not underestimate this course. One member who played regularly to a handicap of 10 moved away after eight years and in no time lowered his handicap to six, playing on a reputedly harder course. If you score well round Largs, you can be classed as a good golfer!

*Largs is a parkland-type course situated beside the sea. The comfortable clubhouse also offers snooker tables and indoor bowls*

Green fees are moderately priced and the club welcomes visitors so you can play any day of the week. It boasts a large comfortable bar, indoor bowls and snooker, so you can relax at the Clubhouse after your game. The holiday town of Largs is just down the road with many interesting leisure activities.

**Helensburgh** is not far from Largs as the crow flies, but, in fact, the two courses are separated by the mouth of the Clyde, which is too wide to span with a bridge. Therefore it takes the visitor at least two hours to drive almost all the way into Glasgow and then back out again to Helensburgh. If you are contemplating visiting this course, you might be well advised to use Glasgow as your base.

But do not avoid Helensburgh for this reason – on the contrary, it is well worth a visit. It is a hilly, moorland course and

after the short par-4 uphill 5th comes the 6th with its spectacular views of the Clyde and beyond to Loch Lomond, Scotland's longest freshwater loch (only 12 miles away). Green fees are moderately priced during the week, but visitors have to be introduced by and play with a member at weekends, although at a substantially reduced fee. After the Open Championship, Helensburgh runs a week-long festival of golf with a variety of competitions for men, ladies, seniors and boys. These are open to everyone and if you are interested in entering you should write to the Club Secretary for an application form (see the list of addresses at the back of the book).

From the clubhouse window you can see the island that is Ardmore Point, now used as a bird sanctuary in the

*Dunaverty is only some 4500 yards long, but it still offers you a challenging test of your golfing skills*

Firth of Clyde. While just across the water are the courses of Gourock and Greenock. Further to the south towards Glasgow are the 18-hole courses of Dumbarton and Cardross, both with low-priced green fees and well worth playing. To visit all these courses, you need not go by car or sea. You could experiment with a more exciting way to travel – a 16-seater deHavilland Otter twin-engined plane. These planes are operated out of Glasgow Airport by Loganair. Flying at a height of about a par-5, it is exhilarating and very speedy, and there are excellent aerial views of the courses themselves and the surrounding countryside and coastline.

**Dunaverty Golf Club** is 20 miles from Campbeltown on Kintyre, immortalized by the McCartney song 'Mull of Kintyre' (Paul McCartney owns a farmhouse nearby). Near the town of Southend, Dunaverty got its name from a rock on which the MacDonalds once had a castle. However, they were overrun and beaten by the Campbells who established Campbeltown in 1682.

From its roots in 1889, the course has evolved into a mixture of heathland, moorland and links. It is quite Spartan compared to many other Scottish courses and the building that passes for a clubhouse is little more than a wooden shack without even a bar! The members, however, willingly undertake projects such as building a verandah round the clubhouse, repairing bridges on the course and cutting the greens themselves. Green fees, not surprisingly, are very low indeed.

The course itself measures 4597 yards, par-64. It has been played by some great golfers and probably its most notable present-day big name is Belle Robertson who has been made a life member and whose picture hangs in the clubhouse.

The narrow peninsula of Kintyre itself is almost tropical in appearance with palm trees and not so badly off weatherwise as you might believe. The Gulf Stream passes close by and keeps the temperature up all the year round. After playing the course, you can take time off to drive the short distance to the local spot where St Columba landed on his way from Northern Ireland to bring Christianity to Iona and the rest of Britain. His footsteps are embedded in a sandstone rock.

**Machrihanish** is the real jewel of golf in this part of Scotland and one of the best Scottish courses. The famous 6228-yards links course is about 12 miles away on the other side of Kintyre and if it were more accessible it would be the perfect venue for a tour event, maybe even the Open Championship itself. However, you must visit it for the golf and may end up staying longer than you planned.

The tee for the first hole is right outside the professional's shop, separated from the clubhouse by the 'main' road which carries hardly any traffic! The drive at this slightly dog-legged 423 yards par-4 is across a sand and shingle bay to a wide expanse of fairway and then on to a semi-plateau of a green.

*The 6th on a fine day at Machrihanish – but the winds can be blustery*

From then on until the 15th you will be just itching to play every hole. They are all gems and although there are a few blind shots both from the tee and the fairway, the challenge does not lessen. It really is a course to remember and one that you will long to play again. The only disappointment is the finishing holes, the 16th being an average par-3, 233-yarder and the last two holes, both par-4s, not quite belonging on the same course as the first fifteen. In the club-house you are quickly made at home and there are very reasonably priced beautifully cooked meals.

**Islay Golf Club**, home of the Machrie golf course, is another unexpected gem. You can reach the island of Islay by Loganair from Glasgow, the flight taking only about 35 minutes. Islay is the place to go if you like malt whisky.

In fact, a little Islay malt is added to practically every big-name blended whisky the world over. Nowadays the number of distilleries has dwindled to a mere half dozen. When you visit the island, take in a trip around one of these distilleries to see the real malt being made in the time-honoured way.

Steeped in history, Islay was once the seat of government for MacDonald, Lord of the Isles. The land was divided into large plots under the ownership of the clans and there were several battles between MacDonald and the King of Scotland. Earlier still, the Norse king Godred had his home on Islay in the sixth century. On the hill on which his settlement was built, there stands a stone monument.

Golf did not arrive on Islay until 1891 when the course was laid out by Willie Campbell. A true links course in every sense, all Campbell had to do was decide where to put the 18 little holes. The sheep in the adjoining fields show where the bunkers came from – hollowed out resting places away from the winds that lash the island in winter.

The course is situated on the west side of the island, skirting the shore of Laggan Bay and the Atlantic Ocean. The first thing that the visitor notices is the freshness and clearness of the air. Even Trevino would not be troubled by 36 holes a day in such an atmosphere. Although it is only a modest 5210 yards in length, it has many blind shots and breaking 90 at the first time of playing is quite an achievement. You will want to play it again and improve on this score,

*The 17th green at Machrie on the historic Isle of Islay, world-famous for its whisky distilleries, which you can still visit*

of course!

The first hole is a straightforward 308 yards, par-4 and may lull the unsuspecting visitor into a false sense of security only to have his illusions shattered at the second, which is a long dog-leg par-5 requiring a drive over the corner of a burn and fence which marks the out of bounds on the left. This out of bounds continues the whole length of the fairway to an elevated green, the ground rising steadily from about 120 yards short. From then on, with many blind shots, every hole is a challenge and some of the huge dunes have to be seen to be believed. If this course was situated on the mainland you might get crushed in the rush to play on it, such are its attractions. It is pure enjoyment to play and a pity in some respects that it has been unknown for so long.

You can stay at the adjoining Machrie

Hotel where all sorts of packages are available in the hotel itself and adjacent cottages – write to the hotel for a price list (see the addresses section at the back of this book). Green fees are low but free to hotel and cottage guests. At the hotel you can dine on delicious fresh local seafood. And if you want a rest from golf, you can go fishing – either to catch brown trout in one of the five local lochs, or sea angling. There are also excellent salmon fishing, local distilleries to visit, hill trails and paths to explore and the island is an ornithologist's dream. Do not be deterred from visiting Islay by tales of dismal weather. During the summer months, temperatures can be high and rainfall low, even when it is raining on the mainland. Yes, it is unpredictable but it can be hot, sunny and dry in the islands.

**Colonsay** and **Vaul** are even further afield on more westerly islands if you are truly adventurous and can be reached by ferry. Whereas on Mull in the Western Isles, there is the 9-hole course of Tobermory and another 9 holes at Craignure.

*This view shows the 10th green at Machrie set in an area of great natural beauty. It may be modest in length but it is enjoyable*

**Glasgow Golf Club** at Killermont back on the mainland is the eighth oldest club in the world, having been founded in 1787. The club has a second course, Glasgow Gailes, which is 35 miles away! This course adjoins Western Gailes and is a true links course. It exists on its own as a separate club as well as being a sort of annexe for the main club at Killermont. Neither club has lady members and although women can play the courses there are few facilities on offer to them.

The Killermont course is set in magnificent parkland only three miles from the city centre. There is plenty of room for sprayed shots in the 5970-yard, par-70 layout, and the course is kept in pristine condition by the dedicated green staff. Although members' guests are always welcome, as a casual visitor you should write to the Secretary seeking permission to play there. Even on the Gailes course where rules are less strict, you are advised to belong to one

of the visiting parties rather than turning up as an individual.

The clubhouse at Killermont is a magnificent building which was once a stately home owned by the Stark family. Stylish and comfortable, it has elegant restaurants and a bar. It is difficult to realise that Glasgow itself is so close when you are surrounded by such quiet elegance.

**Hagg's Castle** is another fine parkland course in Glasgow and home of the PGA's European Tour's Glasgow Classic. It is well worth a visit and many of the Tour's stars speak highly of this course. There are 20 courses within the city's outer boundary which are all easily accessible by the excellent motorway and road network. The other private courses in Glasgow are **Pollok, Ralston, Sandyhills** and **Williamwood**. There are no visiting restrictions however at the city's public courses – **Alexandra Park, Deaconsbank, King's Park, Knightswood, Lethamhill, Linn Park, Littlehill** and **Ruchill**. The choice is endless in this part of Scotland and the welcome genuine and warm.

## Key to map

1 Portpatrick (18)
2 Stranraer (18)
3 Wigtonshire & County (9)
4 St. Medan (9)
5 Wigton & Bladnoch (9)
6 Newton Stewart (9)
7 New Galloway (9)
8 Gatehouse of Fleet (9)
9 Kirkcudbright (18)
10 Castle Douglas (9)
11 Dalbeatie (9)
12 Colvend (9)
13 Southerness (18)
14 Powfoot (18)
15 Dumfries & Galloway (18)
   Dumfries & County (18)
   Crichton Royal (9)
16 Lochmaben (9)
17 Lockerbie (9)
18 Langholm (9)
19 Thornhill (18)
20 Newcastleton (9)
21 Moffat (18)
22 Biggar (18)
23 Carnwarth (18)
24 West Linton (18)
25 Penicuik (18)
26 West Calder (18)
27 Fauldhouse (18)
28 Whitburn (9)
29 Bathgate (18)
30 Polmont (9)
31 Grangemouth (18)
32 Bo'Ness (18)
33 Linlithgow (18)
34 Uphall (18)
35 Livingston (18)
36 Pumpherston (9)

37 South Queensferry (9)
38 Edinburgh:
   Baberton (18)
   Braids 1 (18)
   Braids 2 (18)
   Broomieknowe (18)
   Bruntsfield (18)
   Carrick Knowe (18)
   Craigentinny (18)
   Craigmillar Park (18)
   Duddingston (18)
   Kingsknowe (18)
   Liberton (18)
   Lothianburn (18)
   Merchants of Edinburgh
   (18)
   Mortonhall (18)
   Murrayfield (18)
   Portobello (9)
   Prestonfield (18)
   Ravelston (9)
   Royal Burgess (18)
   Silverknowes (18)
   Swanston (18)
   Torphin Hill (18)
   Turnhouse (18)
39 Ratho Park (18)
40 Dalmahoy East (18)
   Dalmahoy West (18)
41 Musselburgh Old Links (9)
42 Monktonhall (18)
43 Dalkeith (18)
44 Royal Musselburgh (18)
45 Longniddry (18)
46 Kilspindie (18)
   Luffness New (18)
47 Gullane 1 (18)
   Gullane 2 (18)
   Gullane 3 (18)
   Muirfield (18)

48 North Berwick East (18)
   Burgh Links West (18)
49 Dunbar (18)
   Dunbar Winterfield (18)
50 Eyemouth (9)
51 Haddington (18)
52 Gifford (9)
53 Duns (9)
54 Coldstream (9)
55 Kelso (18)
56 Jedburgh (9)
57 Hawick (18)
58 Minto (9)
59 Selkirk (9)
60 St Boswells (9)
61 Melrose (9)
62 Galashiels (18)
   Torwoodlee (9)
63 Lauder (9)
64 Peebles (18)
65 Innerleithen (9)

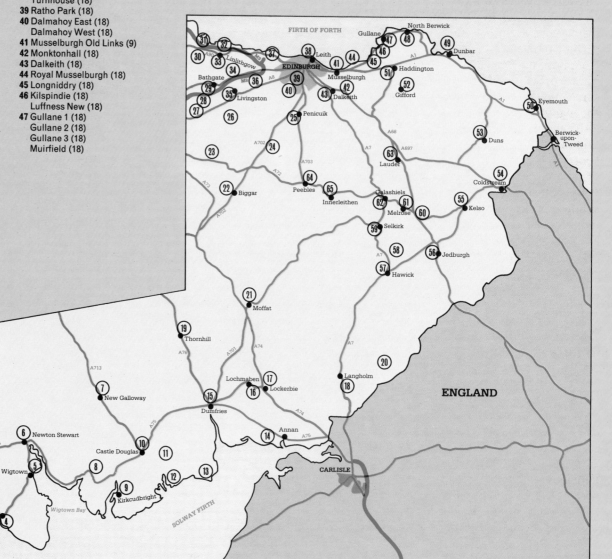

# The Borders, Lothian, Dumfries and Galloway

Until they get to know this region of Scotland and the superb golf on offer, many touring golfers plump instead for the known glories of the Western coast and Isles or the tranquillity and beauty of the Highlands with its great coastal links and inland moorland courses. However, what few people realise is that this is classic golf country with some fine courses and some of the friendliest people you could ever hope to meet. You should never bypass this part of Scotland on your drive northwards to the glamorous big Championship courses.

The Borders, with its rolling hill country and beautiful valleys cut out of the landscape by the winding River Tweed and its many tributaries, are steeped in history and tradition. The area has had a turbulent past when marauding bands from both north and south of the border between Scotland and England fought some bloody battles and laid waste to the many castles and abbeys. The area is also famous for its excellent trout and salmon fishing, and there are many sports and leisure activities on offer for visitors in the beautiful Border country. It has golf courses in abundance and you should not be put off by the fact that the majority are nine-hole layouts. Many are real golfing gems and can even be played as 18 holes by the use of additional tees.

**Peebles** is situated almost in the centre of this golfing region and is a good place to start your tour as it is reasonably close to Edinburgh and its fine surrounding courses. The municipal course is only a few minutes' walk from the town centre but it gently climbs its way up into the hills overlooking the town. Thus its 6137 yards offers some spectacular panoramic views of the Borders landscape. There is enough challenge for golfers of all standards to enjoy a game, and it is a popular course with visitors.

Although the course was first laid out in 1908 by James Braid, it has subsequently undergone numerous changes. Green fees are relatively low – very reasonable indeed if you purchase a special seven-day ticket or stay at the nearby Hydro Hotel which offers its residents a reduction in fees. The licensed clubhouse has a bar and also caters for lunches and teas. Like nearly all of the Scottish courses, you should book in advance although the only restrictions to visitors apply during times of competition.

**Innerleithen** is a nine-hole course situated on the main road between Peebles and Galashiels. However, it can still offer the visitor an enjoyable game of golf. Measuring just under 3000 yards, green fees are inevitably modest, and you collect your starting ticket either from the greenkeeper or from Smail's Shop in the High Street!

**Galashiels** boasts two courses – the 18-hole municipal **Ladhope** course which is but a stone's throw from the town, and the nine-hole **Torwoodlee** course which is a couple of miles out of town on the main road to Edinburgh.

Many of the Ladhope greens are perched precariously on the hillside with some very steep inclines. However, the smaller Torwoodlee layout runs along beside Gala Water through some beautiful flat parkland. Its sheer natural beauty makes it worth a visit. Green fees are low and there is a pleasant clubhouse with full catering facilities.

**Selkirk** is a few miles down the A7 to the south of Galashiels. The course dominates the old town and the surrounding hillside. Another nine-holer, its 2780 yards provide spectacular views and wonderful value – the green fees are very reasonable indeed. Tickets are available from the greenkeeper or the clubhouse when open. Otherwise you pay by means of an honesty box on this pleasant course which celebrated its centenary in 1983.

**Hawick** on the A7 to the south of Selkirk is the centre of the world-famous Scottish woollen industry with such great names in golfing sweaters as Lyle & Scott, Pringle, Braemer and Barrie all located within the town's boundaries. Hawick Golf Club was founded back in 1877 and the original nine-hole course was designed by Robert Purdom. A fine clubhouse and an additional nine holes were completed in 1920, and now the club has an active membership.

The spectacular 5929 yards course is built on and around Vertish Hill and you might be forgiven for thinking that you had entered mountain goat country. However, although the inclines look ferocious, they are gentler when you come to play them and spiked shoes, rather than crampons, are sufficient. The inclines criss-cross the hill itself and you will find a stunning view when you eventually reach the top. Almost all the holes are memorable but the downhill par-4 16th is particularly good as

you are tempted to fly the ball to the green. Miss the putting surface at your peril, as the hole's name – the 'Pit' – warns you of the dangers awaiting you.

Local knowledge really is beneficial when you play this course. If you play with a regular you may find that he deliberately puts his first shot short of the green on the 210 yards 18th, and then proceeds to chip up onto a slope at the back of the putting surface. The ball is then ideally placed to skirt around the top, roll back down onto the green and disappear neatly into the hole.

There is a clubhouse which offers a wide range of catering facilities, and green fees are very low – possibly the best value for money in the area.

**Minto**, a few miles to the north of Hawick, is another 18-hole course set in pleasant parkland surroundings. The gently undulating course is 5460 yards long and from the first tee you drive straight across a fence to the open land beyond. Again, green fees are low, and there is a clubhouse which can even cater for parties by prior arrangement.

*On top of the world – the 16th at Hawick with the town below. This club had one of the first club histories published*

**Jedburgh** is nearby with its nine-hole course. It is only a mile outside the town on the main road which passes the old Jedburgh Castle. Built on the side of a hill, the course measures 2764 yards and is relatively open with little to trouble the odd wayward shot. Although the clubhouse bar is open only at weekends, Jedburgh still offers an enjoyable round of golf and low green fees.

**St Boswells** is further to the north again. The lovely nine-hole course is only a mile down the road from the ruined abbey and is set amid pictures-que hills close to the running waters of the River Tweed, which stretch the length of the course. It is a peaceful setting for a quiet round of golf. Apart from the downhill 1st hole, the remain-der of the course is flat with few hazards to worry you. At only 2527 yards the green fees are almost unbelievably low, and you can obtain tickets from Laing

the newsagents in town or by putting money in the honesty box in the club-house. This is an informal, friendly part of the world.

**Melrose**, three miles further north, is the setting for a pretty nine-hole course and a ruined abbey where Robert the Bruce's heart is reputed to be buried. This fine course, like many others in the area, is laid out on a hillside and, again, green fees are low, the club is welcom-ing to visitors and the course is un-crowded at most times.

**Duns** is another nine-holer situated on the outskirts of the ancient Burgh of Duns which used to be the old county town of Berwick County. On the edge of the Lammermuir Hills the course has fine views of the valley below and is open all the year round. There is a licensed clubhouse and green fees are relatively low.

**Eyemouth** on the east coast of the Borders is worth a visit as it offers wonderful sea views and a relatively flat course – a welcome relief after the climbing involved on the hillside courses!

The compact nine-hole 2748 yards layout is open all the year round to visitors with restrictions only on competition days.

**Dunbar** in East Lothian is a picturesque fishing village with two clubs – the lesser known **Dunbar Winterfield Golf Club** and the older, more famous **Dunbar Golf Club** which is one of the finest links in Scotland and a superb test of golf for golfers of any standard. The former course was built in the 1930s and is a short but enjoyable 5200 yards, whereas the latter was founded in 1856 and now measures 6441 yards off the back tees. It is laid out on a narrow strip of land bordering the North Sea and stretches out for what seems like an eternity until you turn for home after the 10th hole. A stone wall runs along the entire course and there are spectacular views of Bass Rock out at sea.

The club has hosted many championships over the years, including the Scottish Amateur and Professional and British Boys championships. The natural links are legendary in golfing circles for the testing holes, sea views and the force of the wind.

Opening with two par-5's followed by a short, slightly downhill par-3 back to the clubhouse, you then pass through the Old Deer Park Wall, playing the next 14 holes by the shoreline. The 9th at 514 yards is one of the best holes on the course needing a drive to an elevated fairway on the left. Beware of the unsighted trouble down the right which can leave you dead and gone. The second shot must be played down the right side leaving you with a tricky pitch to a long green. The best hole on the course is the 464 yards, par-4 12th with the shore by your right-hand side throughout the hole. Here you are faced with a long drive and an even tougher second shot, especially into the wind, because the fairway doglegs round to

the right, often forcing you to play a precarious shot across the beach. With a stiff breeze against, you have to play the hole as a par-5. Finally the 18th at 441 yards is a tough and fitting finishing hole with out-of-bounds to the right over the wall and thick rough down the left-hand side.

The course has a fully licensed clubhouse with good catering facilities. As well as lunches and snacks, you can eat breakfast and dinner, too. Visitors are made welcome at this friendly club and the green fees are still reasonable although higher at weekends than during the week. However, even so it is recommended that you book ahead, especially if you are organizing a party.

**Gifford** is a uniquely challenging nine-hole course not far from Dunbar. One of its great attractions is the woodland setting with the Lammermuir Hills

*The River Tweed beyond the 1st green at St Boswells. The hole plays downhill*

close by. It has beautiful rolling fairways, well manicured greens, grass bunkers and a burn which has to be negotiated on four holes. Although it is not a long course, the greens are difficult to hit, quick to play and hard to read. The two closing holes are excellent: the 8th at 403 yards demanding that you carry the burn with your second shot; and the final par-5 hole where you drive back over the burn and then thread through the cross bunkers guarding the way towards the green just in front of the charming little clubhouse.

The course is always open to visitors and a round will cost only a modest green fee. Juniors are charged even less. If you find yourself travelling through this part of East Lothian, you should not miss out on the opportunity to try this unusual course. It is worth the diversion.

**North Berwick**, further up the coast from Dunbar, has two courses: the East

and West links. The East is a shorter layout at 6079 yards, whereas the West is famous throughout the world. Measuring 6317 yards, it is no monster in length but such is its trickery that it demands a full repertoire of shot-making from even the most accomplished golfer.

Every hole here is memorable – in fact, two of them, the 382 yards 14th named 'Perfection', and the 192 yards 15th called 'Redan' have been copied at courses the world over. You almost feel as though you are stepping back in time as you tackle the course's little idiosyncrasies. There are blind shots, drives over walls and burns, shots across the bay and bunkers from which you can disappear from view. So this is how golf

used to be played – it is an enjoyable experience, great fun and a real test of skill which will leave you with the feeling of wanting to come back and play again.

Founded in 1832, North Berwick Club is one of the oldest and most distinguished clubs in Britain. A former British Prime Minister, Lord Balfour, was captain of the club from 1891–92. Play here and you will tackle a classic natural links extending alongside the Forth Estuary with nine holes out and nine holes back. Visitors are always welcome and green fees are still modestly priced.

A good place to stay is at the Marine Hotel which overlooks the course and the spectacular coastline with views

across the sea to Bass Rock. Be sure to book the course as well as the hotel in advance as it may get crowded in the busy summer months.

**Muirfield** is another celebrated course, only five miles onwards down the road to Edinburgh. This is hallowed turf indeed, and it belongs to the Honourable Company of Edinburgh Golfers. This historic links course has hosted numerous Open Championships but it is still a very private club. Rules are strict and visitors must play either with a member or write to the secretary for

*No architect would get his fee if he designed the West Course at North Berwick today – but it is great fun to play*

*Dusk at North Berwick. Its most famous hole, the Redan, has probably been more imitated than any other golf hole but Perfection is not far behind*

permission. Male golfers must belong to a recognised Golf Club with a handicap of no more than 18. Ladies must have a handicap of 24 or less but have to be accompanied by a gentleman golfer. If your heart is set on playing there, a letter of introduction from your own club might prove useful. Write to the Secretary for details, but be prepared to be charged some exceptionally high green fees for the privilege of playing there.

The outer and inner loops of the course add interest and it is a hefty 6601 yards off the Medal Tees with a par of 70. In 1987, the Open Championship will have been staged at Muirfield 12 times with such well-known winners over the years as Harry Vardon, James Braid, Henry Cotton, Gary Player, Jack Nicklaus, Lee Trevino and Tom Watson. Opened back in 1891, the unusual course design consists of the first nine holes being arranged in a circular shape round the boundaries of the club, with the back nine forming an inner circle.

Bunkers abound almost everywhere and it has been said that there is one for every day of the year. However, in reality, there are only 151! The 19th hole is, of course, the Clubhouse which requires a jacket and tie to be worn at all times in public rooms. There, you can eat lunch or afternoon tea.

Muirfield was the scene of the 1987 British Open with a British winner in Nick Faldo who won despite the appalling weather conditions – gale-force winds, driving rain and mist. All the golfing stars have always held Muirfield in the highest esteem. Tom Watson once said that there was "not a weak hole on the course", and even Jack Nicklaus himself said of Muirfield that: "You can see where you are going and you get what you hit." In fact, Nicklaus admires the course so much that he named his own Ohio course 'Muirfield Village' after it.

One of Muirfield's outstanding features is its turf which is very fine and tends to dry out quickly as it lies on top of pure sand. It is the perfect links course where you will have to play an iron instead of a driver from the tees on over one-third of the holes (Nicklaus only used his driver 17 times in 72 holes in the 1966 Open). The first and last holes are some of the toughest and best. According to Nicklaus, the 449-yards, par-4 1st "is as tough an opening hole as there is anywhere in championship golf". The left of the fairway is dominated by one of the many large bunkers for which Muirfield is notorious. The 2nd and 3rd holes are both par-4's, but the par-3 4th hole which is only 181 yards is littered with bunkers and more shots are dropped here than on any other hole on the course.

The par-5 5th hole at 558 yards is a candidate for birdies, whichever way the wind happens to be blowing. One of

*The 5th at Muirfield. During the 1987 Open, the hole had to be shortened because players could not reach the fairway. This par-5 is the longest hole on the course*

Muirfield's most difficult tee shots is the par-4 6th with a split-level fairway. To avoid a blind shot to the green, you must place the ball on the right-hand side of the fairway. After the par-3, 185-yards 7th, there follow three really challenging holes which will influence your overall score and make or break your game if you are not careful. No less than 12 bunkers guard the par-4 8th and your drive needs to be right on target to escape them. The classic 9th that follows is a treacherous par-5 with a bunker concealed in the middle of a fairway and an out-of-bounds wall running along the left side. Things do not improve at the 10th either where you must drive accurately between the rough on the left and the bunkers on the right if you are not to drop valuable shots.

The 11th is a par-4 with good views of Edinburgh in the distance and across the Firth of Forth. As usual, the green lies seductively within a semi-circle of bunkers. The 12th hole looks deceptively simple but even here things can go wrong and you must keep to the left on your approach shot to the green. You can lose ground on the 13th which Nicklaus regards as a golfing gem. The narrow green is lined on both sides with bunkers and although this is only a

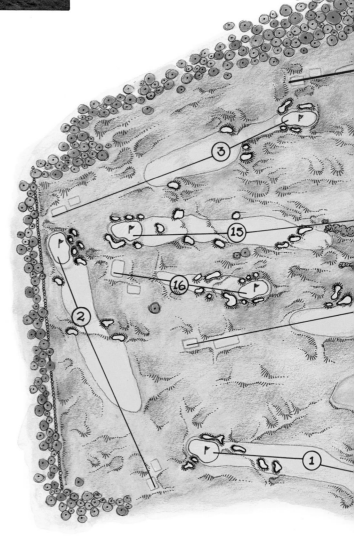

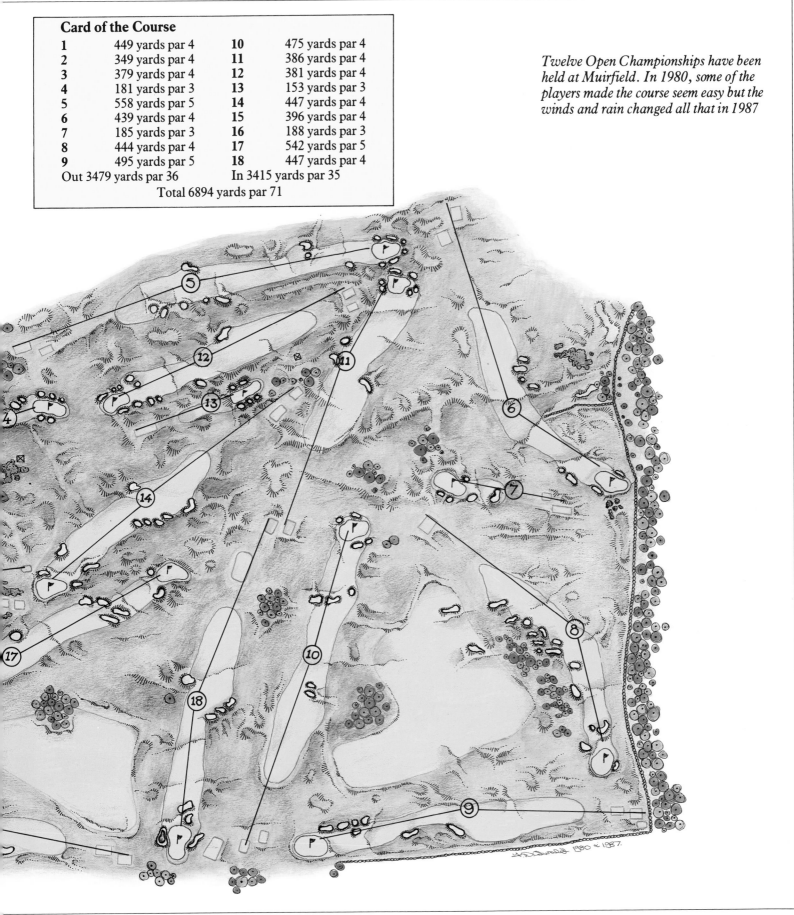

## Card of the Course

| | | | | |
|---|---|---|---|---|
| **1** | 449 yards par 4 | | **10** | 475 yards par 4 |
| **2** | 349 yards par 4 | | **11** | 386 yards par 4 |
| **3** | 379 yards par 4 | | **12** | 381 yards par 4 |
| **4** | 181 yards par 3 | | **13** | 153 yards par 3 |
| **5** | 558 yards par 5 | | **14** | 447 yards par 4 |
| **6** | 439 yards par 4 | | **15** | 396 yards par 4 |
| **7** | 185 yards par 3 | | **16** | 188 yards par 3 |
| **8** | 444 yards par 4 | | **17** | 542 yards par 5 |
| **9** | 495 yards par 5 | | **18** | 447 yards par 4 |

Out 3479 yards par 36   In 3415 yards par 35

Total 6894 yards par 71

*Twelve Open Championships have been held at Muirfield. In 1980, some of the players made the course seem easy but the winds and rain changed all that in 1987*

*Bunkering is the greatest feature at Muirfield. The one on the 12th needs a good shot just to escape from it*

par-3 some people find difficulty in extricating themselves in less than five shots!

After the 14th where many pros manage to birdie the hole, comes the par-4 15th. This hole has been lengthened by a new back tee to 417 yards. Together with a new right-hand bunker, this has had the effect of tightening up what used to be one of the course's less demanding tee shots. However, birdies are still possible. The 16th is notable for its numerous bunkers and the 'sea' of rough. The long par-5 17th has achieved fame because of the 1972 battle between Tony Jacklin and Lee Trevino who sank a difficult chip from the back of the green against the lie of the grass to win the Open Championship.

The last hole is a great one and a fitting finish for one of the world's best Championship courses. This par-4 of 447 yards caught out the great Gary Player in 1959 when he had a six but he still managed to win the Open by two strokes.

To play at Muirfield is one of every golfer's most memorable golfing experiences. The course and the clubhouse evoke the hallowed traditions of the past and the club's glorious history.

**Gullane**, a little further down the road towards Edinburgh, has three courses – No. 1, No. 2 and No. 3. You will have a new golfing experience as you are confronted by courses from all sides. Golf has been played here for over two centuries, with official records showing that the East Lothian Golf Club played over the Gullane Hill in 1854.

The toughest of all the courses is probably Gullane No. 1, a real test in a stiff breeze at 6461 yards. It has been used for the pre-qualifying rounds of the Open Championship on a number of occasions which gives you some idea of its testing nature. No. 2 is a little shorter

*At Muirfield's 7th (above) any shot off-line will be trapped, whereas this bunker at the 18th (left) is almost unique*

and slightly easier at 6021 yards, while No. 3, even though it is only 5079 yards, still requires a high degree of skill and accuracy if it is to be negotiated safely. Between these three courses is as wide a variety of links golf as you could wish to find. Green fees are quite moderately priced, especially on the No. 2 and No. 3 courses.

**Luffness New** is just down the road from Gullane and it is a friendly, peaceful club. It is a comparatively flat links course which calls for accurate driving and strong approach shots. The greens are quick and difficult to read while the bunkers are placed very cunningly – likewise the penal rough! All in all, this course is a test to your ability and self-perceptions as a golfer.

The first two holes are rather generous and should not cause too many problems for the experienced club golfer. However, after this the course starts to hot up and get more interesting. The 9th, in particular, a par-4 of 425 yards, is a great hole with a tough drive onto the edge of a downslope with thick rough threatening down the sides. In a slight breeze, playing this to par will take everything that you have got.

As for the second nine, there is not one weak hole among them. The two par-3's are of medium length but tricky to play within regulation figures, and the remaining seven par-4's are all fine tests demanding great accuracy in getting close to the pins.

It might not be the longest course that you will encounter in this part of Scotland but it is a real delight to play, and if the wind blows hard, the course

*Some rate Gullane Number One, the championship course, the superior of its more famous neighbour, Muirfield*

becomes a monster. Its credentials are spoken for when you realise that it has been used as an Open Championship pre-qualifying course on a number of occasions.

In the friendly clubhouse only double measures of spirits are served but jackets and ties are compulsory. If you would like to play on this course, you should obtain a letter of introduction from your own Club Secretary or write in advance.

**Kilspindie** Golf Club in Aberlady is literally across the road from Luffness New and the two clubs have long been friendly rivals. When the club first opened in 1898, the members had to

have their wits about them when they played to cross a rifle range! This is borne out by some of the holes' dangerous sounding names including 'The Target' and 'The Magazine'. This is a relatively short course at 5423 yards but nevertheless it has gained a reputation for itself that stretches far beyond the county boundaries.

Visitors always enjoy playing the links course, especially lady golfers; the facilities are excellent, and green fees on the low side.

**Longniddry** Golf Club is situated further down the coast road towards Edinburgh. Since it was founded in 1922, it has played host to a number of notable tournaments. Although you might like to call it a links course, because of its proximity to the nearby Firth of Forth, in fact the grass is so lush that it tends to resemble an inland course. There are also more trees than you would expect to find on a links course of 6240 yards with every hole enjoying a sea view. It is well worth a visit and you can play here without an introduction. However, like most other superb courses in the region you are well advised to make an advanced booking by contacting the starter. You can play on any day of the week for a reasonable fee, and enjoy another British Open qualifying course.

**Musselburgh Links,** perhaps the first proper course on which golf was played, are the last stage before you enter the city boundaries of Edinburgh. The early records show that golf was played here

*Luffness has some of the best greens in the British Isles. Golfers have been known to visit to regain their touch.*

as long ago as 1672 – maybe even earlier. In fact, it was only a short distance away near Seton that Mary Queen of Scots is reputed to have played.

Although the historic nine-hole links fell into disrepair long ago, a Heritage Trust has been formed in an effort to restore the course to its former glory. The course, which is the former home of three of Scotland's most famous clubs – the Honourable Company of Edinburgh Golfers, the Bruntsfield Links Golfing Society and the Edinburgh Burgess Golfing Society – is now presided over by the East Lothian District Council and is open to the public at all times apart from when race meetings are held on the surrounding race track. The amazingly low green fees make Musselburgh the bargain of the century. However, the course really comes into

its own and lives up to its fearsome reputation when the wind is blowing.

**Royal Musselburgh** can be found on the outskirts of the town on the road back to Prestonpans. Officially opened in 1926 and laid out by the great James Braid, the course now runs to 6284 yards. It is an attractive and interesting course, set in splendid parkland with many fine trees. The club is guaranteed to give visitors a warm welcome.

**Monktonhall** lies a mile south of Musselburgh town on the road to Dalkeith. This is another course designed by James Braid (in 1938) and it is set out on gently rolling terrain against a backdrop of woods. Bordered by the River Esk, the course is quite heavily wooded thanks to a tree planting operation in the 1950s and 1960s, and it now stands

at 6620 yards. Visitors are welcome throughout the year and the reasonably priced green fees are higher at weekends.

**Newbattle** Golf Club on Abbey Road is further down the road to Dalkeith. It is a pleasant enough test at 6012 yards but you should beware of the River Esk which can come into play on the 2nd and 17th holes. Visitors are usually welcome apart from weekends and public holidays, so check in advance if you are contemplating including this course in your itinerary.

**Edinburgh,** the great capital city of Scotland, has no less than 28 golf courses within its boundaries offering a wide variety of challenges to test golfers of all abilities. However, it is a popular destination for golfers and holidaymakers alike and gets very crowded in the summer months, particularly during the renowned Edinburgh Festival, so it is important to book hotel accommodation and your golf in advance of your visit to avoid disappointment. You would be well advised to invest in a street guide such as the Bartholomews pocket book guide to find your way around the city and between the courses. Another useful publication is *Capital golf* which is published by the City of Edinburgh and lists more than 35 courses.

**Dalmahoy Country Club** is just one of Edinburgh's beautiful courses. Set at the foot of the Pentland Hills only seven miles south-west from Edinburgh on the A71, it is only three miles from the airport and ideally situated for the visitor. This wonderful sporting complex is set in 1100 acres of rolling

*Prestonfield's parkland course lies within Edinburgh's city limits below some gorse covered mounds – Arthur's Seat*

wooded countryside. Apart from two great golf courses, there are also three squash courts, horse-riding, trout fishing, clay pigeon shooting and archery. There is even a sauna and a solarium.

If you feel like treating yourself to some enjoyable self-indulgence, then stay at magnificent Dalmahoy House which was completed in 1725 for the thirteenth Earl of Morton. It is now owned by the twenty second Earl and his Countess, and is a luxurious place to stay while you play.

The real experience, however, is to play golf here, especially on the 6664 yards par-72 East course which has been the venue for many major tournaments. Created by James Braid in 1927, it is a great test with well manicured quick greens, good tees and fairways, which are meticulously maintained in excellent condition.

One hole to watch out for is the 423

*Mrs Forman's at Musselburgh, the historic course which has hosted six early Open Championships*

yards 7th, which demands a very tight tee shot with trees and a lake down the right-hand side. Hit a good drive and you are still left with a formidable second shot, over a quarry, to the green itself.

The majority of the holes are memorable with some exacting par-3's and, no doubt, when the wind blows it can be a very exacting course indeed. However, in good condition, you have a good chance for low scoring as can be seen by

*The clubhouse at Dalmahoy is one of the most splendid in British golf. There is superb parkland golf on the two courses*

the course record of 62 which was shot by Brian Barnes during a Haig Tournament Players' Championship. The course is usually open to visitors, but a time sheet is normally in operation so try and book up in advance.

The West course is slightly shorter at 5212 yards but still offers an enjoyable challenge. You can get professional coaching, and hire clubs and buggies if wished. And there is excellent seven-days-a-week catering on offer back at the clubhouse.

**Ratho Park** is a mere five minutes' drive away down the A71 back in the direction of Edinburgh. This splendid parkland course was designed by James Braid in 1928 and stretches to 6028 yards. There are no restrictions on visitors here, green fees are moderately priced and catering is available every day. The clubhouse is a fine old mansion and regulations stipulate that a jacket and tie must be worn.

**Bruntsfield Links** Golfing Society lies to the west of the city and is one of the oldest golf clubs in the world. It finally came to rest at its present site at Davidson's Main in 1895. Set in a majestic parkland setting with superb views across the rolling countryside and the waters of the Firth of Forth, it measures 6407 yards.

The club has 1000 members, and you must wear a jacket and tie in the clubhouse. Take them with you if you want to sample the food and drink. It is excellent value with a reputation for quality that attracts visitors from far and wide. Although non-members are welcome at most times to play the course, it is still preferable to contact the club in advance. This is certainly one of Edinburgh's top three clubs.

**Edinburgh Burgess** Golfing Society is literally round the corner, bordering Bruntfield Links just off Queensferry Road. This claims to be the oldest golfing society in the world, having celebrated its 250th anniversary in 1985.

The beautifully maintained parkland course was designed by Tom Morris and measures 6604 yards with a par of 71. The club is open to visitors on application to the Secretary although it is unlikely that you will be able to play at weekends. Although there are no women members, ladies can play on weekday mornings. The fine old purpose-built clubhouse offers excellent catering and bar facilities, and you can hire clubs or trolleys.

**Silverknowes** municipal course is a fairly recent addition to the area, having been opened to play in 1947. Measuring 6200 yards with a par of 71 after an additional nine holes were laid in 1957, this parkland course is relatively open with little trouble off the tees, the premium being placed on accuracy for the second shots. Again, there are great views across the Firth of Forth and the green fees are good value for money. Juniors and seniors are both offered reductions, and restaurant facilities are available.

**Braid Hills** has two municipal courses – and only two and a half miles from Edinburgh's city centre off the A702. Braids No. 1 is the toughest of the two and weighs in at 5731 yards with a par of 70. From the top of the course, there are magnificent views all round but you must be prepared for a great deal of hard physical exertion if you tackle this course. Often you will be playing from one hilly crag to another with valleys to be negotiated in between and plenty of hills to climb.

Braids No. 2 is even higher, but at only 4832 yards there should be less strain on the legs. There are no restrictions on visitors at either course, although both are closed on Sundays. There is a professional's shop and clubs are available for hire. Moreover, the green fees are so low that these two courses represent some of the best value in Scottish golf.

**Mortonhall** is just a few minutes away on the south side of Braid Hills and is a challenging 6557 yards layout. Visitors are advised to have a letter of introduction from their own club but are not allowed to play at weekends. There are clubs and trolleys for hire, and catering and bar facilities are available.

**Craigmillar Park,** founded in 1896 and designed by James Braid, is just a short drive away and is worth a visit if you are in the area. A 5846 yards layout set around Blackford Hill, site of the Royal Observatory, you can be assured of some magnificent views, especially from the 10th tee, on this well-contoured parkland course. There are few restrictions on visitors and catering is available on all days of the week.

**Prestonfield** and **Liberton** are two more courses that lie within the confines of the city boundaries, within five minutes of each other near the old Dalkeith road. Both are private clubs but welcome visitors with certain restrictions. Prestonfield has a wonderful setting, lying just below the mounds known as Arthur's Seat. It is a parkland course of 6216 yards and was substantially redesigned by James Braid in 1928. Visitors of recognised clubs are welcome at restricted times of the day and meals are readily available.

As for Liberton, you will have to look carefully to find its concealed entrance which lies just off the old Dalkeith Road. Founded in 1914, this well-kept parkland course, measuring 5299 yards, was built around Kingston Grange, an eighteenth century mansion, which is now the clubhouse. Meals and snacks are available by arrangement and visitors are welcome at most times.

**Moffat** lies south-west of Edinburgh down the A701. Set high among the

*Some courses end with an uphill slog to the clubhouse but not the 18th at Moffat*

beautiful Annandale Hills with marvellous views to the town below, Moffat Golf Club offers you some great scenery. It is not a long course at only 5218 yards, but it is quite open and a real test of your golfing skills when the wind blows and you have to hit the small greens. Although the present course was designed by Ben Sayers in 1904, the club recently celebrated its centenary. Visitors are warmly welcomed, and the club offers special golfing breaks with accommodation arranged in neighbouring hotels. Telephone the club for further details.

**Thornhill,** south-west of Moffat on the A76, is the perfect place for a golfing 'break'. The club was founded in 1883 as a nine-hole course and only became a full 18 holes in 1979. It is a relatively open course with some interesting par-3's, but the 15th is easily the best hole on the course. A par-5 of 497 yards, it

plays every inch of that distance. With out-of-bounds running part of the way down the right-hand side and some penal rough to the left, a well-placed drive is the most important shot on this dogleg left hole. The only way to play this vicious hole is as a par-5. The length of the course is 6011 yards with a par of 71. Green fees are very reasonable and the clubhouse provides the best in local cooking.

If you want a peaceful resting place you can stay in the beautiful old Buccleugh and Queensberry Hotel on the town's high street. It is frequented not only by golfers but also by keen anglers, for Thornhill has excellent salmon and trout fishing to attract fishermen. Of course, if you enjoy a spot of fishing as well as a game of golf, then you will enjoy staying here.

**New Galloway,** heading even further south-west on the A713, is a short 2509 yards nine-holer lying on the edge of the small town of that name. It is particularly hilly and could be fun if you are energetic with plenty of stamina. In fact, the inclines are so steep that you will be filled with amazement. But green fees are very low – you just pay on trust by placing your money in an envelope and depositing it in a box. Juniors are half-price.

**Newton Stewart** is close to Wigtown Bay and has a new nine-hole course on the edge of town. Although the 2789 yards layout is only a few years old, it has matured quickly into an enjoyable, undulating parkland course. Green fees are low and, once again, you pay on trust and juniors are half-price.

**Wigtonshire County** Golf Club lies near Glenluce north of Luce Bay. It is a fairly open links-type course which was founded in 1894. This pleasant course is ideal for holiday golf. You pay on trust and it is half-price for everyone after 6 pm as well as juniors. You can book meals in advance during the summer months from April to October, and dine in the clubhouse.

**Portpatrick** has to be one of the best golfing holiday destinations in the south-west of Scotland. It is a picturesque little fishing port with a population of only 600, although this swells to a peak of 2000 during the high holiday season. There is plenty of first-class accommodation and a marvellous golf course at Portpatrick (Dunskey) Golf Club. In addition, there is wonderful bracing sea air and some breathtaking views for you to enjoy.

A good place to stay is the Fernhill Hotel, set high on the cliffs above the village and only a 4-iron from the golf course. The atmosphere is friendly, the rooms comfortable and the food delicious. The hotel offers special golf 'packages' throughout most of the year which include free golf.

The course itself is an 18-holer of only 5644 yards but do not be misled by the length and look on this as an easy game. In a stiff breeze blowing in off the sea, scores can soar. The links-type course is set high up on the cliff-tops and offers you some of the most majestic scenery and spectacular views that you could hope to find on any links course in the British Isles.

Two holes to watch out for are the 7th, named 'Gorsebank', and the 13th, called 'Sandeel'. The former is a par-3 of 165 yards but it plays longer than the yardage suggests as it is slightly uphill. The green is narrow and there is potential trouble lurking at the back and the right-hand side. Club selection here really depends on the elements, and as

*Portpatrick's 13th – this par-4 of 283 yards played from a very elevated tee can be reached in one by many golfers*

you can experience most weather conditions on this windswept open course it is an exhilarating experience.

As for the 13th hole, it is a shortish par-4 of 283 yards, but it is one of the great sights of any course in the world. The tee is situated high up on a cliff-edge with the green lying a long way below and the Irish Sea bordering the left-hand side. In a stiff sea breeze, you can actually launch the ball right out across the water and let the wind bring it back on target!

The course is perfect for holiday golf and when a gale blows it is a challenge for even the very best golfers. The modern clubhouse offers good catering facilities all week with the exception of Mondays, and a round of golf is reasonably priced. There is also even a nine-hole course at the club. Portpatrick has everything you could wish for on a golfing holiday and part of its essential charm seems to be that it never feels really crowded.

**Stranraer** is only 10 minutes' drive away. This is the major port for ferry services to Northern Ireland (only 19 miles away across the Irish Sea) and also the home of a fine golf club. The course, which was designed by James Braid, measures 6300 yards and although it stretches out beside the sea, it could be more accurately described as rolling parkland rather than a typical links. You should look out for wonderful views at the 5th and 14th holes. Green fees are reasonable, juniors are half-price and catering is available every day bar Mondays.

**St Medan** Golf Club lies off the A747 coast road just a couple of miles from the little village of Port William. If you stick to the coast, you cannot miss it, which you certainly should not do as it is a stunning nine-hole layout. Built round a hillside almost by the shoreline, it extends to 2277 yards and, although not a long course by any standards, it is

*Only 227 yards, the 4th at St Medan is an exhilarating hole to play but it can ruin some golfers' score cards*

well worth a visit.

Try your luck on the 4th hole, a par-4 of 274 yards and aptly named the 'Well'. It is played from the top of the hillside back down to sea-level. Big hitters can keep their fingers crossed and go for the green but could run into trouble if they do not make the putting surface. Short of the green is a line of railway sleepers backed up against the dunes and from behind them you could be faced with a blind shot.

Green fees are incredibly low and it is open all year round for play. A bar and catering are both available from April through to October.

**Southerness** lies eastwards along the coast on the Solway Firth. The course is one of the finest yet least well-known links in the British Isles. Opened as recently as 1947, it was designed by the late Mackenzie Ross and measures 6548 yards with a par-69.

This really is a course for accurate driving with heather, bracken and gorse confronting you on all sides. The two par-5's can be reached in two shots for the long-hitter, but the par-4's are very testing indeed and are often at the mercy of the ever-changing wind. One hole that really stands out and will make a lasting impression is the 12th at 419 yards with bunkers to the left and right

of it to catch poor drives. If you take a chance and drive over the right-hand bunkers, you can make the second shot much shorter but it is a brave line to take, still leaving you with a long iron to the green on the edge of the beach. When the wind is blowing off the sea, you have to play this hole as a par-5.

The par-3's are all first class and demand anything from a medium iron to a driver depending on the conditions. The whole course is fairly flat and a pleasure to walk and play. The friendly clubhouse caters for golfers on every day of the week except Wednesdays and visitors are welcome at most times.

**Dumfries** boasts three courses, one of which, the Dumfries and County Golf Club, is only two minutes' drive from the town centre on the A701 Edinburgh road. Founded in 1912, the course was designed by Willie Fernie, who won the Open in 1883 at Musselburgh. It is a pleasant, attractive parkland course and totals 5914 yards. Willie Fernie must have been thinking of the more celebrated St Andrews when he built a double green for the 1st and 6th holes. The large clubhouse offers full catering and visitors are made most welcome although there are some restrictions on the times they may play, so check ahead of your visit.

**Lochmaben** is the last stop for many golfers heading south out of Scotland. It is a picturesque nine-hole course, only 10 miles east of Dumfries on the A709, but it is worth visiting if you have some spare time or want to break your journey. Set in rolling parkland beside a lake, it offers beautiful scenery as well as an enjoyable game of golf. If nobody is in the clubhouse, the pay on trust system operates as with many smaller Scottish clubs. And in addition to playing golf, you can obtain an angling permit from the clubhouse and fish in the lake just a pitch shot away.

*The great 12th hole at Southerness on the Solway Firth*

You may be surprised to learn that Northern Ireland is the home of some great golf courses and fantastic scenery. If you are visiting Ireland, do not miss the fabulous landscape of the Causeway Coast with its eerie rock formations formed long ago by a legendary Irish giant and the famous links courses of Royal Portrush, Portstewart, Castlerock and Ballycastle. The beautiful coastline is dotted with picturesque fishing villages and wide sweeps of long sandy beaches where you can relax after golf. You will be pleasantly surprised by the sheer beauty and brilliance of the golf courses and the ease and comfort in which they can be played and enjoyed. Do not be deterred by what you may read about this beautiful country in the newspapers or see on your television screen. You will still receive a warm and friendly welcome wherever you go in this land of glorious, uncrowded golf courses.

*Royal County Down*

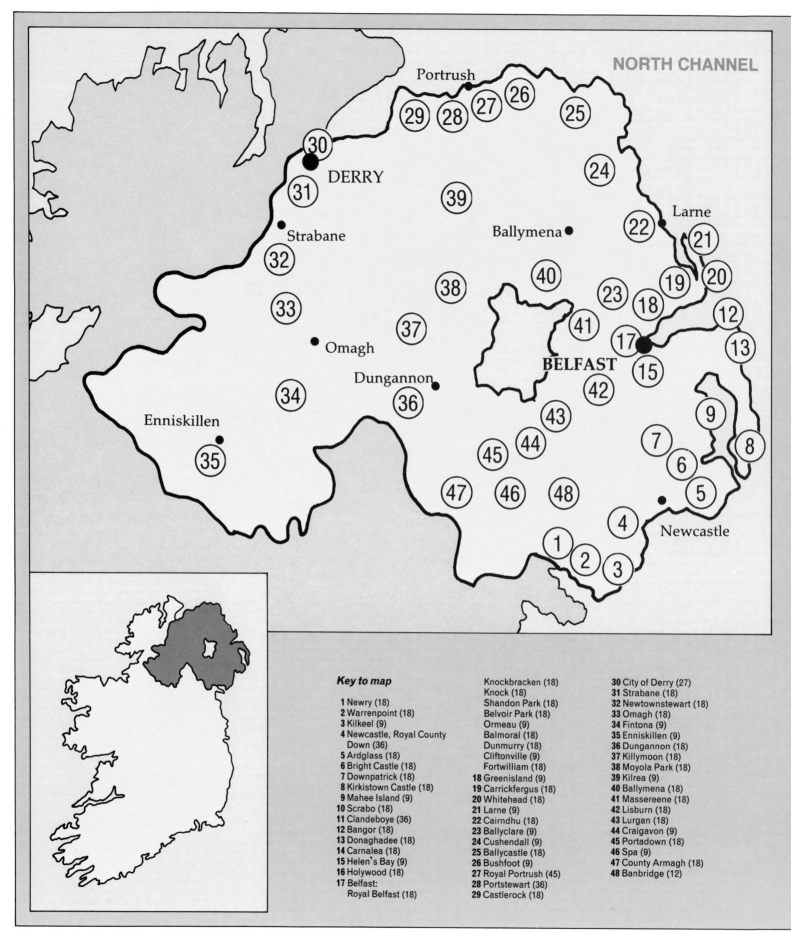

**NORTH CHANNEL**

Portrush

㉙ ㉘ ㉗ ㉖ ㉕

㉚ DERRY

㉛

Strabane

㉜

Ballymena

㉒ Larne
㉑

㉞ ㉓ ⑲ ⑳
㉝ ⑱

㊳ ⑫

Omagh ㊲ ⑰ ⑬
㊶ ⑮

Dungannon ㊷
㊴ ㊱ ㊸

Enniskillen ⑨

㉟ ㊸ ⑦
㊹ ⑥
㊺ ⑤

⑧

㊼ ㊻ ㊽
④ Newcastle

① ② ③

## Key to map

1 Newry (18)
2 Warrenpoint (18)
3 Kilkeel (9)
4 Newcastle, Royal County
  Down (36)
5 Ardglass (18)
6 Bright Castle (18)
7 Downpatrick (18)
8 Kirkistown Castle (18)
9 Mahee Island (9)
10 Scrabo (18)
11 Clandeboye (36)
12 Bangor (18)
13 Donaghadee (18)
14 Carnalea (18)
15 Helen's Bay (9)
16 Holywood (18)
17 Belfast:
   Royal Belfast (18)

Knockbracken (18)
Knock (18)
Shandon Park (18)
Belvoir Park (18)
Ormeau (9)
Balmoral (18)
Dunmurry (18)
Cliftonville (9)
Fortwilliam (18)
18 Greenisland (9)
19 Carrickfergus (18)
20 Whitehead (18)
21 Larne (9)
22 Cairndhu (18)
23 Ballyclare (9)
24 Cushendall (9)
25 Ballycastle (18)
26 Bushfoot (9)
27 Royal Portrush (45)
28 Portstewart (36)
29 Castlerock (18)

30 City of Derry (27)
31 Strabane (18)
32 Newtownstewart (18)
33 Omagh (18)
34 Fintona (9)
35 Enniskillen (9)
36 Dungannon (18)
37 Killymoon (18)
38 Moyola Park (18)
39 Kilrea (9)
40 Ballymena (18)
41 Massereene (18)
42 Lisburn (18)
43 Lurgan (18)
44 Craigavon (9)
45 Portadown (18)
46 Spa (9)
47 County Armagh (18)
48 Banbridge (12)

90

# Northern Ireland

Few people are aware of the beauty and sheer brilliance of the golf courses of Northern Ireland and the ease and comfort in which they can be played and enjoyed. Despite its recent turbulent politics, it is a great holiday destination for golfers. Do not be swayed from visiting this beautiful country by what you see on the news and read in the papers. Any violence tends to be confined to predetermined areas into which you will never venture. On the contrary, you will receive a warm welcome from the local people.

Generally, green fees are very cheap, and so are accommodation and food. And what is reassuring for the visitor is that every hotel, guest house, boarding house and other establishment which offers any type of accommodation has to be inspected and licensed by the Northern Ireland Tourist Board. So does every restaurant and eating house, right down to fish and chip shops. Thus owners and managers know that they have to maintain high standards and provide good service or their licences

will not be renewed. Thus you can book in anywhere and know that you will be looked after well. The Tourist Board even produces an annual guide to the places where you can stay.

**Clandeboye** Golf Club lies between Belfast and Bangor on the A21, and was

*The Mountains of Mourne, which make Royal County Down at Newcastle one of the most beautiful places to play golf in the British Isles*

the home of the Smirnoff Ladies Irish Open in 1984. There are two courses, the Ava and the Dufferin, the latter being the main course with a most tempting opening hole. From an elevated tee, gorse bushes stretch for almost 100 yards with out-of-bounds all the way down on the right.

Gorse is a predominant feature of the course which undulates gently through some spectacularly beautiful countryside with the 6th probably being one of the best holes. It is a par-5 of 530 yards

off the back tees with the fairway completely wooded on the right, the inevitable gorse encroaching from the left for 200 yards. An open stream crosses the fairway at 225 yards to cause headaches for anyone contemplating a driver from the tee. Even then your problems are not over, because a fairway bunker crosses the fairway 105 yards from the green which is itself heavily bunkered to left and right.

Spend the whole day at Clandeboye and after battling with the Dufferin in the morning, try the Ava in the afternoon. Although it is a shorter course, it is almost as challenging and just as much fun. It also has breathtaking views over Strangford Lough and out to the Isle of Man. Societies are most welcome with special green fee rates on weekdays with the exception of Thurs-

day. The clubhouse itself is superbly appointed with full meals available in the dining room, and filling bar snacks in the lounge.

**Shandon Park** Golf Club lies north of Belfast with a course of 6249 yards. This

is the home of the old Ulster Open Championship and here, from the course, players have a good view of Stormont Castle on the hill – this was once the seat of government in the province. This is a challenging course which is well worth visiting. Visitors are welcome on any day of the week except Saturdays and will find the green fees very reasonable.

**Belvoir Park** lies three miles south of Belfast in rolling parkland and was founded in 1927. It was laid out by Harry Colt – the man who designed Sunningdale and many other great courses – using teams of horses and hand ploughs. In 1949, it hosted the Irish Open won by Harry Bradshaw who earlier that year had missed out in the Open Championship itself when his ball came to rest in a broken bottle!

More recently, Belvoir Park has played host to the WPGA and the women professionals admired the course. From the back tees, it measures an impressive 6276 yards with most of the holes wending their way through mature and

*The 9th hole at Royal County Down, which plays towards the clubhouse and the beautiful Mountains of Mourne which are an ever-present feature*

majestic trees. Visitors are nearly always welcome, and, again, green fees are low.

**Balmoral** Golf Club, with its flat parkland course, is close to the centre of Belfast. Young trees line the fairways of this course and the clubhouse has a special Fred Daly corner as the former British Open champion has been a regular there for many years. Green fees are modest and meals are usually available in the clubhouse.

**Dunmurry** Golf Club's new course is only a few miles away. At 5832 yards with an SSS of 68, it is an impressive layout despite its youthfulness, and a good test of golfing skills. However, it probably needs just a little more time to mature. On the adjoining land is the Lady Dixon Park, home of the International Rose Trials, so in the summer months a wonderful fragrance pervades the course.

**Malone** Golf Club is four miles south of the city centre. The attractive course winds its way round a series of trout lakes, and the first hole goes down almost to the River Lagan's edge. During its history, the club has had a number of changes of site, the current one having been in use since 1962. In

1966 a further nine holes were opened, leading to some adjustment to the original layout, but the only change since then has been to the short par-3 15th to bring in more of the trout lake. This was done in 1984, and since then the hole, even at a mere 147 yards, has been regarded as a card wrecker, so be warned! You can play on any days except Tuesdays and Saturdays.

**Royal Belfast,** surprisingly, is classed as being in County Down rather than in the city itself. A real beauty of a course, it has a stiff, uphill opening hole with the 8th, 9th, 10th and 11th following the shoreline of the picturesque Belfast Lough. Many golfers regard the 10th as the best hole out of the 18. This is a little honey of 312 yards to a plateau fairway and the green beyond, with perils awaiting you on the left and an extremely difficult target to hit from the right.

Royal Belfast Golf Club is the oldest in Ireland having celebrated its centenary in 1981. The course is excellent and any visitor who misses it out of his itinerary is depriving himself of a rare treat. However, letters of introduction are necessary, and one from your own Club Secretary will probably be suf-

*The clubhouse, at Royal County Down, is welcoming after playing a course which has been rated among the world's best*

ficient. Moreover, green fees are very modest, making it excellent value for money and worth visiting.

**Fortwilliam** Golf Club, established in 1903, is three miles north of Belfast with a fairly short course of 5275 yards. **Knockbracken** with its floodlit driving range lies south-east of the city, and there are nine-hole courses at **Ormeau, Gilnahirk** and **Cliftonville.**

**Knock** Golf Club is further east with a parkland course set in 100 acres. Although there is no rough, there are plenty of well-established trees and 75 bunkers – probably more than any other course in Ireland. It is tight but well-manicured with a par of 69.

**Royal County Down** golf course is one of the best three or four courses to be found anywhere in the British Isles. To get there, travel south from Belfast on the A24 or A21. The roads link at Ballynahinch where you take the A24 and then the A2 to Newcastle. This course is an old-fashioned links at its very best – grandeur supreme with huge sand dunes. The course is overlooked by the majestic Mountains of Mourne which really do sweep down right to the edge of the sea.

**Warrenpoint,** the home club of Ronan Rafferty, lies further south. This club has a happy, friendly atmosphere and the members are very welcoming to visitors. The course is sited within view of southern Ireland from which it is separated by Carlingford Lough which extends to the border town of Newry, about five miles away.

*A short par-4 but the 5th green at Royal Portrush is dangerously close to the sea and needed protection from it*

**Ardglass, Downpatrick** and **Bright Castle** golf courses are further back out of Newcastle along the A2 and A25. Ardglass, set on the rocks beside the sea, is well worth visiting. Look out especially for the 2nd and 11th holes, both par-3's by the water's edge.

**Kirkistown Castle** Golf Club is on the Ards Peninsula. To reach it, you have to cross on the little ferry at Strangford and motor up the A20. The journey is worth it and you will be well rewarded. The legendary James Braid carried out the bunkering on the then newly laid out course, and sighed, "Ah, if only I had this within 50 miles of London".

The course has two distinct loops of nine holes starting and finishing at the clubhouse, and the whole atmosphere of club and course is what real golf in Northern Ireland is all about. It is golf right down to the basics, and how the members love it! Visitors pay a very modest fee to sample the delights of the 'Tower,' the 'Quarry' and the 'Moat,' to name but three of the interesting holes. The whole course overlooks the Irish Sea and is located towards the bottom of the Ards Peninsula on the outskirts of the little town of Cloughey.

**Royal Portrush** and its fabulous links course is only an hour or so from Belfast. Situated on the beautiful scenic Causeway Coast it is almost within spitting distance of three other great links courses – those at Portstewart, Castlerock and Ballycastle. You can play all four courses and stay at any number of delightful hotels in the little resorts and fishing villages. The Causeway Coast gets its name from the spectacular and awe-inspiring Giant's Causeway which looks like gigantic boulders and sculptured stone pillars rising out of the sea. You will hear this described as a geological freak or as the work of the giant Finn McCool, who threw a clod of earth at a fleeing enemy and where it landed in the sea became the Isle of Man! McCool then fell in love with a lady giant on the Hebridean Island of Staffa and started to build the Giant's Causeway as a road to fetch her back across the sea. It is worth breaking off from your golf to go and visit this amazing stone monument.

Royal Portrush is along the coastal road from the Giant's Causeway past the burned-out ruins of Dunluce Castle. It is the only course in Ireland to have hosted the Open Championship – in 1951 when the winner was Max Faulkner. It still remains as one of the best links courses in the world.

Bernard Darwin, the doyen of golf writers, wrote in *The Times* of July 3rd 1951: 'It is a truly magnificent course and Mr H.S. Colt who designed it in its present form, has thereby built himself a monument more enduring than brass. The course does not disdain the spectacular, such as the one-shot hole called "Calamity Corner" with its terrifying sandy cliffs and its gadarene descent into unknown depths to the right of the green; for the most part the course does not depend on any such dramatic quality, but rather on the combined soundness and subtleness of its architecture. There is a constant demand for accuracy in driving, the more so at present as the rough is really worthy of its name and

the approaches are full of varied interest. In particular, there are one or two holes of the despised length called "drive and pitch" which are entirely fascinating, such as the 5th, with its green almost on the brink of the sea, and the 15th. The greens are full of interesting undulations and altogether I find it hard to imagine a more admirable test of golf.' Times have not changed even over 30 years later. It is still an outstanding course.

The 5th hole almost sank into the sea a few years ago as the Atlantic gales lashed the cliffs but the club's members rallied round and, with outside support,

*The ruined Dunluce Castle which gave its name to the championship course at Royal Portrush, where the 1951 Open Championship was played*

*Royal Portrush – Harry Colt's masterpiece*

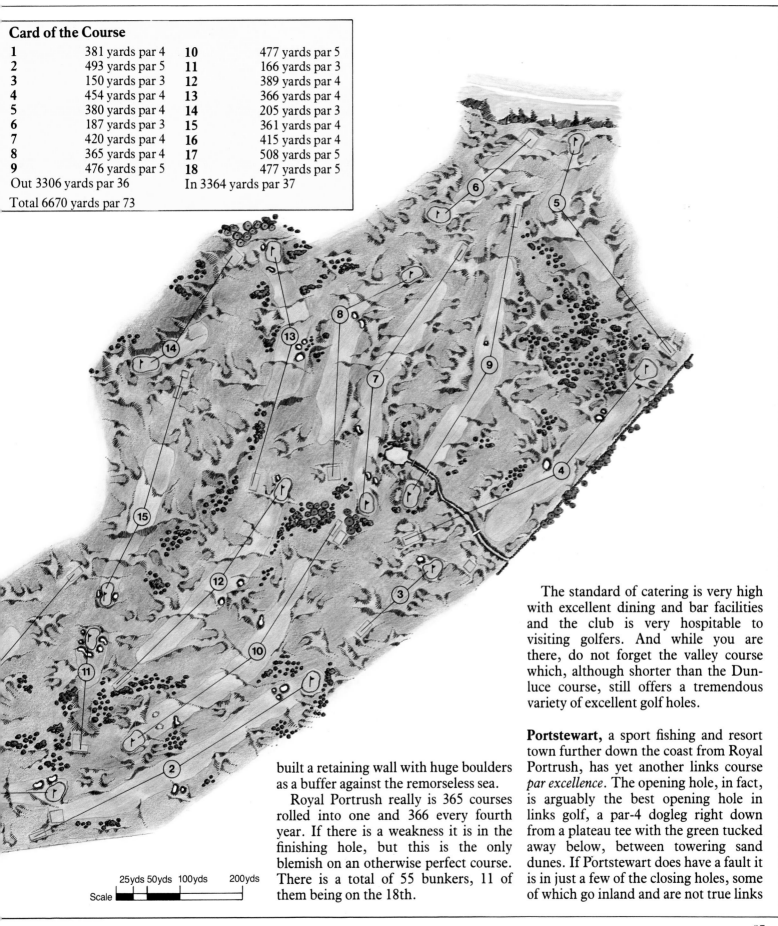

## Card of the Course

| | | | |
|---|---|---|---|
| **1** | 381 yards par 4 | **10** | 477 yards par 5 |
| **2** | 493 yards par 5 | **11** | 166 yards par 3 |
| **3** | 150 yards par 3 | **12** | 389 yards par 4 |
| **4** | 454 yards par 4 | **13** | 366 yards par 4 |
| **5** | 380 yards par 4 | **14** | 205 yards par 3 |
| **6** | 187 yards par 3 | **15** | 361 yards par 4 |
| **7** | 420 yards par 4 | **16** | 415 yards par 4 |
| **8** | 365 yards par 4 | **17** | 508 yards par 5 |
| **9** | 476 yards par 5 | **18** | 477 yards par 5 |
| Out 3306 yards par 36 | | In 3364 yards par 37 | |
| Total 6670 yards par 73 | | | |

Scale 25yds 50yds 100yds 200yds

The standard of catering is very high with excellent dining and bar facilities and the club is very hospitable to visiting golfers. And while you are there, do not forget the valley course which, although shorter than the Dunluce course, still offers a tremendous variety of excellent golf holes.

**Portstewart,** a sport fishing and resort town further down the coast from Royal Portrush, has yet another links course *par excellence*. The opening hole, in fact, is arguably the best opening hole in links golf, a par-4 dogleg right down from a plateau tee with the green tucked away below, between towering sand dunes. If Portstewart does have a fault it is in just a few of the closing holes, some of which go inland and are not true links

built a retaining wall with huge boulders as a buffer against the remorseless sea.

Royal Portrush really is 365 courses rolled into one and 366 every fourth year. If there is a weakness it is in the finishing hole, but this is the only blemish on an otherwise perfect course. There is a total of 55 bunkers, 11 of them being on the 18th.

holes. The 16th, for instance, brings the players back to the clubhouse and then they have to drive directly away for the 17th and back parallel for the 18th. This is not the best of situations, especially if it is raining!

However, plans are in hand to build new holes in the dunes beyond the first green and it is hoped that the work will be completed by the time of its centenary in 1994. Although green fees are modest, societies can take advantage of further reductions.

**Castlerock** with its impressive links course is further along the main A2 coastal road six miles west of Coleraine. The informal atmosphere in the clubhouse ill-prepares you for what is to follow. Far from being an easy relaxing game, this is a case of one challenging hole after another with hardly any let up in concentration or enjoyment.

**Ballycastle** is the fourth links on the Causeway Coast, along the A2 back past Portstewart, Portrush and the little town of Bushmills with its world-famous whiskey distillery. Together these four courses are the natural setting for any visiting golfer or society.

*A magnificent setting for the 5th green at Castlerock – another Irish golfing gem on the Causeway Coast*

We have only highlighted the major areas of golf in Northern Ireland. Of course, there are many other courses where you will receive a warm welcome and an enjoyable game of golf. Do not be afraid to try them and discover the natural beauty of the countryside, the spectacular coastline and the high quality of the courses.

*Portstewart (left) and Ballycastle (bottom left) are two of the spectacular links courses on Northern Ireland's beautiful Causeway Coast. Enjoy the scenery while you play a challenging round*

## Bushmills Distillery

No visit to Northern Ireland is complete for a whiskey lover without an outing to Bushmills, the oldest distillery in the world. It is the home of the famous Bushmills Irish Whiskey and the famous 'Black Bush' label. Wherever you go in Northern Ireland, it is everybody's favourite drink.

There are organized tours around the distillery and all visitors are invited to sample a whiskey in the bar. Try a drop of Jimmy Kane's Special – Old Bushmills mixed with water, cloves and cinnamon and served hot – which is sometimes known as a 'hot bush'. For more information on distillery tours, contact Bushmills on (0265) 731521 (tours are Mondays to Thursdays and Friday mornings).

Bushmills Whiskey is linked with the golf world, too. It sponsors the Black Bush Causeway Coast Tournament which is held every year in the first week of June. This is a 72-hole Stableford competition played off handicap on the four spectacular courses of Royal Portrush, Portstewart, Ballycastle and Castlerock. For further details write to the organizer, John Dalzell, at 155 Coleraine Road, Portstewart (Tel. (0265) 832417).

*I*n Ireland you will discover some real golfing gems, whichever area
you visit. The popular courses of Ballybunion, Killarney, Waterville, Tralee and
Portmarnock are just some of the precious jewels in Ireland's golfing crown.
To play on these celebrated courses is a memorable experience, but take time also to
discover some of the more remote courses – the ones you have never encountered in
your reading or travels. The green fees are often incredibly low, and you

will receive a remarkably friendly welcome wherever you go.
The western coastline is particularly wild, rugged and beautiful and
here you will find some of the world's finest links courses. Kerry, in particular, could be
described as the best endowed golfing county in the whole of the British Isles. The golf
courses are magnificent and a challenging test for every golfer, whatever
his handicap. The scenery is among the most spectacular in Ireland with precipitous
cliffs, long expanses of golden sand and a backdrop of high mountains. You
approach the courses through winding country lanes between lush green
fields in a quintessentially Irish landscape. Here you will discover
lesser-known courses which are admired by the top professionals.

A lady who came from Drogheda
where the golfing pro often annogheda
She soon was at scratch,
and won every match,
So the golf club sacked him and emplogheda

This gent is young Seamus O'Kelly
who invariably gives it some welly
When he slices his ball
We can't find it at all
And he's been in a pro-am on telly

A pint sir? I'm sure that you oughter
Have a drink of the fine Liffey water
Me n' my cousin's brother
will buy you another
And you can buy one for my daughter

Dave F. Smith

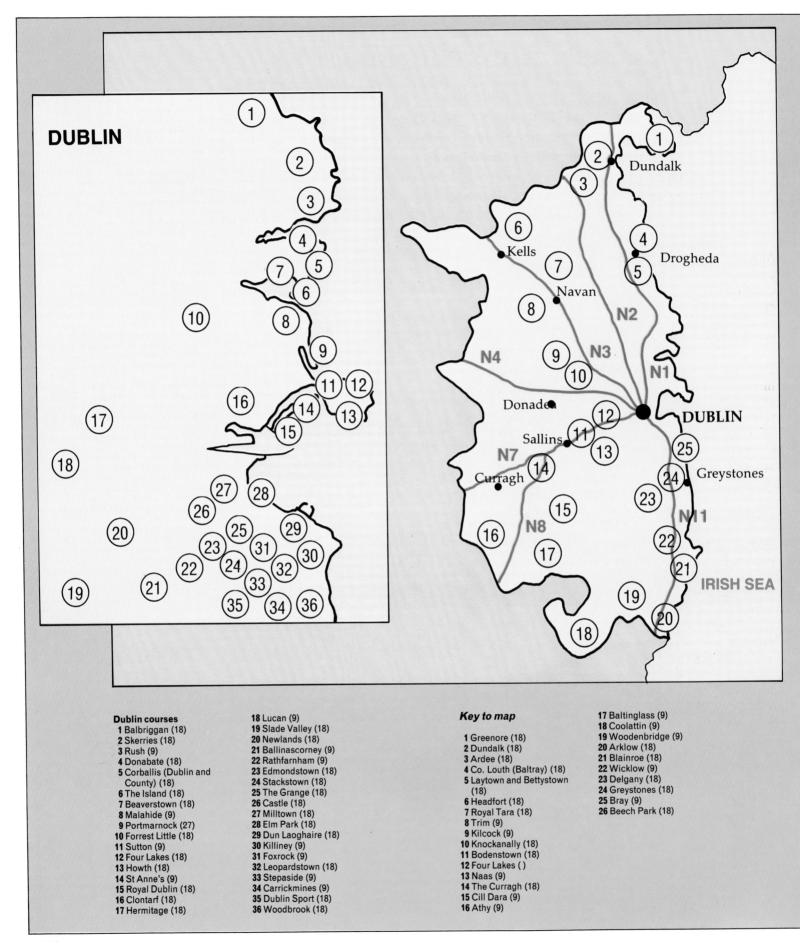

# DUBLIN

**IRISH SEA**

Dundalk
Drogheda
Kells
Navan
Donadea
Sallins
Curragh
Greystones
DUBLIN

N1 N2 N3 N4 N7 N8 N11

**Dublin courses**
1 Balbriggan (18)
2 Skerries (18)
3 Rush (9)
4 Donabate (18)
5 Corballis (Dublin and County) (18)
6 The Island (18)
7 Beaverstown (18)
8 Malahide (9)
9 Portmarnock (27)
10 Forrest Little (18)
11 Sutton (9)
12 Four Lakes (18)
13 Howth (18)
14 St Anne's (9)
15 Royal Dublin (18)
16 Clontarf (18)
17 Hermitage (18)

18 Lucan (9)
19 Slade Valley (18)
20 Newlands (18)
21 Ballinascorney (9)
22 Rathfarnham (9)
23 Edmondstown (18)
24 Stackstown (18)
25 The Grange (18)
26 Castle (18)
27 Milltown (18)
28 Elm Park (18)
29 Dun Laoghaire (18)
30 Killiney (18)
31 Foxrock (9)
32 Leopardstown (18)
33 Stepaside (9)
34 Carrickmines (9)
35 Dublin Sport (18)
36 Woodbrook (18)

*Key to map*

1 Greenore (18)
2 Dundalk (18)
3 Ardee (18)
4 Co. Louth (Baltray) (18)
5 Laytown and Bettystown (18)
6 Headfort (18)
7 Royal Tara (18)
8 Trim (9)
9 Kilcock (9)
10 Knockanally (18)
11 Bodenstown (18)
12 Four Lakes ( )
13 Naas (9)
14 The Curragh (18)
15 Cill Dara (9)
16 Athy (9)

17 Baltinglass (9)
18 Coolattin (9)
19 Woodenbridge (9)
20 Arklow (18)
21 Blainroe (18)
22 Wicklow (9)
23 Delgany (18)
24 Greystones (18)
25 Bray (9)
26 Beech Park (18)

# Dublin and the East

Golfing in and around Dublin presents you with an immensely enjoyable dilemma. Incredibly, here are nearly 60 courses within an hour's drive of the city centre making the visiting golfer spoilt for choice. From the classic links tests of celebrated Portmarnock and Royal Dublin, to the peaceful, yet exhilarating, parkland layouts of the Grange and Hermitage, Dublin has it all for the visitor together with some of the most friendly and hospitable golf clubs that you will encounter anywhere in the world.

Although only a few of the courses are public, Dublin's private clubs actively encourage visitors – almost without exception. It is always advisable to book in advance wherever you play and to avoid Tuesdays and weekends. Tuesday, more often than not, is Ladies' Day, and at weekends most clubs organize competitions which are invariably over-subscribed. But where do you start this voyage of discovery? At the courses of Dun Laoghaire to the south, or Clontarf to the north of the city which are both near the ferry terminals if you sail across the Irish Sea, or at Forrest Little Golf Club at the end of Dublin's International Airport's main runway?

**Forrest Little** was founded in 1971 by players from the nearby Corballis public links course. It is a pleasant fairly open, tree-lined course with a river crossing a number of holes. However, you may need to wear earplugs on the 440 yards 8th which just happens to be directly under the flight-path. The club has full catering and is ideal for the businessman wanting to get in a few holes before a meeting or flying home.

**Beaverstown** is located near the village of Donabate to the north of Dublin up the N1 road. This relatively new course was opened in 1986 and is the work of Ireland's leading course architect, Eddie Hackett. It is a parkland course with surprisingly links-type greens, which has been laid out over a former fruit farm. With mature trees all the way round and a canal crossing the course, it is a beautiful setting for a round of golf.

**The Island** is not far away on a peaceful peninsula with majestic dunes. This real gem of a course was founded back in 1890, and until 1973 it could be reached only by a small boat from the village of Malahide. However, it is now connected to the mainland by a road bridge, although such is the tranquillity of the place that it is hard to believe that the airport is less than 15 minutes' drive away from its solitude.

This really is a superb test of golf, the only problem being the number of blind shots. There are plans for five new holes and when they are built, the Island will rank among Ireland's finest courses. Even now there are many good holes and one of the best is the 5th, a par-3 situated right on the tip of the peninsula. With out-of-bounds along the shoreline to the right, heavy rough to the left and a big dip in front of the green, it can take anything from a 6-iron to a driver to reach the putting surface, depending on the wind. You can look across Broad Meadow Estuary to the attractive village of Malahide beyond the nine-hole parkland course of **Malahide Golf Club** nestling on the hillside. This is where Philip Walton learnt his

*An aeroplane coming in to touch down at Dublin Airport, viewed from the neighbouring course at Forest Little*

game.

The Island has an active membership boasting no fewer than 80 single figure players, and the course is usually full at weekends. Green fees are in the middle range but half-price if you are accompanied by a member. The clubhouse facilities are excellent, and although the course is not particularly long at just over 6300 yards, players of all standards will enjoy a game of golf here. And there is a special card for winter competitions – the 13-hole scorecard makes it unusual, to say the least.

**Corballis** backs on to the Island. It is a superbly maintained public course of just under 5000 yards running within a narrow strip of linksland. Golfers have a multitude of options with 18 greens and 36 tees. Green fees represent excellent value for money at very low rates indeed. But the facilities on offer are at a minimum and if you want a drink or something to eat, you will have to go next door into the neighbouring clubhouse of **Dublin & County**, a private club that plays over Corballis. You

would be hard pressed to find better greens than these, making Corballis well worth a visit.

**Donabate** is further inland but not too far away. This private club was formed by players from Corballis back in 1925. It is a fairly flat parkland course and Mary McKenna, Ireland's most renowned lady golfer, has been a member there since 1963.

**Rush** is a journey back inland to the N1 highway, a short drive north and then back out towards the coast again. It is a pretty fishing village with a memorable nine-hole links course that any visitor is guaranteed to enjoy. Although it is difficult to find owing to the sad lack of signposts, it is worth looking and asking for there are marvellous views to Lambay Island in the distance and a superb beach that runs alongside the course. Founded in the 1940s, Rush is built on a

*Corballis, which has the unusual feature of 36 tees to serve 18 holes so that you can really take your pick when you play*

narrow strip of rolling duneland and stretches to over 6000 yards by the device of using 18 tees. It has many tricky holes, none more so than the 1st – a par-4 of 320 yards which can soon land you in trouble. A quarry on the right invariably catches errant tee shots. Green fees are modest but visitors cannot play on Sundays. Full catering is available.

**Skerries**, another attractive fishing village, is reached by following the coast road for another 10 miles northwards. The golf course is a couple of miles inland from the village itself with 18 holes of parkland. Green fees fall in the middle range but are marginally higher at weekends than on weekdays.

**Balbriggan**, a parkland course, lies a few miles further north just off the N1, while further on beside the Irish Sea are the 18-hole links of **Laytown and Bettystown**. This is Des Smyth's home club and is a tricky but enjoyable layout, finishing with a blind approach to the 18th. The club has a reputation for friendliness and does a lot to foster junior golf. Visitors are always welcome and green fees are modest.

**County Louth** Golf Club is one of the best well-kept secrets of Irish golf. Cross over St Mary's bridge and the historic River Boyne from Drogheda and turn immediately to the right. Drive back alongside the river for another four miles and you will find it. Sometimes referred to also as **Baltray**, this has got to be one of the most enjoyable links in Ireland and undoubtedly represents superb value. The club even has its own accommodation if you fancy getting away from it all and just living and breathing golf for a few days. It provides 14 bedrooms with full Irish breakfast at extremely low prices – a golfing bargain! The restaurant is marvellous and with the prospect of a round over the testing 6798-yards course, County Louth is not to be

missed.

There is not a weak hole on the course and some of the holes merit greatness. Two of note are the 12th which dictates a tough drive into a valley and a slightly blind second shot to the green 418 yards away; and the 339-yards 14th which is quite a carry off the back tees with a tantalizing second shot to a green surrounded by humps and hollows. The par-3's are excellent, too.

Many of Ireland's top amateur players hail from County Louth – not surprisingly. And at the well-stocked pro's shop you can hire clubs.

**Dundalk** Golf Club is another 20 minutes' drive northwards close to the border between Northern Ireland and the Republic. This friendly club has a pleasant 18-hole parkland course recently designed by Peter Alliss and Dave Thomas although the club itself was founded back in 1905. Visitors are welcome every day except Sundays.

*Portmarnock has often hosted the Irish Open and, once, in 1949, the British Amateur – the only time that it was not held in the United Kingdom. The 15th, one of the finest holes, is shown here*

Full catering is available and from the clubhouse verandah there are splendid views of Dundalk Bay with a backdrop of the Cooley and Mourne Mountains.

**Greenore** Golf Club is 16 miles away near the tip of the Cooley peninsula. Founded back in 1897 when British Rail owned the small port, village and course, Greenore's fairly flat 18 holes are a mixture of links, heath and parkland. Green fees are exceptionally low, although marginally higher at weekends than on weekdays, but there is no catering at the club.

**Portmarnock**, one of the most famous courses in the world, lies to the south back down the N1 some 10 miles north

of Dublin. It lies on a narrow peninsula and has 27 great holes to choose from for the visiting golfer. It is a marvellous links terrain surprisingly dotted with a few trees. Founded in 1894, it has played host to many famous championships over the years. It is expensive for a day's golf – green fees are unusually high – but it is worth it for at over 7000 yards it is the supreme test of your skill as a golfer with knee-high rough in the late summer months and a par-5 6th hole of 605 yards.

**Sutton** lies on a larger headland to the south of Portmarnock's peninsula. This nine-hole links bordering the Irish Sea, was founded back in 1896. Tricky to play, especially in a sea breeze, Sutton is not over-long but it is quite tight. If you want to take advantage of the full catering facilities you must book in advance, although you can always buy tea and sandwiches.

**Deer Park** and **Howth** both offer marvellous scenic views further to the south on the coastal road where it starts to climb. Whereas Deer Park has four public courses to choose from, Howth has panoramic views back towards Dublin Bay. Howth's hilly 18-hole course is reminiscent of heathland and the greens are kept in excellent condition. Green fees are very reasonable, but at weekends, visitors can play only with a member.

Whereas Howth is a private club, Deer Park is golf for the masses with the largest golf complex in the whole of Ireland. It boasts an 18-hole course, another of nine, a short 12-hole layout plus an 18-hole pitch and putt. At weekends, it is extremely crowded indeed with the overflow from nearby Dublin, and a tannoy system is used to summon golfers to the 1st tee. The main course is set in open, undulating parkland and is an enjoyable, although not too difficult, challenge. As you might expect on a public course, green fees are low although, as usual, higher at weekends. And the club has facilities for food and drink. Special golfing packages are available from nearby Deer Park Hotel.

Take the coastal route back to Dublin and you will pass Bull Island, three miles of low duneland hiding a wonderful beach and two tremendous links courses. Back in 1819 the island did not exist, but that same year a one-and-three-quarter miles sea wall was built out from the Clontarf shoreline to prevent Dublin Harbour silting up. After the wall was completed, sand started to collect naturally behind it, moved there by the tides. The result is Bull Island which has literally grown out of the sea.

**St Anne's** links lies at the northern end of Bull Island. You approach it on a road which runs across a salt marsh. It is a terrific test of just under 3000 yards, but the land is being reclaimed and landscaped to create an additional nine holes which have been designed by

*The elevated green on the 12th hole at Portmarnock's great links course*

Eddie Hackett. There are splendid views from the clubhouse, and the course is well worth a detour. Unfortunately, visitors cannot play at weekends, but catering is available through the week, and green fees are modest.

**Royal Dublin** backs onto St Anne's and is reached by a narrow causeway. Founded over a century ago, the club moved from Phoenix Park, Dublin, to its present site at Bull Island back in 1889, receiving the 'Royal' distinction two years later. This truly great links has hosted many major events including the Carrolls Irish Open. Look out for the 18th, a par-5 of just over 500 yards and a dogleg right with out-of-bounds on that side. It is a difficult decision whether to try and carry the 'garden' and get to the green in two shots. It is open to visitors every day except Saturdays and Wednesday afternoons. Green fees are in the higher bracket and you should always book in advance rather than turn up on the offchance. It has

also one of the best pro shops you are likely to see. A special room with a wide array of instructional videos is set aside for teaching. The tournament pro at Royal Dublin is Christy O'Connor himself – one of the greatest names in Irish Golf and a great attraction.

**Clontarf Golf and Bowling Club** is just a couple of miles away. An attractive tight tree-lined course, it has a treacherous par-4 12th played across a quarry and a pond. It is the club that is closest to Dublin's city centre.

**Hermitage** Golf Club lies west of the city heading out on the N4. It is a truly beautiful parkland course surrounded by majestic trees. At just over 6500 yards, you will really enjoy the golf here as well as the excellent clubhouse facilities and catering. However, do book in advance as it is a popular venue.

One of the finest holes of many is the 11th at 556 yards. It runs alongside the River Liffey. But for something completely different, it is the par-3 10th that gets all the publicity and attention. For there is not one, but two par-3's! One is

for the winter and the other for the summer, and both are tremendous little tests. The one that backs onto the Liffey is the better of the two but as it was prone to frequent flooding, the other hole was brought into play. The hole has now been moved back and the green raised slightly.

**Lucan** and **Kilcock** both have nine-hole layouts as you head westwards towards **Knockanally** in County Kildare. Just over 20 miles out of Dublin and only four miles from the village of Prosperous, this fairly open parkland 18-hole layout features an attractive 120-years-old Palladian mansion as the clubhouse. Full catering is available at weekends.

Travelling south through the coun-

*The 18th at Royal Dublin: a par-5 that gives the gambler a chance of an eagle if he cuts across the out-of-bounds*

try, the N7 is the next big arterial road out of Dublin. It takes you through Ireland's famous 'horse country' with the legendary Curragh racecourse and surrounding stud farms. In fact, the Curragh also refers to a large area of heathland, and within its boundaries is the Irish Republic's oldest golf course.

**Curragh** Golf Club was formerly a 'Royal' club until the land on which it lies was handed over to the Irish Free State Army in 1922. It has an interesting history and for many years it was believed to have been built well after 1855, the year the nearby military Curragh Camp was established to expand the training requirements for the Crimean War. Now, thanks to Commandant William H. Gibson, a prominent club member, the true history has been unearthed. A recently found newspaper report from 1942 actually revealed that a match between an Alexander Lowe and a David Ritchie had been played at the links near Donnelly's hollow (a former outdoor boxing arena next to the present-day course) in 1857. Furthermore documents found by Ritchie's granddaughter revealed that he had been a member of Musselburgh and came to Ireland in 1851, laying out the course soon after his arrival – before the army came!

In any event, today the army plays a

*The River Liffey flows close by a green at the Hermitage. The course is famous for its superb trees – and good golf, too. It is popular with many Dubliners*

big role in the club, forming a sizeable share of the membership. The club's president is always the General Officer Commanding, whether a golfer or not.

Set out in gently contoured heathland, the Curragh, which is a good test, is noted for one or two local hazards. Local farmers have grazing rights which means that you are never alone for long with sheep on the fairways. And when interclub competitions take place many believe that it is more than a coincidence that the nearby army range is often open. Try playing with hand grenades and machine guns going off at the top of your backswing!

Ireland's great golfing discovery, Lillian Behan, who became an international after playing for just two years, is a member here, and for visitors to play on

help of professional Tommy Halpin, the courses are built on former farmland. But back in 1983, some of the members broke away and formed their own club at Beech Park near Rathcoole in County Dublin. The scenic tree-lined layout is interesting, enjoyable to play and green fees are very low.

**Slade Valley**'s 18 holes are situated high in the Dublin mountains and offer stunning views across five counties. Although they are challenging to your golfing skills, they test your strength and your legs, too, so be warned.

**Stackstown** and **Dublin Sport** are two more hilly courses to the south of the city. Stackstown was built in 1976 with over 50 per cent of its membership coming from Dublin's Garda (police force). It is tough finding a level lie but the views of Dublin are unbeatable. Dublin Sport has advantages of a different kind – in addition to the golf course, there are a dry ski slope, a swimming pool and hotel. In **Dublin** there are many fine hotels catering for a wide range of budgets. The Tourist Board will be happy to supply you with details (see the address section). Dublin also has its fair share of top restaurants and places of interest if you enjoy sightseeing. Not to be missed is the wonderful Georgian architecture of Fitzwilliam Square. And, of course, it goes without saying that if you really want to get a taste of Dublin and meet the people, you should visit the pubs and try the famous local brew in its home town – Guinness.

the Curragh's 18 holes, the green fees are very reasonable indeed. Three miles away across the race track lies the flat nine-hole course of **Cill Dara**.

**Naas** has a pleasant nine holes of rolling parkland just off the N7 back towards Dublin, while Four Lakes Golf and Country Club is a new 18-hole parkland course even closer to the city.

*Clontarf is the nearest course to the city centre of Dublin. It caters for bowls players as well as golfers and is worth a visit if you play both sports*

**Bodenstown** Golf Club, founded in 1971, is close to the nearby village of Sallins. Owned by entrepreneur Dick Mather, who recently designed the club's second 18-hole course with the

**Dublin** has many attractive courses on its southside, the majority of which are parkland. They include **Elm Park**, an appealing layout with a stream crossing many of the holes (and tennis, too, if you are a keen player); **Milltown**, an exclusive club which boasts wonderful catering but a fairly flat course; **Castle** which is more undulating and a marginally stiffer test; **Edmondstown; Dun Laoghaire** in a peaceful setting behind the port and the scene of Tommie Campbell's record drive of 392 yards in 1964 when he attempted to bring the par-5 18th to its knees; and **Newlands** to the west.

**The Grange** lies directly south of the city centre and was established in 1911. James Braid was involved in the original layout, and it is a deceptively tricky and demanding course. Walter Sullivan has been the club's pro for many years and none other than Eamonn Darcy was once a former assistant.

Laid out over mature rolling parkland, it has a gentle introduction with two par-3's opening the card. However, by the time you reach the 18th, the course will have presented you with a

formidable test. The 18th itself is a challenging 420 yards requiring an accurate drive downhill to the left opening up an entrance to the green beyond a stream. Green fees are average for Dublin and the clubhouse is very friendly. In such a quiet, peaceful setting, it is difficult to remember that the bustling centre of the city is only a short drive away.

**Rathfarnham, Ballinascorney, Killiney** and **Carrickmines** are all nine-holers on Dublin's southside. In and around the well-known horse racing track at **Leopardstown** is an 18-hole par-3 cir-

*The Grange is quite close to Dublin's centre. James Braid, the course architect, set the golfer some challenging tests as always on this course*

cuit plus driving range to complement a full nine-hole course. **Foxrock** is another enjoyable nine-holer with a very amiable club. Set in attractive parkland, John O'Leary started his golf here.

**Stepaside**, run and funded by the Golf Union of Ireland, gives a marvellous indication of what can be achieved by reclaiming land from a rubbish tip. Designed by Eddie Hackett and landscaped by the council, it is a delightful place and a lesson as to how public courses should be run and built. With special rates for senior citizens, juniors and the unemployed, the basic green fee is very low.

**Woodbrook** is reached by the main road south from Dublin (the N11). This is yet another of the capital's famous clubs

which has hosted the Carrolls Irish Open. Founded as recently as 1927, the course is a subtle mixture of parkland with a links flavour to some holes. A railway line separates 13 holes close to the sea (the most interesting) from the remaining five. The clubhouse has superb facilities and the course is a popular venue for societies. Green fees are

*This view of Greystones gives a good feel of the heath and parkland mix of this pleasant and enjoyable course*

slightly on the high side, and visitors are not encouraged to play on Saturdays.

**Bray**, with its nine-hole course is nearby and there are plans for a new club to be

built close to the town. In 1986 the river that meanders past Bray's second fairway burst its banks in the aftermath of Hurricane Charlie. The result was a few feet of water on the course, and some stranded salmon were left when the waters eventually receded!

**Woodenbridge** to the south of County Wicklow suffered a similar fate. This picturesque nine-holer was covered in hundreds of tons of silt when the River Avoca decided to look for a new route. However, the members rallied round and cleared the course within days.

**Arklow** and **Blainroe** are both 18-hole links courses while **Wicklow** has a nine-holer. But for really good holiday golf you need look no further than Delgany and Greystones on the coast 40 minutes' south of Dublin. This area has the proud boast of having produced some of Ireland's finest players including the Bradshaws, Jimmy Martin, Christy Greene, Ray Hayden, Bill Kinsella, Eamonn Darcy and the Dalys. There are numerous hotels, inns and guest houses where you can stay.

**Delgany** is an attractive, hilly parkland course which was founded in 1908. It is open to visitors at most times and has full catering facilities. The green fees are reasonable and there is a well-stocked pro shop where you can hire clubs if wished.

**Greystones** is just a couple of miles away and although it is difficult to find, it has all the right ingredients for great holiday golf. With a charming clubhouse, friendly staff and a good course combining some of the best elements of parkland and heath, few visitors leave disappointed. Furthermore, there are great views of the Wicklow Mountains and the Irish Sea, especially from the tee at the 367-yards 18th (the highest point on the course). Try driving the 13th – over 300 yards and uphill all the way.

It is a small club with a big heart and the warmest of welcomes. Green fees are reasonable, too, so make sure you pay it a visit.

From the classic links courses in the north to the scenic parkland layouts in the South, Dublin offers the visitor a feast of golf and at reasonable prices. With so much golf to choose from, wonderful hospitality from the friendly people and an exciting city to discover, Dublin should not be missed.

*Dublin is a beautiful city with graceful Georgian buildings and historic churches. Stay there and combine the best of golf with great entertainment, shopping and sightseeing. Some of the sights of Dublin include Christchurch (right), the Merchant's Arch (bottom left), and St Patrick's Cathedral (bottom right)*

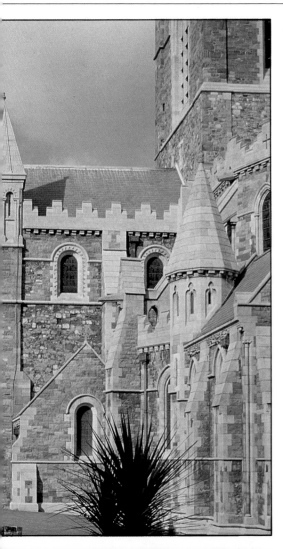

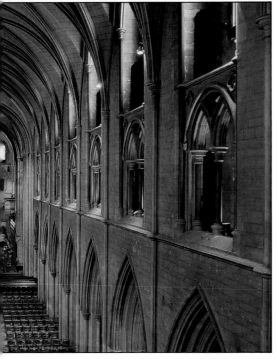

# Guinness – a taste of Ireland

It is as close to an Irishman's heart as Scotch is to a Scotsman. Guinness, that unique blend of barley, hops, water and yeast, is undoubtedly the taste of Ireland and has been for over 200 years.

It was Arthur Guinness who founded the brewery in Dublin in 1759 after being left £100 by his godfather. Arthur arrived in the city at St James' Gate, took over a small disused, ill-equipped brewery and made it prosper when other Dublin brewers were going through hard times. He took on the premises on a 9000-year lease, at an annual rent of just £45!

In the 1770s a new drink, popular with porters at London's Covent Garden and Billingsgate markets, was being exported to Dublin. It was served from a single barrel and contained roasted barley which gave it a distinctive dark colour. Arthur Guinness had been brewing ale served from a blend of several barrels but decided to put all his hops in one basket, so to speak, taking on the English brewers with his own 'porter'. He obviously made the right choice for that decision set the seal on the world's largest porter and stout brewery.

Now drunk at a staggering rate of nine million glasses a day, the Guinness empire stretches to all corners of the globe. There are now sister breweries in five other countries, including one at Park Royal in London, licensing agreements in a further 16 countries, and two ships, the Lady Patricia and Miranda Guinness which constantly carry their thirst-quenching liquid cargo from the banks of the River Liffey in the centre of Dublin through the waterways of the world.

In Ireland, 80 per cent of their sales are on draught and for the Irishman who cannot bear to be away from his pint for too long, Guinness have come up with a unique answer; for as well as the ordinary bottled variety they can now obtain bottled *draught* Guinness! What's more, it tastes just like the pint lovingly pulled at the bar.

What makes Guinness so special? Well, it is the barley that makes the malt, lupulin in the hops which gives that familiar bitter flavour, the roasting that provides the ruby tint and yeast that makes the creamy head.

Guinness is always favoured in Ireland with seafood. However, you will not hear many complaints in the clubhouse when it is drunk on its own after a challenging round of golf.

**1** Carlow (18)
**2** Borris (9)
**3** Waterford (18)
**4** Tramore (18)
**5** Dungarvan (9)
**6** Lismore (9)
**7** Clonmel (18)
**8** Cahir Park (9)
**9** Tipperary (9)
**10** Carrick-on-Suir (9)
**11** Callan (9)
**12** Kilkenny (18)
**13** Castlecomer (9)
**14** Thurles (18)
**15** Templemore (9)
**16** Nenagh (18)
**17** Roscrea (9)
**18** Birr (18)
**19** Moate (9)
**20** Athlone (18)
**21** County Longford (18)
**22** Mullingar (18)
**23** Edenderry (9)
**24** Tullamore (18)
**25** Portarlington (9)
**26** Heath (18)
**27** Mountrath (9)
**28** Rathdowney (9)
**29** Abbey Leix (9)
**30** Courtown (18)
**31** Enniscorthy (9)
**32** New Ross (9)
**33** Wexford (18)
**34** Rosslare (18)

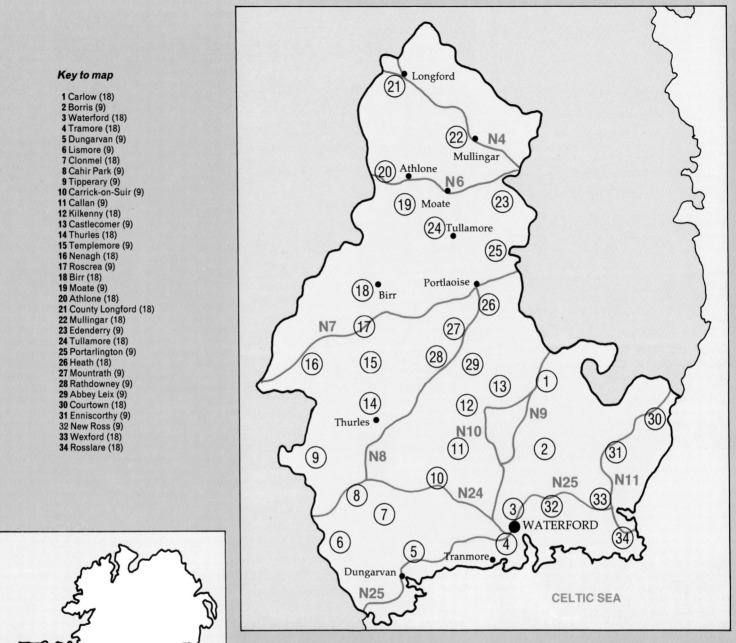

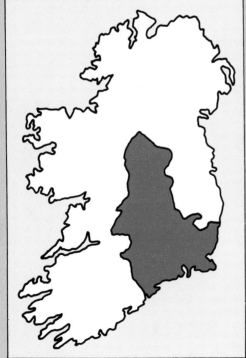

# South~east Ireland

Although the south-east of Ireland does not have the magnificent Championship courses of the neighbouring south-west, it does offer challenging, inexpensive and uncrowded courses in some of the friendliest places you could possibly visit. One of the region's benefits is that this right-hand corner of Ireland boasts more hours of sunshine and less rain in summer than any other region, thus earning its name as the 'sunny south-east'. And it is a great area for holidays with superb sandy beaches and a wide range of sports and leisure activities on offer for golfers and golf widows alike. There are sightseeing tours to places of historical interest and local landmarks.

It is easy to get to this part of Ireland, whether you fly to Cork or Dublin and then hire a car, or drive your own and take the ferry between Fishguard in Wales and Rosslare in County Wexford. And when you arrive, there is something for everyone to keep the whole family occupied so that you can all enjoy your holiday in this beautiful corner of Ireland.

**Carlow** is the ideal place to tee off a

*The 17th at Carlow with its green set at the top of a rise – only 150 yards but further than it looks so take enough club*

golfing holiday. The course is hailed by many as the finest inland layout that Ireland has on offer. You will soon discover why if you play there.

Situated within a rich, agricultural region, Carlow was built on good land and, as a consequence, is able to boast of excellent turf which proves playable

almost all the year round. The beauty of this 6350-yard course is that no two holes play the same. It is now all the better since the club acted on advice from Jim Arthur, the renowned agronomist, regarding the positioning of bunkers and trees. They add to the overall challenge of the course which continues to attract some of the best names in amateur golf to compete in the annual Midland Scratch Cup. Walker Cup player Peter McEvoy is among these. He has competed in three of these events, during which he shot 11 consecutive rounds under 70 (the SSS from the championship tees is 71), including two 66's – the joint course record.

The tighter of the two halves at Carlow is the back nine. After the dogleg right 10th, which plays over water, the trees lining the fairways become thicker, demanding greater accuracy from the tee. The closing stretch from the 14th, an exacting par-4 of 456 yards, will draw on the resources of every golfer to the bitter end.

Worthy too of mention is the 16th. At 431 yards, this par-4 requires a good blow from the tee to give the player any chance of success with the approach shot. This leads through a narrow, tunnel-like entrance to a raised green which only accommodates the most accurate of strokes. Making par here

*Although Borris has just 9 holes, they are all good ones, with two sets of tees and some excellent greens*

deserves a well-earned pat on the back, but beware! Do not relax because the 17th is no less a test of skill. Deceptively short at 151 yards, this, the best of Carlow's four par-3's, calls for more club than you might at first assume by virtue of the amply bunkered green which sits way up a steep hill. Completion of the 18th will leave you more than ready to pay a visit to the comfortable, friendly clubhouse for refreshment and, before long, you will be ready to go out again in an attempt to gain revenge on the course.

**Borris** is the only other golf course in County Carlow – it is reputedly one of the best nine-holers in the country and is renowned for the excellence of its

*The 13th at Rosslare, a par-4 of just 280 yards which can be challenging*

greens. With two tees on each hole to give a different perspective the second time round, the 6041 yards track is built around a hill in the shadow of the majestic Blackstairs range which includes Mount Leinster. On a nearby hill sits the splendid Borris House, seat of the MacMurrough Kavanaghs, former kings of the Leinster province who date back to Norman times.

**Kilkenny** is an 18-hole course situated to the west of Carlow over the border in County Kilkenny. It is about a mile outside the Medieval City of Kilkenny which was once the capital of Ireland and home of the Irish Parliament.

It is an excellent parkland layout of 6369 yards and, although mostly flat, it has a few interesting holes on hills and slopes. There are a number of short par-4's and par-3's. However, to compensate for them, there are also such holes as the 436 yards par-4 11th, and the 211 yards par-3 10th. These are both challenging propositions for any stan-

dard of golfer. Green fees are very reasonable, and the course is worth a visit if you are in the region.

The county of Kilkenny is also home to two nine-hole courses at **Castlecomer** and **Callan**, but the county's best-known game is hurling – Ireland's national sport. The locals learn to swing a hurling stick while still young children and, since hurlers often make excellent golfers, this may account for the many natural golf swings seen throughout the area. If you are staying here, you should not miss a spot of sightseeing, especially Kilkenny Castle and Kyteler's Inn in the Medieval City itself.

This was established in the early fourteenth century by Dame Alice le Kyteler who was famous for her charm, immeasurable wealth and her four husbands. However, she died tragically having been whipped through the streets and then burned at the stake for

witchcraft – no doubt the charges brought against her were provoked by jealousy. Kyteler's still stands and you can enjoy a drink or a meal under the ancient beams that were old even before Christopher Columbus discovered America.

**Rosslare** Golf Club lies to the east in the county of Wexford. Formed in 1905, it is one of Ireland's oldest clubs. This true links course, although it cannot profess to championship status, is nevertheless an extremely testing challenge and one of the most enjoyable golf venues in the south-east.

Rosslare is the old Irish name for Middle Peninsula, a sandbank which originally ran out across the mouth of Wexford Harbour. When Rosslare Harbour was built, it changed the tidal behaviour of the sea and resulted in the bank being eroded away completely. This is a problem that Rosslare Golf Club also had to wrestle with because of the proximity of the course to the sea.

Some holes have already been washed into the briny, and now railway sleepers have been used as a barrier to save any further loss of the precious links.

With two sets of tees, Rosslare can play to either 6502 yards with a par of 74 or 6066 with a par of 69. The course can become quite a different proposition from the back tees, especially when the wind whips in off the sea. Covering a narrow strip of land running parallel to the beach, Rosslare is blessed with natural rolling duneland, wispy rough and furze.

Also in County Wexford are the 18-hole courses of **Courtown** and **Wexford**, and the nine-holers of **New Ross** and **Enniscorthy**. Crossing back westwards into County Waterford, you will come across more courses and some attractive beach resorts on the south coast of Ireland.

**Tramore** Golf Club is an 18-hole layout built on marsh and bogland on Newtown Hill. You would not realise this from the beautifully conditioned greens which make it one of Ireland's better inland courses. It was not always like this, however. The original links built in 1894 was totally swamped by the sea in 1912 when it broke through the protective sandbanks. A second nine-holer was then built within a racecourse but having some of the tees outside the walls of the track was hardly conducive to good golf so the club moved to its present site in 1935.

It took four years to drain the land and prepare the holes for play. The planting of a multitude of trees served at the time to draw the water out of the ground, and now provides an attractive backdrop to the 6560-yards, par-71 course. There are some tough doglegs and tight drives on this lush, firm parkland terrain, and the greens are of such a size that three putts can often seem quite respectable. But the great feature of Tramore is its ability to provide any standard of golfer with an appropriate test for his personal level.

The relatively new clubhouse, built in 1970, is unrivalled in the area. It accommodates visitors and members alike and full catering is always available. There are even squash courts and five double bedrooms if you feel like staying overnight.

Tramore itself is a wonderful little holiday town with three miles of golden

*The 13th at Clonmel, a long par-4 on a course that is very much a mixture of uphill and downhill shots, making judgement of distance difficult*

beaches and a wide range of accommodation including high-quality hotels, bed-and-breakfast houses and self-catering chalets.

# Waterford glass

Although Waterford can boast a fine 18-hole golf course, there is no question that the county town is of worldwide renown for its crystal, arguably the finest produced anywhere in the world.

The Waterford Crystal Company does, however, hold strong links with the local golf club, and vice versa. About 80 per cent of the golf membership work at the glass factory, which means that the club is able to host Ireland's biggest annual open golf day, when over £17,000 worth of crystal is put up in prizes. Also, in 1956, Waterford Crystal presented the famous Waterford Scratch Trophy, now one of the most prestigious amateur events in Ireland and Britain. The magnificent trophy, which resides permanently at Waterford Golf Club, took three-and-a-half months to make, stands three feet high and weighs 56lb.

The Waterford Trophy is undoubtedly the showpiece of the crystal company's association with golf. A replica of it adorns the plush, new display room where it stands proudly among other replicas, including the US Tournament Players' Championship, Kemper Open, USF&G Championship, USLPGA Championship, World Championship of Women's Golf, Carrolls Irish Open and Australian Open.

Despite its fame throughout the world, Waterford Crystal did not really become a big name in golf until 1975 when the BBC presented souvenir crystal pieces during the popular Pro-Celebrity TV series at Gleneagles. Bing Crosby, one of the guest celebrities, was so taken with the glass, he started using it as prizes for his own USPGA tournament, the Bing Crosby Pro-Am. From then on, the popularity of the crystal in America grew to such a point that the United States now imports 80 per cent of all the products manufactured at the Waterford factory.

The exceptionally high quality of workmanship that has given Waterford Crystal its tremendous reputation can be witnessed, right from the molten glass stage through to the engravers' room, where the senior cutters are required to have undergone a 10-year apprenticeship. Organized tours are available for visitors and can be booked in advance by phoning the glass factory at Kilbarry on (051) 73311.

**Waterford** is the only other 18-hole course in the county. This 6323 yards, par-71 parkland layout is the work of Willie Park Jnr. with later modifications by James Braid and Hamilton Stutt. Although there are no apparent problems for the visiting golfer, Waterford is deceptively tough and deserves its reputation as a great inland course.

And a trip to the town could not possibly be complete without a visit to the world-famous Waterford Crystal factory where the renowned Waterford Scratch Trophy, permanently housed at the golf club, was made. Tours of the factory covering every aspect of its manufacturing processes and the chance to buy some beautiful glassware, are available.

The only other two golf courses in County Waterford are the nine-holers at **Dungarvon** and **Lismore**.

**Clonmel** is a hilly 6349-yards layout just north of the county boundary in County Tipperary. It is a highly enjoyable course which remains largely unknown and unrecognised due to its isolated location which is off the usual tourist beaten track. And you certainly will not have to queue for the first tee here as it rarely gets busy. Once out on the course, you can feel quite alone and isolated, with only the sound of streams babbling down from the mountains and the singing of birds to interrupt the quiet and tranquillity. The layout was designed by the great Irish course architect Eddie Hackett, and it offers a great variety of holes which climb up and down the slopes and hillsides. Accuracy is essential if you are to avoid trees, streams and the odd sprinkling of gorse and heather. Severe slopes also mean that strategic placing of shots will keep the ball from rolling off line.

The three-year-old clubhouse is reminiscent of Switzerland or Austria with its Alpine design and the superb backdrop of pine and fir covered mountains. Full catering is available at lunchtime and dinner for visitors as well as members. Green fees are reasonably priced.

**Nenagh** and **Thurles** are the two other 18-hole layouts in County Tipperary, both situated in the northern half. Nenagh is a quiet club with a course of only just over 5500 yards and an SSS of 68. Although it may not be much of a challenge to play, it is great exercise for your leg muscles with hills to climb from many of the tees to the greens. No

catering is available.

Thurles is flatter and much busier. Established in 1944, it has nine holes on either side of a main road. It makes a pleasant outing although it is not the most demanding of courses. However, it is advised that you book in advance by phoning the Secretary to be sure of a

*Note the clever siting of the 5th green at Nenagh, which is a 170-yard par-3. A challenge for every player*

game.

There are five other courses in Tipperary, but they are all nine-holers, situated at **Carrick-on-Suir**, **Cahir**, **Tipperary**, **Templemore** and **Roscrea**.

**The Heath** is the only 18-hole course in County Laois (pronounced 'leash'). Situated on common land, it has to share its home with flocks of wandering sheep. However, the 6256 yards, par-71 layout is immensely enjoyable, especially if you manage to avoid some of the immovable hazards that dot the fairways! Most of the course is flat, although the humps and hollows on some holes give the impression of a links layout. Visitors are always welcome in this hospitable club and the catering is excellent. Green fees are reasonable, too, making it well worth a visit.

The neighbouring golf clubs of **Rath-**

*The clubhouse at Thurles, flanked by fine trees, is busy and popular*

**downey**, **Mountrath**, **Abbeyleix** and **Portarlington** all have nine holes apiece.

**Birr** in County Offaly is a good test of golf with 18 holes set out over a 6262-yards layout of rolling terrain with a number of blind shots on offer. The tumbling land is owned by the Earl of Rosses, whose grandfather originally offered the land to the club at a minimal rent of just two shillings a year as a gesture towards the people of the town. The cost is still just a token fee. Birr enjoys visitors as it rarely gets the opportunity to welcome them.

**Tullamore** is another good 18-holer situated near the old Grand Canal linking Dublin and Shannon. The town is also the home of Irish Mist, Ireland's legendary liqueur, and is an excellent base for exploring the mystical Slieve Bloom Mountains. The club has been at its present site since 1926, leased from a private estate and dotted with ancient trees. James Braid himself worked in an advisory capacity on the 6314-yards, par-72 parkland course which is a fair but flat test of golf. Visitors are welcome but they should book in advance of their visit.

**Athlone** is another magnificent setting with the course set on a peninsula jutting out into Lough Ree. Despite this it has inland-type turf with some enjoyable holes and great potential for expansion. The most demanding hole is the 16th, a long par-4 with the Lough on the left and trees to the right. For a modest green fee, it is a real golfing bargain, the view from the clubhouse being worth the expenditure alone.

**Mullingar** in County Westmeath is another of Ireland's great inland courses. It sits among some of the picturesque countryside of the Irish Midlands where the beautiful lakes, or loughs, of Ennell, Owel and Derravaragh are located.

Having struggled with the layout of the course for some time, the members employed the services of James Braid in 1937. He took the rough plans that had already been drawn up, 18 tee pegs and 18 stakes out with him for a day, and by evening had already laid out the skeleton of the 6461-yard layout that is still played today. On a later visit to Mullingar, Braid admitted that he regarded it as one of his better pieces of work, especially as it was designed in only one day!

As well as the annual Mullingar Scratch Cup, which boasts such prestigious names as Joe Carr, Peter McEvoy, Tom Craddock and Peter Townsend among its champions, the club has hosted many major national tournaments, including the Irish National Championship and Carrolls Irish Matchplay Championship.

Mullingar is fortunate in having a close association with the neighbouring Bloomfield House Hotel. Golf packages can be arranged from the hotel, as well as windsurfing on the adjacent Lough Ennell.

*Rocks and sheep are amongst the hazards at the Heath in County Laois. This is the 11th, a par-3, on a flattish links-type course*

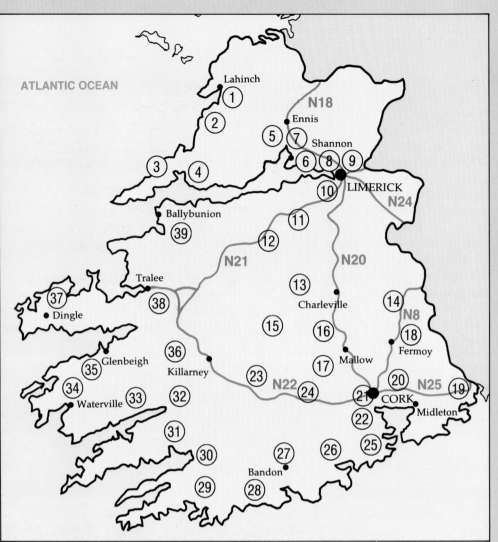

ATLANTIC OCEAN

## Key to map

1 Lahinch (36)
2 Spanish Point (9)
3 Kilkee (9)
4 Kilrush (9)
5 Ennis (18)
6 Shannon (18)
7 Drumoland Castle (9)
8 Clonlara (9)
9 Limerick (18)
10 Castletroy (18)
11 Adare Manor (9)
12 Newcastle West (9)
13 Charleville (18)
14 Mitchelstown (9)
15 Kanturk (9)
16 Doneraile (9)
17 Mallow (18)
18 Fermoy (18)
19 Youghal (18)
20 East Cork (9)
21 Cork (18)
22 Douglas (18)
23 Macroom (9)
24 Muskerry (18)
25 Monkstown (18)
26 Kinsale (9)
27 Bandon (18)
28 Dunmore (9)
29 Skibbereen (9)
30 Bantry (9)
31 Glengarriff (9)
32 Kenmare (9)
33 Parknasilla (9)
34 Waterville (18)
35 Dooks (18)
36 Killarney (36)
37 Ceann Sibeal (9)
38 Tralee (18)
39 Ballybunion (18)

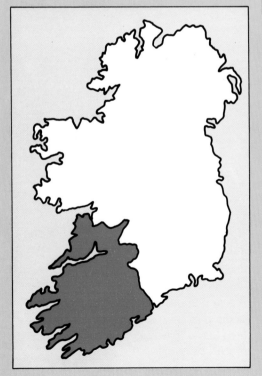

# South~west Ireland

This area encompasses the great golf country of Ireland – the counties of Kerry, Clare, Cork and Limerick which are home to some of the best courses in the Emerald Isle. Kerry is the most famous throughout the world and is on a par with the great golfing areas of Scotland. In fact, it is regarded by some as the best endowed golfing country in the British Isles with such meccas as Ballybunion and Tralee. And once again, as elsewhere in Ireland, the people are friendly and hospitable and you are certain of a warm welcome. It is a beautiful area of outstanding natural beauty with lush green countryside, magnificent lakes and mountains and a spectacular coastline.

**Ballybunion** is a 'must' for all golf enthusiasts and no visit to the south-west would be complete without playing here. It collects compliments like philatelists collect stamps. For instance, the great American writer Herbert Warren Wind described it as the "finest seaside course I have ever seen". And Tom Watson says: "Ballybunion is a

course on which golf architects should live and play before they build golf courses." Both these comments refer to Ballybunion Old. There is now a New

*The 16th green with its entrance between dunes, one of the best holes on the famous Old Course at Ballybunion*

Course, too, the creation of a man who heeded Tom Watson's advice. Robert Trent Jones, the doyen of the present-day course architects, said of the land at his disposal: "It was the finest piece of linksland that I had ever seen and perhaps the finest piece of linksland in the world". Peter Dobereiner, the well-known and internationally respected

golf writer says: "I have no hesitation in proclaiming that this course is a masterpiece, the greatest links course in the world, and by a clear margin."

So most people recognise that Ballybunion is a good place for a decent day's golf. The only hazard is the unpredictable weather, or rather the volume of wind and rain in this part of Ireland. Even the Irish Tourist Board admits that 'There is not much climate in Kerry – temperatures normally range between 7°C to 8°C in winter to 15.5°C in summer, but there is a great deal of weather, strong winds from the Atlantic and much rain.' The wind alone can be severe enough to reduce the most resilient golfing umbrella to a tattered wreck within a few minutes, so do take your waterproof, even in the summer months.

However, having said that, Ballybunion remains one of the world's great golf courses. Situated in the remotest of the south-western counties, it is approached mainly by winding country roads from Cork or Shannon airports. When you get there, you will soon discover that Ballybunion is indeed brilliant, but which course should you play? Well, as the old dictum runs, age before beauty, and so the Old takes precedence over the New, even though it can justifiably boast of both.

It began life late in the nineteenth century but was only extended to 18 holes in 1926. The renowned British architect Tom Simpson was brought in to recommend alterations prior to the course hosting the Irish Amateur Championship in 1937. Simpson's reputation is not only deserved for what he could do but also because he recognised when to leave well alone. He was given *carte blanche* but chose only to move three greens and insert one fairway bunker.

The visual appeal of Ballybunion rests primarily on the marvellous use of its land by the sea to create several outstanding holes. Herb Wind perceptively noted what he called "undoubted-ly the secret of its character and charm – it is the only links I know of where the sandhill ridges do not run parallel with the shore but at a decided traverse." Add to this Ballybunion's merited claim to be the stiffest test of the approach shot in links golf (perhaps only Dornoch, with its invariably raised greens, can compare with it) and you can readily appreciate why so long as Guinness is dark the Old Course will be a cast-iron certainty for inclusion in the top 10 courses in the British Isles.

Since Wind made his assessment in 1967, the course has undergone two notable alterations. The bad news is that the 7th green has had to be moved. The cliff-top upon which it was so lovingly and precariously sited has succumbed to that hazard of many spectacular links holes – coastal erosion. The green was originally moved inland but today it has been shifted again to recapture something, if not all, of its former glory nearer the pounding waves.

A change for the better in recent times has been the building of a new clubhouse, causing the old 14th to become the 1st. This means that two relatively mundane short par-5s, now the 4th and 5th, are no longer the closing two holes of the round.

Describing any of the holes at Ballybunion as mundane is a risky business, even in the convivial atmosphere of the bar. The members do not lightly accept criticism of their pride and joy, but it is an inescapable fact that though neither the 4th or 5th are poor holes, they are more fittingly enjoyed as a kind of entrée than as a pair of *petit fives*. Sadly the present 18th, which requires an iron off the tee to be short of a huge bunker, followed by an approach to a completely hidden green, is not exactly the finest of finishing holes either.

*The 15th at Ballybunion Old. It gives real satisfaction to find the green at this outstanding and much admired par-3, rated one of the best in the world by Tom Watson*

Having knocked the only three mediocre holes on the Old, there is insufficient space to do justice to the rest. Three of those that are justifiably most lauded are the 6th, 9th and 11th. There is not a sand bunker on any of these tremendous par-4's but the second shot to all of them has to be as true as a bullet to hold the target. To err left or right, short or long, is to ensure an exacting piece of wedge practice with absolutely no guarantee of holding the target with the resultant chip shot. The 11th is a particularly heroic hole from the back markers (449 yards) and hardly less stimulating from the ordinary plates at 400 yards. The view from the tee is both magnificent, with the crashing

waves not far below, and awesome. A nest of sandhills protects the green as if it were a precious jewel.

The 15th, 16th and 17th (respectively a long par-3 back towards the beach, a par-5 where the green beckons at the far end of a narrow alley between the dunes, and a dogleg left par-4 with a vertigo-inducing tee and Himalayan-like sandhills) bring the round to a tumultuous climax, the 18th being regarded as merely an intriguing walk back to the clubhouse.

*Robert Trent Jones seldom had the chance to work on links land. He rejoiced in what he found for his New Course at Bally-bunion. Here are the 4th, 6th and 7th*

The smart thing to do on leaving the 17th green is to walk the few yards to the 11th tee on the New. Obviously we cannot advocate that you do that but, nevertheless, one cannot help but ponder what a composite course that would make: holes 1, 2 and 10 to 17 on the Old and 11 to 18 on the New. Since there are many more than 18 great holes in the 36 at Ballybunion this would deny you the privilege of playing gems like the 6th and 7th on the Old or the 4th and 5th on the New, these two being classic examples of the Trent Jones philosophy of easy bogey, tough par. You would also miss out on the 328-yard 10th of which Jones said: "There is no more natural golf hole in the world, an outrageously

beautiful stretch of God-given terrain." The driving zone is wide enough to be almost visible to the naked eye and the green is at least half the size of Troon's 'Postage Stamp' 8th. In other words, when the wind is against you, it is one of the most difficult par-4's in the world.

The land is magnificent, lending itself to holes like the 13th where it does indeed appear as if the Lord Himself decided on the position of the green. Work only began on the New in the winter of 1981 and the members held the first competition over it in December 1982. It is now in superb condition, and the greens are especially excellent: some of the best putting surfaces you will ever see in the British Isles.

The New owes its existence to the foresight of the club in buying the adjoining land in the 1970s and its development, ironically, has inevitably been assisted by the phenomenal success of the erosion appeal and life

*The holes through the dunes at Tralee are magnificent. The combination of sea, sand, bays and headlands were the scenic backdrop for 'Ryan's Daughter'*

membership scheme launched 10 years ago to help build the defences necessary to safeguard the Old from the ravages of the Atlantic.

Whichever is the better of the two courses, the members at Ballybunion are fortunate to have at their disposal the best 36 holes of links golf anywhere. Visitors are greeted with genuine warmth and a day's golf is worth the high green fees.

**Tralee** Golf Club is about 40 minutes' drive south of Ballybunion on a finger of land bravely jutting out into the Atlantic Ocean, near the hamlet of Barrow. Tralee is the principal town of County Kerry, but the members of the original golf club were disillusioned with their

marshy nine-holer at Mounthawk which was virtually unplayable during the winter months. So they sold it as a building plot and purchased a property eight miles away at Barrow. The new Tralee was opened in October 1984 at enormous cost. The clubhouse is still a well-equipped Portakabin, and a full programme of bunkering is still in the process of being implemented, but do not let that put you off.

Now assuming that a golf course consists of two elements – its attraction as a place and the quality of the holes themselves – Tralee is another masterpiece. It is impossible to conceive of a more marvellous setting. The course rests upon the steep majestic cliffs made famous in the film *Ryan's Daughter*, and beneath them is a vast expanse of golden sand and a spectacular bay. Across the estuary is the Dingle Peninsula, and the Slieve Mish Mountains dominate the skyline behind you. It is impossible not

to draw comparisons with the beauty of Pebble Beach and Cypress Point. But Peter Dobereiner writes: 'Robert Louis Stevenson was wrong, and by a long chalk, when he described the Monterey Peninsula of California as the finest conjunction of land and sea that this earth has to offer. As a spectacle Tralee is in a different class.'

The course was designed by Arnold Palmer and his indefatigable colleague, Ed Seay. Their plans were approved by the club after a tender competition. There are those in the business who allege that Palmer cannot design a cup and saucer but he has certainly produced a golf course which is a treat to play. He has resisted the urge to go for excessive length. At 5912 metres off the whites and 6210 from the blues it is not

*Dooks is one of the oldest courses in Ireland. For many years, little more than rabbits kept the turf cut close until it was later extended to 18 holes*

inordinately long and some of the cliff-top holes, especially the long 2nd and short 3rd, are heroic. But like Trent Jones, Palmer was granted a tract of 'God-given terrain' to work with, and one wonders if the 6th, 8th and 15th make the most of the land and whether the generally prosaic inland holes around the clubhouse might be improved.

Tralee is mercilessly exposed to the elements and the wind and salt water have conspired to hamper attempts at nurturing the turf. But the members are a resilient and ambitious bunch and

they will no doubt conquer adversity to bring their course on and erect the clubhouse it deserves. The green fees make a day's golf at Tralee rare value – and remember to take a camera.

**Dooks** is not on such a grand scale as Tralee but the panorama takes in the peaks of the Kingdom of Kerry and the long promontory of Dingle. To get there, you must follow the Tralee road (the N70) through Killorglin and look for Cromane which is signposted to the right. Turn left at Cromane church and when you see a small bright red building on the right you have arrived, for this is the clubhouse.

Quaint and humble it may look on the outside but inside the clubhouse is a real beauty with an excellent bar. The whole

club has recently undergone a facelift and many improvements have been made.

The club was founded in 1889 with a nine-hole course which was extended to 18 holes in 1970. The turf is half-links, half-meadowland in nature, and the course's status as a sporty holiday test is soon to be upgraded as a result of plans to increase its length, but no doubt idiosyncrasies like the 13th green, which resembles a creased envelope, will be retained.

Considering that there are no permanent greenstaff, the course is in fine condition, totally belying its name (Dooks is the Gaelic word for rabbit warren). Unusually, most of the trouble is behind rather than short of the greens, but Dooks' most singular appeal

*Many say that neither of the two Killarney courses are really great golf. But the few other courses that match the setting can be counted on the fingers of one hand*

is that it is a haven for the Natterjack Toad. This protected animal features prominently on the club's logo.

**Killarney** lies approximately the same distance to the other side of Killorglin. This resort offers much more than golf, with fishing and walking being other popular pastimes in this lakeside paradise at the foot of the Macgillicuddy Reeks chain of mountains. Killarney is often claimed by its devotees as the 'Irish Gleneagles' – a claim that is thoroughly justified. It is arguable whether Gleneagles offers marginally

better golf and Killarney better scenery, but they are both top-class courses in beautiful locations.

Golf was introduced to Killarney in 1891 but it was during the 1930s that it enjoyed a renaissance under the supervision of the Viscount Castlerosse, a large man with a large bank account who achieved fame, and presumably notoriety, as the gossip columnist on the *Sunday Express*. Henry Longhurst, the revered golf correspondent of *The Sunday Times*, was one of his closest friends and with his advice and under the direction of Sir Guy Campbell, already established as a course architect of considerable credentials, Castlerosse's dream 18 was laid out around the shores of Lough Leane in this idyllic location.

That masterpiece has since been split

up into two courses: Mahony's Point and Killeen. This move has brought much needed revenue to Killarney over the year but it is aesthetically disappointing. It is probably beyond argument that the best 18 holes at Killarney are the original 18.

The 185-metre, par-3 18th hole at Mahony's Point, which was also the climax to Castlerosse's project, so appealed to Longhurst that he modestly dubbed it "the best short hole in the world". He may have been biased but Frank Pennick, another esteemed architect, was equally complimentary.

There are several great holes other than that gorgeous finale, with the 387-metre 8th at Killeen being as good as any on that course. Like many holes on both layouts it is devoid of sand but not of peril. The overall lure of Killarney was summed up by Pat Ward-Thomas – another late, venerable British golf writer – when he urged that "all golfers should make a pilgrimage to this truly enchanting place".

In conclusion it has to be said that Killarney is maintained in superior order, and the courses are in perfect shape. The best grasses have been introduced onto the greens and the course is generally as firm as a links. Surprisingly, green fees are not all that expensive, and 18 holes on each course are a must. Do be sure to visit Killarney even if it means making a detour. You cannot help but fall in love with the place.

**Waterville** lies at almost the southernmost point of Kerry and to reach it the road winds through the glorious scenery of the Ring of Kerry. The course itself measures 7257 yards from the back tees but reduces to 6049 off the 'society' plates. When the wind whips up off the sea, some of the carries can be too demanding for even the strongest hitters in golf.

It is the brainchild of Jack Mulcahy, a wealthy Irish-American. Each July, the Jack Mulcahy Classic is contested there

*The Killeen course at Killarney, which followed the original course opened early in World War II, known as Mahony's Point*

– a European Tour 'satellite' event. The course itself, designed by Jack and Eddie Hackett, provides a game of two halves. The outward nine is quite ordinary with the exceptions of the 3rd and 4th which are both excellent. However, the homeward half is outstanding bar one or two holes. The 11th, a 477-yard teaser of a par-5 from the middle marker under the deceiving name of 'Tranquillity', may be the best long hole in Ireland. It epitomizes all that is wonderful about Waterville – Birkdale-type

sandhills and a sinuous stretch of immaculately groomed, tumbling fairway winding between the rough grass of the dunes.

The members take particular pride in two short holes on the back nine, the 12th and 17th. The former is 'The Mass Hole', in honour of the priests who used to celebrate the service in the deep hollow in front of the green in the days when praying was a capital offence. The 17th is 'Mulcahy's Peak' because the elevated tee now stands on the spot from

which the boss would survey his site while plotting the routing of the holes. Some purists complain that Mulcahy should have opted for sandy-based links turf rather than deliberately choosing strains of grass more often associated with parkland courses and which inevitably appear a trifle incongruous when set against the proximity of the ocean and the indigenous sandhills. Maybe but it is, after all, Mulcahy's course and any visitor will be grateful that he built it. Green fees, incidentally, are exactly

*While he made his money in the United States, Jack Mulcahy dreamed of building a magnificent course on the west coast of Ireland – he did it at Waterville*

the same as at Ballybunion, even down to the extra fee for overseas visitors.

If you wish to stay for a few days, the nearby Waterville Lake Hotel has extensive and luxurious facilities and is a great golfing holiday destination.

**Lahinch** is located further north in County Clare, and only 30 miles north-west of Shannon Airport. The small town overlooks Liscannor Bay and the Cliffs of Moher, and its fabric is inextricably interwoven with the life of the golf club – hence its nickname as the Irish St Andrews. It is another great course and is not eclipsed by the riches of neighbouring Kerry.

The Scots introduced golf to Lahinch in 1893, but it was in 1928 that Dr Alister Mackenzie, who had recently completed work in Cypress Point and was soon afterwards to build Augusta National in collaboration with Bobby Jones, revised the links. He eventually left the job contented with what he had done. "Lahinch will make the finest and most popular course that I, or I believe anyone else, ever constructed", he said. Although that has to be an overstatement of Lahinch's worth, it does indicate the calibre of the place, and Mackenzie was demonstrably not a man whose opinion can be easily ignored.

Good golf holes abound at Lahinch.

*A view up in the dunes at Lahinch, with the ruined O'Brien's Castle in the distance*

Some of the par-4s utilize the fabulous terrain to absolutely optimum advantage. The stretch from the 7th to the 10th is especially memorable in this respect. Two holes that Mackenzie was not permitted to touch were the 5th and 6th, a long hole and a short one, respectively known as 'Klondyke' and 'Dell'. The former measures 453 metres

and the second shot has to clear a central mound very much in the fashion of the 16th hole at Southport & Ainsdale. The 6th is that ultimate horror, a blind par-3, where the only clue as to the direction of the flag is a white stone which is shifted every time a new cup is cut. These two holes are anachronisms, but not without charm unless you have run up a double-bogey.

Like Killarney, the course has been subject to a few modifications, notably the adding of new tees at the 9th and 13th and the moving back of the greens on the 7th and 12th. This has primarily been done according to plans drawn up by Donald Steel. And if competitors baulk at the prospect of playing the 'Dell', the club could always use its genuine 19th hole; a fine new par-3 inserted between the 8th and 9th in case of emergencies.

The South of Ireland Amateur Championship was inaugurated at Lahinch in 1895 and the club has remained the permanent home to this prestigious event. It is played over the Cham-

*Most golfers reckon that the holes running close to the Atlantic are the best at Waterville – superb golfing country*

pionship Course, to which one is always referring when talking of Lahinch. There is also a short holiday 18, the Castle Course, across the road, encircling the solitary tower of O'Brien's Castle.

Green fees are lower, of course, on the Castle Course but even on the Championship one they are not unreasonable, although higher at weekends and on bank holidays.

**Shannon** Golf Club is close to the international airport and the River Shannon's estuary. This excellent inland course was laid out by John Harris and, in common with all the courses in the region, it is open 12 months of the year. However, because it is so close to the river, it can suffer in the wake of a long wet spell. On such occasions its 6900 yards plays uncomfortably longer than suggested by the card. Green fees are reasonably priced and it is the pick of the remaining three 18-hole courses and four nine-holers in County Clare.

**Cork** Golf Club, overlooking the town's harbour on Little Island, lies south of Clare and east of Kerry. Cork is the largest county in Ireland. Not only is it

an area of outstanding beauty and history but it also has 19 golf courses.

The present site was found only after four previous removals. Cork was another course worked upon by Alister Mackenzie in the 1920s and he combined an old quarry and the undulating terrain to characteristically splendid effect. The greens are large but always in fine fettle and the members can boast an impressive pedigree of important tournaments, both professional and amateur. A round at Little Island concludes with a severe five-hole examination of tough par-4's but perhaps the 455-yard 4th is the best of the bunch. It is a classic of the 'he who dares' genre. The more of the carry across the hazard you are able to chew off, the more chance there is of reaching the green in two.

Little Island's most famous son was Jimmy Bruen. His portrait adorns the

*The 9th tee at Cork. The course looks at its very best when the huge clumps of golden gorse are in bloom*

clubhouse lounge, a tribute to a fellow who as a young man was in the victorious Walker Cup team against the Americans at St Andrews in 1938 and later, in 1946, was the British Amateur Champion.

**Douglas** Golf Club lies on a hillside above the city of Cork. At 6131 yards it is 500 yards shorter than nearby Cork but is possesses picturesque views also – over Cork itself and out to the surrounding countryside. **Monkstown** and **Muskerry** are two other courses in the immediate vicinity. The former was extended to 18 holes in 1970 while the latter, seven miles to the north-west of Cork, is a riot of colour when the furze is in bloom. The River Shournagh

comes devilishly into play on the 429-yard 17th. Muskerry is situated less than two miles from the world-famous Blarney Castle which is an obvious detour if you fancy kissing the world-famous Blarney Stone for luck and conversational prowess!

**Mallow**, 21 miles north of Cork city, is unusual among Irish golf clubs in that it also offers squash, tennis, an indoor games room and a sauna. The golf course is an exacting test of nearly 6800 yards and is widely considered to be the best course in the county outside the city itself. There are five other 18-hole layouts in County Cork at **Bandon, Charleville, East Cork, Fermoy** and **Youghal**. The shorter courses of **Kanturk** and **Macroom** have alternative tees so that their nine holes present the visitor with a slightly different challenge on the second circuit.

**Castleroy** is one of only two 18-hole courses in County Limerick. It was remodelled extensively in the early 1980s and consequently has not yet had the opportunity to mature fully. However, even now it can be acclaimed as a tough, tight course of 6559 yards with several vantage points from which to enjoy the views.

**Limerick** Golf Club is three miles south of Limerick town and was founded in 1891 by Scottish officers of the Black Watch Regiment. These same soldiers were the ones who moved 40 miles north-west to take golf to Lahinch two years later. The pleasant parkland setting of the Limerick course at Ballyclough has been enhanced in recent times by the cultivation of dozens of trees and shrubs. It is a sufficiently stern examination of the game to have been selected to host the Irish Professional Championship in the past.

To summarize, the cost of golf in Ireland represents excellent value for money and, as always, you get what you pay for. Five of the clubs featured in this region – Ballybunion, Tralee, Killarney, Waterville and Lahinch – have eight courses between them. They have combined their considerable forces in an organization called South West Ireland Golf which is based at Tralee. This caters for holiday golfers and is worth contacting if you are thinking of visiting the area and spending some time there.

And even apart from the Famous Five themselves, there are plenty of interesting and challenging courses with good golf on offer. As everywhere in Ireland, the people are unforgettable with their astonishing hospitality, courtesy and friendliness, and you are almost assured of a great golfing holiday.

*So many of the greens on both courses at Ballybunion occupy totally natural sites, some with the sea close at hand*

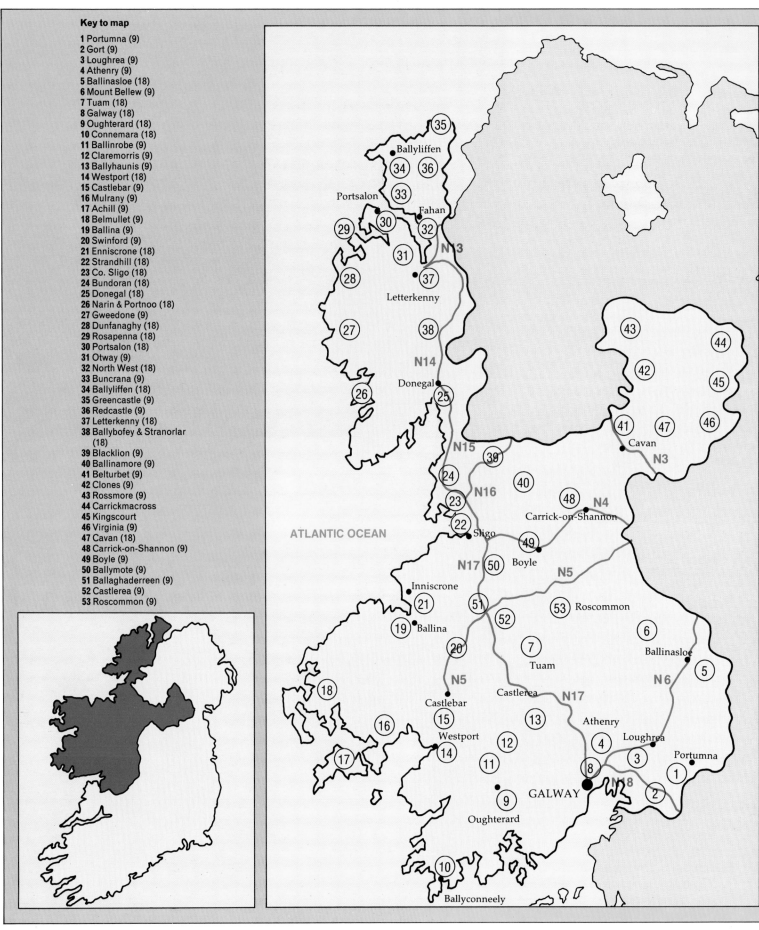

# North~west Ireland

The north-west of Ireland has a great deal to offer the golfer apart from a wide and varied number of excellent tests for his game. There is magnificent scenery, the people are friendly and welcoming, green fees are exceptionally reasonable, and if you enjoy seafood then this area is heaven on earth for you. There are plenty of little-known golfing gems, especially on the beautifully rugged coastline between Galway in the south and Donegal in the north. And because the courses generally fall into close-knit groupings, it is easy to play three or four over a couple of days before moving on to the next clump.

**Portumna** in County Galway has had a golf course since 1897, although the present one has only been in use since 1934. It is a bunkerless nine-holer which is soon to be extended to 18, with interesting, rolling fairways. However, because of the lack of sand-traps, the greens lose out somewhat. Nevertheless, it is very pleasant even with the ever-watchful sheep that freely roam over the course. Green fees are exceptionally low and to find the club, all you have to do is to follow the signs for two miles out of town.

**Athenry** is 25 miles away, and the course itself is three-and-a-half miles down the Galway road from the little town of that name. The new nine-hole layout is still immature but has plenty of potential with the passing of time. Green fees, again, are very good value and, like most clubs in the area, it has the advantage of being quiet and peaceful without the crowds that throng the more famous Irish courses. You do not have to allocate a whole day to a game of golf, and even allowing for motoring between courses, it is still easy to play more than one course in a single day – a positive boon for those players who get frustrated by slow play.

**Tuam** is 20 miles north of the N17 highway. It has an extremely flat parkland course whose biggest claim to fame is the crows that plague the local membership by stealing balls from the 11th fairway! The green fees are low but you will need some ammunition!

**Galway** is one of the few courses in the north-west where you will have to book a game in advance rather than just turning up and trusting to luck. The scene of the 1984 Celtic International Pro-am won by Gordon Brand Jnr, it has nearly 1000 members and caters for 20,000 visitors every year.

The course itself is inland in character, despite its close proximity to the Atlantic Ocean, with lots of gorse and fir trees forming the main hazards to be avoided. It is amazing the number of Irish clubs that are no longer playing over their original homes and Galway is another of these, having been at the present course only since 1923 despite being formed as early as 1893. This 'new' course, in the Salthill area of the town, was laid out by Dr Alistair Mackenzie, a short time before he emigrated to the United States where he went on to more lasting fame as the designer of Augusta National and Cypress Point, and was the place where the adolescent Christy O'Connor learned the game. Older members can, even now, remember the young O'Connor honing his short game by the light from one of the street lamps on the edge of the course. Maybe that was the secret of his wonderful touch – playing in daylight was easy after practising in the dark! Playing to a stiff par of 70, especially when the prevailing wind sweeps in off the sea, Galway is well worth a visit and a real bargain.

**Oughterard**, on the road to Clifden, is a relatively new course where golf has been played only since 1974. Here you can enjoy a quiet, relaxing game after the hurly-burly of Galway – not too taxing, not too easy. However, the club provides what must be the most unique walk to the first tee in the world of golf – straight through a still-to-be-converted cowshed! From Oughterard, you should continue on the road to Connemara and just let the scenery take your breath away. If you are a film buff, you may recognise this beautiful part of County Galway as the setting for the John Wayne movie, *The Quiet Man*.

**Connemara** golf course, located near the small village of Ballyconneely about nine miles from Clifden, lives up to its glamorous situation. It was opened as recently as 1973 and is one of the many Irish courses designed by Eddie Hackett. At first sight it appears to be a real monster measuring well over 7000 yards from the back tees and winding its way through some very rugged terrain indeed. Play from these championship tees if you need a real challenge or are in desperate need of practice with your 3-wood. However, there is no need to be overawed by the course, for it is immensely enjoyable.

The first nine holes are generally weaker than those later on, being rather flat and slightly monotonous. In fact, you cannot help feeling that the venerable Mr Hackett has missed an opportunity here as the opening holes are unimaginative, to say the least, considering what he had to work with. There has been some attempt to break up the flatness of the land, but the use of some rather incongruous man-made mounds which can rarely, if ever, come into play does nothing for the aesthetic value of the holes. Having said that, it is easy to forgive the course because the back nine more than makes up for this. The par-3's in particular live on in the mind's eye along with the by now almost compulsory spectacular view over to the mountains, the 12 pins of Connemara, in the distance. Green fees at Connemara are modest and there is a special weekly ticket with concessionary tickets for students and husband and wife 'teams'. Full catering is also available in the lavish new clubhouse where visitors can sit back with a relaxing drink and enjoy the scenery.

**Ballinrobe** in County Mayo is about an hour's drive away heading north-east. You will find the nine-hole course in the middle of the local race-track, and the clubhouse even has scales for weighing jockeys! Although there is a slightly unreal atmosphere about the place, it cannot be beaten for real 'get away from it all' golf, and for a very small financial outlay, green fees being a pittance.

*This is typical of the rocky terrain at Connemara and this hole, the 13th, is one of the best on this long course*

**Westport** is the best course in County Mayo and here you are assured of a warm welcome. This testing course of almost 7000 yards from the championship tees was the scene of the 1977 and 1985 Irish Amateur Championships. Again, it is fairly new, only coming into existence in 1973. Designed by Fred Hawtree on land purchased from Lord Sligo for a bargain £60,000, the course has quickly become a 'must' for all visitors to the area. You should not be fooled, however, by the relative straightforwardness of the opening holes for there is a sting in the tail. The back nine is a great test of golf for even the best players and contains one of the

*The view from the tee at the 580-yard 15th at Westport. The carry is not enormous – at least, not until the wind is blowing straight at you*

most scenic holes to be encountered anywhere. The 580 yards 15th bends around the edge of Clew Bay after a very intimidating drive over an inlet which tends to get wider with every glance. Anyone securing a par from the back tee can feel proud of a job well done.

Because of its slightly remote location Westport's membership is fairly widespread and so the club is only really busy at weekends when visitors are recommended to call up in advance. Full catering is available, although it is better to order your meal before playing to avoid delays, and the low green fees are an undoubted bargain for a course of this class.

**Castlebar** is only a short drive from Westport and its gently rolling parkland course is welcome relaxation if you are still feeling shell-shocked from the

rigours of the former. A comfortable length at 6100 yards, this former holiday home of the late British prime minister Clement Attlee is not too much of a strain for the average player and is only really busy at weekends. Bar snacks are available in the clubhouse, and green fees are low in keeping with other courses in the area.

**Inniscrone** is set on the shores of Killala Bay and is the home of one of the hidden gems of the north-west. It has been discovered by the fortunate few who return every year, including former 'James Bond', Sean Connery.

Laid out on classic links terrain the

course has all the normal characteristics of sea-side golf – sand dunes, humps and hollows, thick rough and lightning-fast greens. It is a real joy for anyone who enjoys playing golf as near as possible to the way it was in days gone by. The best holes are found at the far end, around the turn. The 7th, known as 'Hogs Back', is appropriately named as the fairway slopes sharply away on either side, while the short 8th is a gem of a hole where the premium is again on accuracy. Pride of place, however, must go to the 9th and 10th, par 4's which would not look out of place on the best of courses. Neither is very long – the 9th is 357 yards and the 10th even shorter at 338 – but the opportunities for disaster are plentiful, the penalties for missing either fairway or green being exceptionally harsh. This is certainly a course not to be missed and as the club is very keen to encourage visitors, a warm welcome is assured. Green fees are reasonable, and married couples can play together very economically indeed.

**Rosses Point**, a little further along the coast near the pretty town of Sligo, is the home of County Sligo Golf Club, and is undoubtedly the best course in this part of the Republic. For many years, it has played host to the West of Ireland Championship. The beautiful links is blessed with that wonderful turf found only by the sea, and offers superb panoramic views across Donegal Bay. In fact, from the 9th tee, it is possible to

*The beautifully sited 10th green at Enniscrone (right) and the 17th at Rosses Point (below) which many of the club's members consider to be the best hole and the most difficult on the course*

facing an almost certain three putts.

You might expect that the green fees would be set at a discouraging level for a course of this superior standard, but at Rosses Point this is not the case. A weekday round is still very reasonable with only a small premium at weekends. For golfing addicts who cannot drag themselves away, there is even a special monthly bargain price which may prove irresistible. Only the remoteness of the course prevents the inclusion of Rosses Point in the British *Golf World* magazine's top 50 courses in the British Isles. Peter Alliss said of the course: "I did think Rosses Point was a gentle sleeping giant and something people should go and look at and I think they will come away marvelling at its beauty. The great test of any golf course is that it can be a tremendous test for the highest quality player and great fun for the modest competitor, and that is where Ross Point has got it made. I have never visited the course before but had heard a lot about Ballybunion, Tralee, Connemara and Lahinch, but Rosses Point stands at the very top of the list of Irish courses, and it is one more people should discover."

**Bundoran** lies further north along the coastal road from Rosses Point through the narrow neck which connects Donegal with the rest of the Republic. Founded in 1894, this fairly exposed links course was altered in the 1930s by six-times Open Champion Harry Vardon. It is owned by the local hotel which leases the course to the club. Hotel guests play for free, but the green fees are still modest for other visitors.

For seven years in the 1950s, Bundoran was home to the legendary Christy O'Connor who is still remembered fondly by the locals. Catering is available in the hotel, and generally there is no need to book ahead for a game on a course which is good enough to have hosted the Irish Professional Championship in the past.

see five counties – Sligo, Donegal, Roscommon, Leitrim and Mayo.

It is difficult to select the best hole on the course, there being so many candidates, but the 8th, a classic par-4, takes some beating. Two perfect shots around the dogleg are required if the hidden burn is to be avoided and a birdie-putt

*Christy O'Connor enjoyed many tournament successes when he was the professional at Bundoran in the 1950s*

to result. The ferociously difficult 17th with its steeply sloping putting surface is another memorable test. Any player finding himself above the hole here is

**Donegal** is the next stop up the N15 road, and if you are intending to play over the local course, you must be careful not to miss the signposts to the club as you approach the town. In fact, it is five miles outside at Murvagh and easily missed if you are driving fast. This is another relatively new course which was opened in 1976. Designed by the ubiquitous Eddie Hackett, the course must be one of the most severe tests of golf and examinations of skill to be found anywhere. Indeed, it is Donegal's proud boast that off the back tees the course is the longest in the British Isles, measuring over 7200 yards.

Exposed to the elements and isolated from the rest of the world, it is a mixture of both inland and links-type terrain with many good holes, but the short 5th will not be forgotten easily by any visitor. Green fees are reasonable and you should not have to book.

*Donegal (top) is a part links, part inland golf course. The view shown here is of the 7th green in links country*

*The sweep of the bay at Tra na Rosann in County Donegal (above). The Donegal coastline has many fine beaches*

*The many splendours of Donegal, a county that combines rugged mountain scenery with a beautiful coastline. You can view the natural beauty of Glengesh (1), see typical cottages (2), visit Glenveagh National Park (3), or the Errigal Mountains (4). Or you can just enjoy the majestic beaches and cliff walks, as shown here near Kilcar (5)*

**Letterkenny** is another Eddie Hackett-designed course and it was opened in 1968. It is an attractive, holiday-type course overlooking Lough Swilly. Not too difficult for even higher handicappers, with very generous fairways and nothing much in the way of rough, it is perfect for a nice soothing round of golf, especially if you have played at Inniscrone, Rosses Point and Donegal and are feeling in need of a slight break! The more interesting holes in Letterkenny are to be found on the hill around the

*The beautiful Lough Swilly (right) is close to Letterkenny golf course. The course is set partly on a hill and partly on the flat. The 18th hole (below) is a good par-5 which plays gently downhill*

clubhouse area, the lower half down by the Lough being on very flat ground, and the 18th is indicative of this. It is a very attractive downhill par-5 with potential disaster lurking both left and right – a great finishing hole and a real test for anyone 'protecting' a score. Visitors are welcome here at any time, green fees are low and bar snacks are available in the extremely attractive clubhouse.

**Rosapenna** stands on the western side of Lough Swilly which splits the top half of Donegal in two. The original course was laid out by Old Tom Morris and opened in 1893, but the design was altered in 1906 by Harry Vardon and James Braid. The barren windswept links overlook Sheephaven Bay and

there are some fine holes, particularly those following the line of the beach. The good sandy soil enables the course to stay open all the year round, even though the hotel that owns it is closed between October and Easter. Green fees are low and if you enjoy battling with the wind and like your golf 'in the raw', you will be in your element here.

**Portsalon** Golf Club, founded in 1897, was one of the four founder members of the Golfing Union of Ireland along with Royal Portrush, Royal County Down and Royal Dublin. Unfortunately, because it really is a wonderful setting and still has enormous potential, the course,

*The superbly natural course at Rosapenna: no earth-moving equipment was used here*

unlike its illustrious partners, has, due to lack of funds, suffered from some neglect over the years. However, the club, which only has 80 members, has recently purchased the course and improvements, combined with proper maintenance, are top of the agenda. Portsalon really is a wonderful place to play and certainly not expensive. Do not let first impressions put you off – there are some great holes out there, and do not be misled by some rather mysterious tee-boxes!

Also, because the club has no clubhouse, visitors are required to pay their green fee at Rita's Bar, a small shop-cum-pub about 300 yards from the 1st tee. A course not to be missed, if only for the wonderful views and the completion of your golfing education.

*The 3rd green at Portsalon. The club has very few members so this is the ideal course for a quiet and relaxing day out*

**Narin and Portnoo**, about one hour's drive west of Letterkenny, is another course suffering from lack of exposure due entirely to its rather remote location. Opened as long ago as 1930, it is a deceptively difficult little links with greens that make elusive targets, exacting severe penalties for even the narrowest miss. It is very old-fashioned in nature, like a cross between Prestwick and North Berwick, both the ultimate in leave-it-as-you-find-it seaside courses. Although it is easy to become rather blasé after a while about the scenery in this part of the world, the views from the far end of the course do not let the rest of Donegal down. They are simply spectacular, as are the greens – a pleasure both to look at and to putt on.

Societies are not allowed to play at Narin and Portnoo in June, July and August because the course is very busy with the influx of holidaying country members staying in the many and varied summer homes overlooking the 1st tee. Casual visitors can pay for a round, but it is advisable to call up beforehand.

**Ballybofey and Stranorlar** is a compact little course south from Letterkenny and split down the middle by the N56 road. The parkland layout has small well-kept greens which are deceptively difficult to hit and hold. The most scenic hole is the 8th where the tee is set out on Loch Alan – a nerve-racking shot for the most experienced golfer. Extended to 18 holes in 1979, it is a pleasant place to play and not too demanding. However, it is sufficiently interesting to capture your complete attention and is very economical for a day's play.

**Carrick-on-Shannon, Boyle, Castlerea** and **Roscommon** are a convenient cluster of nine-holers in the counties of Leitrim and Roscommon. Although they are all relatively undemanding in nature, they are worth a visit if you are passing through the area. The best is probably Roscommon which has the distinction of being a nine-hole course

*Tumbling ground at Narin and Portnoo. Probably the original club members just chose natural sites for greens and tees and began playing. This is the 10th hole*

with 11 greens and 14 tees. It also has a very strong junior section which produced the 1986 Irish Boys' and Girls' Champions.

*There is a superb beach at Narin (1) as well as a golf course. While you are staying in the region, you could visit the ruins of Roscommon Abbey (2). If money is no object and you have always wanted to stay in a real castle, you could enjoy the luxurious splendours of Ashford Castle Hotel at Cong in County Mayo (3)*

Like all the other areas of Ireland, both in the Republic and the North, the clubs in this area were remarkably hospitable and it is difficult to envisage a more enthusiastic and knowledgeable group of people than you will encounter here. There are plenty of friendly hotels, guest houses and bed-and-breakfast establishments where you can stay and it is easy to plan a hugely enjoyable golfing itinerary that takes in a wide range of courses – inland and links; demanding and relaxing; Championship and little-known. As in Scotland, golf in Ireland is still the game of the people and they will want to share it with you wherever you go.

# Discovering beautiful Ireland

*Ireland is a marvellous place for a holiday and offers you a wide range of sports, activities and sightseeing. In addition to playing golf you can enjoy the trout and salmon fishing, horse-riding, swimming and watersports, bowls and tennis. Many of the larger hotels and even some golf clubs have their own sports facilities. Ireland is a country of outstanding beauty with a spectacular coastline, wild and rugged mountains and national parks, and astonishingly green hills and meadows. The beaches are relatively uncrowded even in high summer.*

*There is more than golf to Ireland and while you are staying there, you should explore the country and see some magnificent places – the Killarney Lakes (1), the Dartry mountains in County Sligo (2) and the holy sites of Kilfenora (3) and Glendalough (4), for instance*

Visit the historic town of Athlone in County Westmeath (1), the breathtakingly beautiful Beara Peninsula in County Cork (2), Connemara National Park (3) and Slea Head in County Kerry (4). Ireland offers excellent fishing as well as good golf. Keen anglers can enjoy good sport all over the country (5), especially trout and salmon fishing for which it is renowned

1

2

4

5

# Useful addresses

## Scottish golf clubs

### Fife, Tayside and Perthshire

**Aberdour**
Seaside Place, Aberdour
Tel. (0383) 860688
**Aberfeldy**
Taybridge Road, Aberfeldy
Tel. (0887) 20535
**Aberfoyle**
Aberfoyle, Stirlingshire
Tel. (087–72) 493
**Alloa**
Schawpark, Sauchie, Alloa
Tel. (0259) 722745
**Alva**
Beauclerc Street, Alva,
Clackmannanshire
Tel. (0259) 60431
**Alyth**
Pitcrocknie, Alyth
Tel. (082–83) 2268
**Anstruther**
Tel. (0333) 310872
**Arbroath**
Elliot by Arbroath
Tel. (0241) 73853
**Auchterarder**
Orchil Road, Auchterarder
Tel. (076–46) 2804
**Auchterderran**
Woodend Road, Cardenden
Tel. (0592) 721547
**Balbirnie Park**
Balbirnie Estate, Markinch,
Glenrothes
Tel. (0592) 752006
**Ballingry**
Lochore Meadows Country
Park, Crosshill, Lochgelly,
Fife
Tel. (0592) 860086
**Blair Atholl**
Blair Atholl, Perthshire
Tel. (079–681) 407
**Blairgowrie**
Blairgowrie
Tel. (0250) 2383
**Braehead**
Cambus Alloa,
Clackmannanshire
(0259) 722078
**Brechin Golf and Squash
Club**
Trinity Brechin, Angus
Tel. (035–62) 4106
**Bridge of Allan**
Sunnylaw, Bridge of Allan,
Stirlingshire
Tel. (0786) 832332
**Burntisland Golf House
Club**
Dodhead, Burntisland, Fife
Tel. (0592) 873247

**Caird Park**
Dundee, Angus
Tel. (0382) 40138
**Callander**
Aveland Road, Callander,
Perthshire
Tel. (0877) 30090
**Camperdown**
Camperdown Park, Dundee
Tel. (0382) 68340
**Canmore**
Venturefair, Dunfermline,
Fife
Tel. (0383) 724969
**Carnoustie** (all courses)
Carnoustie Golf Links
Management Committee,
Links Parade, Carnoustie
Starter's box:
Tel. (0241) 53249
Links Management
Committee:
Tel. (0241) 53789
**Comrie**
Comrie
Tel. (0764) 70544
**Craigie Hill**
Cherrybank, Perth,
Perthshire
Tel. (0738) 24377
**Crail Golfing Society**
Balcomie Clubhouse, Crail,
Fife
Tel. (0333) 50278
**Crieff**
Perth Road, Crieff
Tel. (0764) 2909
**Cupar**
Hillarvitt, Cupar, Fife
Tel. (0334) 53549
**Dalmunzie**
Glenshee, Blairgowrie
Tel. (025–085) 224
**Dollar**
Brewlands House, Dollar,
Clackmannanshire
Tel. (025–94) 2400
**Downfield**
Turnberry Avenue, Dundee,
Angus
Tel. (0382) 825595
**Dunblane New**
Dunblane, Perthshire
Tel. (0786) 822343
**Dunfermline**
Pitfirrane House, Crossford
by Dunfermline, Fife
Tel. (0383) 723534
**Dunkeld & Birnam**
Fungarth, Dunkeld
Tel. (035–02) 524
**Dunnikier Park**
Dunnikier Way, Kirkcaldy,
Fife
Tel. (0592) 261599

**Edzell**
High Street, Edzell by
Brechin, Angus
Tel. (035–64) 235
**Forfar**
Cunninghill, Forfar, Angus
Tel. (0307–81) 62120
**Glenalmond**
Trinity College, Glenalmond,
Perthshire
Tel. (073–888) 270
**Gleneagles**
Gleneagles, Perthshire
Tel. (076–46) 3543
**Glenrothes**
Golf Course Road,
Glenrothes, Fife
Tel. (0592) 758686
**Golf House Club (Elie)**
Elie Leven, Fife
Tel. (0333) 330327
**Green Hotel**
Beeches Park, Kinross
Tel. (0577) 63467
**Killin**
Killin, Perthshire
Tel. (056–72) 312
**Kinghorn**
Macduff Crescent, Kinghorn,
Fife
Tel. (0592) 890345
**King James VI**
Moncrieffe Island, Perth
Tel. (0738) 25170
**Kirkcaldy**
Balwearie Road, Kirkcaldy,
Fife
Tel. (0592) 260370
**Kirriemuir**
Kirriemuir, Angus
Tel. (057–52) 72729
**Ladybank**
Annsmuir, Ladybank, Fife
Tel. (0337) 30320
**Leslie**
Leslie, Fife
Tel. (0592) 742158
**Leven Links**
Leven, Fife
Tel. (0333) 23509
**Lochgelly**
Cartmore Road, Lochfelly,
Fife
Tel. (0592) 780174
**Lundin Links**
Golf Road, Lundin Links,
Fife
Tel. (0333) 320202
**Milnathort**
South Street, Milnathort,
Perthshire
Tel. (0577) 64069
**Monifieth**
Monifieth Golf Links
Committee of Management,

45 Ferry Road, Monifieth,
Dundee
Tel. (0382) 532767/8
**Montrose**
Starters Box, Traill Drive,
Montrose
Tel. (0674) 72634
**Muckhart**
Muckhart by Dollar,
Clackmannanshire
Tel. (025–981) 423
**Murrayshall**
Murrayshall, New Scone,
Perth
Tel. (0738) 51173
**Muthill**
Peat Road, Muthill,
Perthshire
Tel. (0764) 3319
**Panmure**
Barry by Carnoustie
Tel. (0241) 53120
**Pitlochry**
Pitlochry, Perthshire
Tel. (0796) 2792
**Pitreavie**
Queensferry Road,
Dunfermline, Fife
Tel. (0383) 722591
**Royal Perth Golfing Society
& County & City Club**
1/2 Atholl Crescent, Perth
Tel. (0738) 22265
**Saline**
Kinneddar Hill, Saline, Fife
Tel. (038–3852) 591
**Scoonie**
North Link, Leven, Fife
Tel. (0592) 260370
**Scotscraig**
Golf Road, Tayport, Fife
Tel. (0382) 552515
**St Andrews**
Links Management
Committee of
St Andrews, Golf Place,
St Andrews, Fife
Tel: (0334) 75757
Old Course: tel. (0334) 73393
New Course: tel. (0334) 73938
Eden Course: tel. (0334)
74296
Jubilee Course: tel. (0334)
73938
**St Fillans**
South Lochearn Road,
St Fillans, Perthshire
Tel. (076–485) 312
**Stirling**
Queen's Road, Stirling
Tel. (0786) 73801
**St Michaels**
Leuchars, Fife
Tel. (033–483) 365
**Strathtay**
Tel. (088–74) 362

**Taymouth Castle**
Kenmore, Tayside
Tel. (088–73) 228
**Thornton**
Station Road, Thornton, Fife
Tel. (0592) 771111
**Tillicoultry**
Tel. (0259) 50741
**Tulliallan**
Kincardine by Alloa,
Clackmannanshire
Tel. (0259) 30396

### The Highlands

**Abernethy**
Nethybridge, Inverness-shire
Tel. (047–982) 305
**Aboyne**
Formaston Park, Aboyne,
Aberdeenshire
Tel. (0339) 2215
**Alness**
Ardross Road, Alness, Ross-
shire
Tel. (0349) 883877
**Askernish**
Lochboisdale, South Uist,
Western Isles
Tel. (087–84) 277
**Auchinblae**
Auchinblae, Kincardineshire
Tel. (056–12) 407
**Auchmill**
Provost Rust Drive,
Aberdeen
Tel. (0224) 714577
**Ballater**
Victoria Road, Ballater
Tel. (0338) 55567
**Balnagask**
Aberdeen
Tel. (0224) 876407
**Banchory**
Kinneskie, Banchory,
Kincardineshire
Tel. (033–02) 2365
**Boat of Garten**
Boat of Garten, Inverness-
shire
Tel. (047–983) 684
**Bonar Bridge & Ardgay**
Bonar Bridge, Sutherland
Tel. (086–32) 577
**Braemar**
Braemar, Aberdeenshire
Tel. (033–83) 618
**Brora**
Golf Road, Brora, Sutherland
Tel. (0408) 21417
**Buckpool**
Buckie, Banffshire
Tel. (0542) 32236

**Carrbridge**
Carrbridge, Inverness-shire
Tel. (047–984) 674
**Cruden Bay**
Cruden Bay, Aberdeenshire
Tel. (077–981) 2285
**Cullen**
The Links, Cullen, Banffshire
Tel. (0542) 40685
**Deeside**
Bieldside, Aberdeen
Tel. (0224) 867697
**Duff House Royal**
The Barnyards, Banff
Tel. (026–12) 2062
**Dufftown**
Dufftown, Banffshire
Tel. (0340) 20325
**Elgin**
Hardhillock, Birnie Road,
Elgin, Morayshire
Tel. (0343) 2338
**Forres**
Muiryshade, Forres,
Morayshire
Tel. (0309) 72959
**Fort Augustus**
Fort Augustus, Inverness-
shire
Tel. (0320) 6460
**Fortrose and Rosemarkie**
Ness Road East, Fortrose,
Ross-shire
Tel. (0381) 20075
**Fort William**
North Road, Fort William,
Inverness-shire
Tel. (0397) 4464
**Fraserburgh**
Philorth, Fraserburgh,
Aberdeenshire
Tel. (0346) 28287
**Gairloch**
Gairloch, Ross-shire
Tel. (0445) 2407
**Garmouth and Kingston**
Garmouth, Fochabers,
Morayshire
Tel. (034–387) 388
**Golspie**
Golspie, Sutherland
Tel. (040–83) 3266
**Grantown-on-Spey**
Grantown-on-Spey,
Morayshire
Tel. (0479) 2749
**Hazlehead**
Hazlehead, Aberdeen
Tel. (0224) 35747
**Helmsdale**
Helmsdale, Sutherland
Tel. (043–12) 650
**Hopeman**
Hopeman, Morayshire
Tel. (0343) 830578
**Huntly**
Huntly, Aberdeenshire
Tel. (0466) 2643
**Insch**
Golf Terrace, Insch,
Aberdeenshire
Tel. (0464) 20363
**Inverallochy**
Inverallochy,

nr. Fraserburgh,
Aberdeenshire
Tel. (034–65) 2324
**Invergordon**
Cromlet Drive, Invergordon,
Ross & Cromarty
Tel. (0349) 853140
**Inverness**
Inverness, Inverness-shire
Tel. (0463) 239882
**Inverurie**
Blackhall Road, Inverurie,
Aberdeenshire
Tel. (0467) 20207
**Keith**
Fife Park, Keith, Banffshire
Tel. (054–22) 2469
**Kemnay**
Kemnay, Aberdeenshire
Tel. (0224) 634684
**King's Links**
Aberdeen
Tel. (0224) 632269
**Kingussie**
Kingussie, Inverness-shire
Tel. (054–02) 374
**Kintore**
Kintore, Aberdeenshire
Tel. (0467) 32631
**Lochcarron**
Ross & Cromarty
Tel. (052–02) 311
**Lybster**
Lybster by Wick, Caithness
Tel. (059–32) 359
**McDonald**
Ellon, Aberdeenshire
Tel. (0358) 20576
**Moray**
Stotfield Road, Lossiemouth,
Moray
Tel. (034–381) 2018
**Muir-of-Ord**
Great North Road, Muir-of-
Ord, Ross-shire
Tel. (0463) 870825
**Murcar**
Bridge of Don, Aberdeen
Tel. (0224) 704354
**Nairn**
Seabank Road, Nairn
Tel. (0667) 53208
**Nairn Dunbar**
Lochloy Road, Nairn,
Nairnshire
Tel. (0667) 52741
**Newburgh-on-Ythan**
Newburgh, Aberdeenshire
Tel. (033–74) 389
**Newtonmore**
Newtonmore, Inverness-shire
Tel. (054–03) 328
**Oldmeldrum**
Oldmeldrum, Aberdeenshire
Tel. (046–75) 238
**Orkney**
Grainbank, Kirkwall, Orkney
Tel. (0856) 2457
**Peterhead**
Craigewan, Peterhead
Tel. (0779) 2149
**Reay**
Reay by Thurso
Tel. (0847) 63035

**Royal Aberdeen**
Balgownie, Bridge of Don,
Aberdeen
Tel. (0224) 702571
**Royal Dornoch**
Golf Road, Dornoch,
Sutherland
Tel. (0862) 810219
**Royal Tarlair**
Buchan Street, Macduff,
Banffshire
Tel. (0261) 32548
**Scalloway**
Berry Farm, Scalloway,
Shetland
Tel. (059–588) 254
**Sconser**
Skye
Tel. (0478) 2275
**Shetland**
PO Box 18, Lerwick
Tel. Gott (059584) 369
**Spean Bridge**
Tel. (0397) 3825
**Spey Bridge**
Spey Bay Hotel, Spey Bay,
Fochabers
Tel. (0343) 820424
**Stonehaven**
Cowie, Stonehaven,
Kincardineshire
Tel. (0569) 62124
**Stornoway**
Lady Lever Park, Stornoway,
Outer Hebrides
Tel. (0851) 2240
**Strathlene**
Buckie, Banffshire
Tel. (0542) 32034
**Strathpeffer Spa**
Strathpeffer, Ross &
Cromarty
Tel. (0997) 21219
**Stromness**
Ness, Orkney
Tel. (0856) 850245
**Tain**
Tain, Ross & Cromarty
Tel. (0862) 2314
**Tarbat**
Portmahomack, East Ross-
shire
Tel. (086–287) 519
**Tarland**
Tarland, Aberdeenshire
Tel. (033–981) 413
**Thurso**
Newlands of Geise, Thurso,
Caithness
Tel. (0847) 63807
**Torphins**
Torphins, Aberdeenshire
Tel. (033–982) 493
**Torveau**
Glenurquhart Road,
Inverness
Tel. (0463) 38541
**Traigh**
Braeholm, Mallaig,
Inverness-shire
Tel. (068–75) 2126
**Turriff**
Rosehall, Turriff,
Aberdeenshire

Tel. (0888) 62745
**Westhill**
Westhill, Skene,
Aberdeenshire
Tel. (0224) 740159
**Westray**
Westray, Orkney
Tel. (085–77) 28
**Wick**
Reiss Wick, Caithness
Tel. (0955) 2726

**Glasgow and the West**

**Airdrie**
Rochsoles, Airdrie
Tel. (02364) 62195
**Alexandra Park**
Alexandra Parade, Glasgow
Tel. (041–554) 4887
**Allander**
Tel. (041–956) 5124
**Annanhill**
Irvine Road, Kilmarnock,
Ayrshire
Tel. (0563) 21644
**Ardeer**
Greenhead, Stevenston,
Ayrshire
Tel. (0294) 64035
**Auchenharvie**
Brewery Park, Saltcoats,
Ayrshire
**Ayr Belleisle**
Ayr
Tel. (0292) 42136
**Ballochmyle**
Ballochmyle, Mauchline
Tel. (0290) 50696
**Balmore**
Balmore by Torrance,
Dunbartonshire
Tel. (041–332) 0392
**Barshaw**
Barshaw Park, Paisley,
Renfrewshire
Tel. (041–889) 2908
**Bearsden**
Thorn Road, Bearsden,
Dunbartonshire
Tel. (041–942) 2351
**Beith**
Bigholm Road, Beith,
Ayrshire
Tel. (05055) 2011
**Bellshill**
Orbiston, Bellshill,
Lanarkshire
Tel. (0698) 745124
**Bishopbriggs**
Brackenbrae Road,
Bishopbriggs, Glasgow
Tel. (041–772) 1810
**Blackwaterfoot**
Isle of Arran
Tel. (077086) 226
**Blairbeth**
Burnside, Rutherglen
Tel. (041–632) 0604
**Blairmore and Dunoon**
Tel. (036984) 486
**Bonnybridge**
Larbert Road, Bonnybridge,
Stirlingshire

Tel. (0324) 812645
**Bonnyton**
Eaglesham, Renfrewshire
Tel. (03553) 2781
**Bothwell Castle**
Blantyre Road, Bothwell
Tel. (0698) 852 395
**Brodick**
Brodick, Isle of Arran
Tel. (0770) 2349
**Buchanan Castle**
Drymen, Stirlingshire
Tel. (0360) 60307
**Caldwell**
Caldwell, Uplawmore,
Renfrewshire
Tel. (050585) 8751329
**Calderbraes**
57 Roundknowe Road,
Uddingston
Tel. (0698) 813425
**Cambuslang**
Westburn Drive, Cambuslang
Tel. (041–641) 3130
**Campsie**
Crow Road, Lennoxtown,
Stirlingshire
Tel. (0360) 310244
**Caprington**
Kilmarnock Municipal,
Ayr Road, Kilmarnock
Tel. (0563) 21915
**Cardross**
Cardross, Dumbarton
Tel. (0389) 841213
**Carluke**
Hallcraig, Carluke
Tel. (0555) 70366
**Carradale**
Carradale, Argyll
Tel. (05833) 624
**Cathcart Castle**
Mearns Road, Clarkston,
Glasgow
Tel. (041–638) 9449
**Cathkin Braes**
Cathkin Braes, Rutherglen,
Glasgow
Tel. (041–634) 4007
**Cawder**
Cadder Road, Bishopbriggs,
Glasgow
Tel. (041–772) 5167
**Clydebank and District**
Hardgate, Clydebank
Tel. (0389) 73488
**Clydebank Overtoun**
Overtoun Road, Dalmuir,
Clydebank
Tel. (041–952) 6372
**Clober**
Craigton Road, Milngavie,
Glasgow
Tel. (041–956) 3293
**Coatbridge**
Townhead Road, Coatbridge
Tel. (0236) 28975
**Cochrane Castle**
Craigston, Johnstone,
Renfrewshire
Tel. (0505) 20146
**Colonsay**
Isle of Colonsay, Argyll
Tel. (09512) 316

**Colville Park**
Jerviston Estate, Motherwell
Tel. (0698) 66045
**Corrie**
Corrie, Isle of Arran
Tel. (077–081) 223
**Cowal**
Ardenslate Road, Dunoon,
Argyll
Tel. (0369) 2216
**Cowglen**
301 Barrhead Road, Glasgow
Tel. (041–632) 0556
**Craignure**
Isle of Mull Hotel, Mull
Tel. (0680) 2370
**Crow Wood**
Muirhead, Chryston, Glasgow
Tel. (041–779) 2011
**Cumbernauld**
Cumbernauld,
Dunbartonshire
Tel. (0236) 28138
**Dalmilling**
Tel. (0292) 263893
**Deaconsbank**
Glasgow
**Dougalston**
Milngavie, Glasgow
Tel. (041–956) 5750
**Douglas Park**
Hillfoot, Bearsden,
Dunbartonshire
Tel. (041–331) 1837
**Douglas Water**
Douglas Water, Lanark
Tel. (055538) 460
**Drumpellier**
Langloan, Coatbridge
Tel. (0236) 24139
**Dullatur**
Dullatur, Glasgow
Tel. (02367) 23230
**Dumbarton**
Broad Meadow, Dumbarton
Tel. (0389) 63051
**Dunaverty**
Southend, Argyll
**Easter Moffat**
Plains by Airdrie,
Lanarkshire
Tel. (0236) 21864
**East Kilbride**
Chapelside Road, Nerston,
East Kilbride
Tel. (03552) 47728
**East Renfrewshire**
Pilmuir, Newton Mearns,
Renfrewshire
Tel. (041–226) 4311
**Eastwood**
Muirshield, Loganswell,
Newton, Renfrewshire
Tel. (03555) 280
**Elderslie**
Elderslie, Renfrewshire
Tel. (0505) 23956
**Erskine**
Bishopton, Renfrewshire

Tel. (050586) 2302
**Falkirk**
Stirling Road, Camelon,
Falkirk, Stirlingshire
Tel. (0324) 21388
**Falkirk Tryst**
86 Burnhead Road, Larbert,
Stirlingshire
Tel. (0324) 562050
**Fereneze**
Barrhead, Renfrewshire
Tel. (041–221) 6394
**Girvan**
Golf Course Road, Girvan,
Ayrshire
Tel. (0465) 4272
**Glasgow Gailes**
Gailes, Ayrshire
Tel. (041–942) 2011
**Gleddoch**
Langbank, Renfrewshire
Tel. (047554) 304
**Glenbervie**
Stirling Road, Larbert,
Stirlingshire
Tel. (0324) 562605
**Glencruitten**
Oban
Tel. (0631) 62308
**Gourock**
Cowal View, Gourock,
Renfrewshire
Tel. (0475) 33696
**Greenock**
Forsyth Street, Greenock,
Renfrewshire
Tel. (0475) 26819
**Haggs Castle**
70 Dumbreck Road,
Dumbreck, Glasgow
Tel. (041–427) 3355
**Hamilton**
Riccarton, Ferniegair by
Hamilton, Lanarkshire
Tel. (0698) 282872
**Helensburgh**
25 East Abercromby Street,
Helensburgh,
Dunbartonshire
Tel. (0436) 4173
**Hilton Park**
Auldmanoch Estate,
Stockiemuir Road, Milngavie,
Dunbartonshire
Tel. (041–956) 4657
**Hollandbush**
Acre Tophead, Lesmahagow
by Coalburn, Lanarkshire
Tel. (055582) 222
**Innellan**
Innellan
Tel. (0369) 3546
**Irvine** (Bogside)
Bogside, Irvine, Ayrshire
Tel. (0294) 78139
**Irvine** (Ravenspark)
Irvine, Ayrshire
Tel. (0294) 79550
**Kilbirnie Place**

Largs Road, Kilbirnie,
Ayrshire
Tel. (0505) 683398
**Killermont**
Killermont, Glasgow
Tel. (041–942) 2011
**Kilmacolm**
Kilmacolm, Renfrewshire
Tel. (050587) 2139
**Kilmarnock Barassie**
Hillhouse Road, Barassie,
Troon
Tel. (0292) 311322
**Kilsyth Lennox**
Tak-Ma-Doon Road, Kilsyth
Tel. (0236) 823213
**Kingarth**
Tel. (0700) 83242
**King's Park**
Glasgow
Tel. (041–637) 1066
**Kirkhill**
Greenlees Road, Cambuslang,
Lanarkshire
Tel. (041–641) 3083
**Kirkintilloch**
Todhill, Campsie Road,
Kirkintilloch,
Dunbartonshire
Tel. (041–776) 1935
**Knightswood**
Lincoln Avenue, Glasgow
Tel. (041–959) 5610
**Kyles of Bute**
Tighnabruaich, Argyll
Secretary's tel. (0700) 811355
**Lamlash**
Lamlash, Isle of Arran
Tel. (07706) 555
**Lanark**
The Moor, Lanark
Tel. (0555) 3219
**Largs**
Irvine Road, Largs, Ayrshire
Tel. (0475) 673594
**Largs Routenburn**
Tel. (0475) 674171
**Larkhall**
Burnhead Road, Larkhall,
Lanarkshire
Tel. (0698) 881113
**Leadhills**
Leadhills, Biggar,
Lanarkshire
**Lenzie**
19 Crosshill Road, Lenzie,
Dunbartonshire
Tel. (041–776) 1535
**Letham Grange Lethamhill**
Cumbernauld Road, Glasgow
Tel. (041–770) 6220
**Linn Park**
Simshill Road, Glasgow
Tel. (041–637) 5871
**Littlehill**
Auchinairn Road,
Bishopbriggs, Glasgow
Tel. (041–772) 1916
**Lochgilphead**

Blarbuie Road, Lochgilphead
Tel. (0546) 2340
**Lochranza**
Lochranza, Isle of Arran
Tel. (077083) 273
**Lochwinnoch**
Burnfoot Road,
Lochwinnoch, Renfrewshire
Tel. (0505) 842153
**Londoun Gowf Club**
Galston, Ayrshire
Tel. (0563) 820551
**Machrie** (Islay)
Tel. (0496) 2310
**Machrie Bay**
Machrie Bay, Brodick,
Isle of Arran
Tel. (0770) 258
**Machrihanish**
Tel. (0586) 2366
**Millport**
Tel. (047553) 311
**Milngavie**
Laighpark, Milngavie,
Dunbartonshire
Tel. (041–956) 5615
**Mount Ellen**
Gartcosh, Glasgow
Tel. (041–776) 0747
**New Cumnock**
New Cumnock, Ayrshire
**Old Ranfurly**
Bridge of Weir, Renfrewshire
Tel. (0505) 613612
**Paisley**
Paisley, Renfrewshire
Tel. (041–884) 2292
**Pollok**
90 Barrhead Road,
Pollokshaws, Glasgow
Tel. (041–632) 1080
**Port Bannatyne**
Port Bannatyne, Isle of Bute
Tel. (0700) 2244
**Port Glasgow**
Port Glasgow
Tel. (0475) 42182
**Prestwick**
Links Road, Prestwick,
Ayrshire
Tel. (0292) 77404
**Prestwick St Cuthbert**
East Road, Prestwick,
Ayrshire
Tel. (0292) 79120
**Prestwick St Nicholas**
Grangemuir Road, Prestwick,
Ayrshire
Tel. (0292) 77608
**Ralston**
Ralston, Paisley, Glasgow
Tel. (041–882) 1349
**Ranfurly Castle**
Golf Road, Bridge of Weir,
Renfrewshire
Tel. (0505) 612609
**Renfrew**
Blythswood Estate, Inchinnan
Road, Renfrew

Tel. (041–886) 6692
**Rothesay**
Canada Hill, Rothesay,
Isle of Bute
Tel. (0700) 2178
**Royal Troon**
Craigend Road, Troon,
Ayrshire
Tel. (0292) 311555
**Ruchill**
Brassey Street, Glasgow
Tel. (041–946) 7676
**Sandyhills**
223 Sandyhills Road, Glasgow
Tel. (041–778) 1179
**Sanquhar**
Sanquhar
Tel. (06592) 577
**Seafield** (Ayr)
Ayr, Ayrshire
Tel. (0292) 41314
**Shotts**
Blairhead, Shotts,
Lanarkshire
Tel. (0501) 20431
**Skelmorlie**
Skelmorlie, Ayrshire
Tel. (0475) 520152
**Strathaven**
Strathaven, Lanarkshire
Tel. (0357) 20421
**Strathendrick**
By Drymen, Strathendrick,
Stirlingshire
**Tarbert**
Kilberry Road, Tarbert
Tel. (08802) 565 (evenings
only)
**Torrance House**
Strathaven Road, East
Kilbride, Lanarkshire
Tel. (03552) 32460
**Troon Darley, Troon
Lochgreen, Troon Fullarton**
Troon, Ayrshire
Tel. (0292) 312464
**Troon Portland**
1 Crosbie Road, Troon,
Ayrshire
Tel. (0292) 314309
**Turnberry** (Ailsa and Arran)
Turnberry, Ayrshire
Tel. (06553) 202
**Vale of Leven**
Tel. (0389) 52351
**Vaul**
Scarinish, Isle of Tiree by
Oban
**Western Gailes**
Gailes Irvine, Ayrshire
Tel. (0294) 311649
**Western Isles**
Tobermory, Isle of Mull
Tel. (0688) 2381
**West Kilbride**
West Kilbride, Ayrshire
Tel. (0294) 823341
**Whinhill**
Beith Road, Greenock,

Renfrewshire
Tel. (0475) 24694
**Whitecraigs**
72 Ayr Road, Giffnock,
Glasgow
Tel. (041–639) 4530
**Whiting Bay**
Whiting Bay, Isle of Arran
Tel. (07707) 487
**Williamwood**
Clarkston Road, Glasgow
Tel. (041–226) 4311
**Windyhill**
Windyhill, Bearsden,
Dunbartonshire
Tel. (041–942) 2349
**Wishaw**
Cleland Road, Wishaw,
Lanarkshire
Tel. (0698) 372869

## Edinburgh and the South

**Baberton**
Juniper Green, Edinburgh
Tel. (031–453) 3361
**Bathgate**
Edinburgh Road,
Tel. (0506) 630505
**Biggar**
Public Park, Broughton
Road, Biggar, Strathclyde
Tel. (0899) 20566
**Bo'Ness**
Tel. (0506) 825923
**Braids 1 & 2**
Edinburgh
Tel. (031–447) 6666
**Broomieknowe**
36 Golf Course Road,
Bonnyrigg, nr. Edinburgh
Tel. (031–663) 9317
**Bruntsfield Links**
32 Barnton Avenue,
Davidson's Mains, Edinburgh
Tel. (031–336) 1479
**Carnwath**
Main Street, Carnwath,
Lanarkshire
Tel. (0555) 4359
**Carrick Knowe**
Glendevon Park, Edinburgh
Tel. (031–337) 1096
**Castle Douglas**
Abercromby Road, Castle
Douglas, Kirkcudbrightshire
Tel. (0556) 2801
**Colvend**
Sandyhills, Nr. Dalbeattie,
Kirkcudbrightshire
Tel. (055–663) 398
**Craigentinny**
Edinburgh
Tel. (031–554) 7501
**Craigmillar Park**
1 Observatory Road,
Edinburgh
Tel. (031–667) 0047
**Dalkeith**
Tel. (031–633) 4197
**Dalmahoy East & West**
Dalmahoy, Kirknewton,
Midlothian
Tel. (031–333) 2055

**Duddingston**
Duddingston, Edinburgh
Tel. (031–661) 7688
**Dumfries & County**
Nunfield, Dumfries
Tel. (0387) 62045
**Dumfries & Galloway**
Laurieston Avenue,
Maxwelltown, Dumfries
Tel. (0387) 63848
**Dunbar**
East Links, Dunbar
Tel. (0368) 62317
**Dunbar Winterfield**
St Margaret's Back Road,
Dunbar
Tel. (0368) 62280
**Duns**
4 Hardens Road, Duns
**Galashiels**
Ladhope Recreation Ground,
Galashiels
Tel. (0750) 21669
**Gatehouse of Fleet**
Gatehouse of Fleet,
Kirkcudbrightshire
Tel. (05574) 654
**Gifford**
Gifford, nr. Haddington,
East Lothian
Tel. (0620) 81267
**Grangemouth**
Grangemouth, Stirlingshire
Tel. (0324) 711500
**Gullane 1, 2 & 3**
Gullane
Tel. (0620) 842255
**Haddington**
Amisfield Park, Haddington,
East Lothian
Tel. (062–082) 3627
**Hawick**
Vertish Hill, Hawick
Tel. (0450) 73183
**Innerleithen**
Leithen Water, Leithen
Road, Innerleithen
Tel. (0896) 830951
**Jedburgh**
Dunion Road, Jedburgh
Tel. (08356) 3587
**Kingsknowe**
326 Lanark Road, Edinburgh
Tel. (031–441) 1145
**Kirkcudbright**
Stirling Crescent,
Kirkcudbright
Tel. (0557) 30542
**Langholm**
Langholm, Dumfriesshire
Tel. (0541) 80061
**Lauder**
Lauder
Tel. (05782) 381
**Liberton**
297 Gilmerton Road,
Edinburgh
Tel. (031–664) 3009
**Linlithgow**
Braehead, Linlithgow
Tel. (050684) 2585
**Livingston**
Carmondeau, Livingston
Tel. (0506) 38843

**Portobello**
Stanley Street, Portobello,
Edinburgh
Tel. (031–669) 4361
**Powfoot**
Cummertrees, Annan
Tel. (046–12) 2866
**Prestonfield**
6 Priestfield Road,
North Edinburgh
Tel. (031–667) 9665
**Pumpherston**
Drumshoreland Road,
Pumpherston
Tel. (0506) 32122
**Ratho Park**
Ratho, Newbridge,
Midlothian
Tel. (031–333) 1752
**Ravelston**
24 Ravelston Dykes Road,
Edinburgh
Tel. (031–332) 4630
**Royal Burgess**
181 Whitehouse Road,
Barnton, Edinburgh
Tel. (031–339) 2075
**Royal Musselburgh**
Prestongrange House,
Prestonpans
Tel. (0875) 810276
**St Boswells**
St Boswells, Roxburghshire
Tel. (0835) 22359
**St Medan**
Port William, Wigtownshire
Tel. (09887) 358
**Selkirk**
Selkirk
Tel. (0750) 20621
**Silverknowes**
Silverknowes, Parkway,
Edinburgh
Tel. (031–336) 5359
**Stranraer**
Creachmore, Leswalt,
Stranraer, Wigtownshire
Tel. (0776) 3539
**Swanston**
111 Swanston Road,
Fairmilehead, Edinburgh
Tel. (031–445) 2239
**Thornhill**
Thornhill, Dumfriesshire
Tel. (0848) 30546
**Torphin Hill**
Torphin Road, Edinburgh
Tel. (031–334) 6052
**Torwoodlie**
Galashiels
Tel. (0896) 2260
**Turnhouse**
154 Turnhouse Road,
Corstorphine, Edinburgh
Tel. (031–339) 1014
**Uphall**
Uphall, nr Livingston
Tel. (0506) 856404
**West Calder**
Harburn, West Calder
Tel. (0506) 871131
**West Linton**
West Linton, Peebleshire
Tel. (0968) 60463

**Lochmaben**
Castlehill Gate, Lochmaben
Tel. (038–781) 552
**Lockerbie**
Corrie Road, Lockerbie
Tel. (05762) 2165
**Longniddry**
Links Road, Longniddry,
East Lothian
Tel. (0875) 52141
**Lothianburn**
Biggar Road, Edinburgh
Tel. (031–663) 8354
**Luffness New**
Aberlady, Nr Gullane
Tel. (0620) 843336
**Melrose**
Dingleton, Melrose
Tel. (089682) 2811
**Merchants of Edinburgh**
Craighill Gardens,
Morningside, Edinburgh
Tel. (031–447) 1219
**Minto**
Denholm, Hawick,
Roxburghshire
Tel. (0450) 87220
**Moffat**
Coateshill, Moffat
Tel. (0683) 20020
**Monktonhall**
Musselburgh
Tel. (031–665) 2005
**Mortonhall**
231 Braid Road, Edinburgh
Tel. (031–447) 6974
**Muirfield**
Muirfield, Gullane
Tel. (0620) 842123
**Murrayfield**
43 Murrayfield Road,
Edinburgh
Tel. (031–337) 3478
**Musselburgh Links**
Monktonhall, Musselburgh
Tel. (031–665) 2005
**New Galloway**
New Galloway,
Kirkcudbrightshire
Tel. (06442) 239
**Newton Stewart**
Kirroughtree Avenue,
Minnigaff, Newton Stewart,
Wigtownshire
Tel. (0671) 2172
**North Berwick East**
East Links, North Berwick
Tel. (0620) 2726
**North Berwick West**
West Links, Beach Road,
North Berwick
Tel. (0620) 2135
**Peebles**
Kirkland Street, Peebles
Tel. (0721) 20153
**Penicuik**
Tel. (0968) 77189
**Polmont**
Manuelrigg, Maddiston,
Falkirk, Stirlingshire
Tel. (0324) 713811
**Portpatrick**
Portpatrick
Tel. (0776) 83215

**Wigtownshire County**
Glenluce, Wigtownshire
Tel. (05813) 420
**Wigtown and Bladnoch**
Wigtown, Wigtownshire
Tel. (09884) 3310

## Scottish travel

**British Caledonian**
Tel. (01–668) 4222
**Loganair**
Tel. (041–889) 3181
**Tayside Aviation Ltd**
(aircraft charter)
Dundee, Tayside
Tel. (0382) 644992

## Distillery tours

Many distilleries in Scotland
operate special guided tours of
their premises and there is the
opportunity to purchase whis-
ky. Two such distilleries are:
**Glenfiddich Distillery**
Dufftown
Tel. (0340) 20373
**Morrisons Bowmore
Distillery**
Bowmore, Isle of Islay
Tel. (049–681) 441

## Scottish hotel guide

There are over 3000 hotels of
all standards, and 7000 other
premises offering both short-
stay and long-stay accom-
modation in Scotland, ranging
from guest houses to self-
catering apartments and crof-
ters' cottages. The regional
Scottish Tourist Boards or
Scottish Tourist Information
Centres will help arrange
accommodation. However,
we have compiled a list of a
few of the hotels which are near
to some of Scotland's best and
most beautiful golf courses
which we believe to be up-to-
date at the time of going to
press. They are just a small
sample of the many hotels that
you will discover.

**Balgarth Hotel**
Dunure Road, Alloway, Ayr
Tel. (0292) 42441
(0292) 42442
Convenient for Belleisle
**Boat Hotel**
Boat of Garten,
Inverness-shire
Tel. (047) 983258
Convenient for Boat of Garten
**Buccleugh and Queensberry
Hotel**
Thornhill, Dumfries and
Galloway
Tel. (0848) 30215
Convenient for Thornhill and
Dumfries

**Buchanan Arms Hotel**
Drymen, Central Scotland
Tel. (041–332) 6538
Convenient for Buchanan
Castle and Strathendrick

**Collearn House Hotel**
Auchterarder, Tayside
Tel. (07646) 3553
Convenient for Auchterarder

**Coul House Hotel**
Contin, Ross-shire
Tel. (0997) 21487
Convenient for Royal
Dornoch, Nairn, Tain and
Strathpeffer

**Craw's Nest Hotel**
Bankwell Road, Anstruther,
Fife
Tel. (0333) 310691
Convenient for St Andrews

**Dalhousie Castle**
Bonnrigg, Edinburgh
Tel. (0875) 2153
Convenient for all Edinburgh
courses

**Dornoch Castle Hotel**
Dornoch, Sutherland
Tel. (0862) 810216
Convenient for Royal
Dornoch

**Dryburgh Abbey Hotel**
St Boswells, Roxburghshire,
Borders
Tel. (0835) 22261
Convenient for St Boswells
and Melrose

**Enmore Hotel**
Marine Parade, Kirn,
Dunoon, Argyll
Tel. (0369) 2230
Convenient for Inellan,
Strone and Cowal

**Fennie Castle Hotel**
Nr. Letham, By Ladybank,
Fife
Tel. (033) 781381
Convenient for Ladybank,
St Andrews, Gleneagles and
Carnoustie

**Fernhill Hotel**
Portpatrick, Dumfries and
Galloway
Tel. (0776) 81220
Convenient for Portpatrick
and Stranraer

**Gleneagles Hotel**
Gleneagles, Tayside
Tel. (07646) 2231
Convenient for Gleneagles

**Glenesk Hotel**
Edzell, Tayside
Tel. (03564) 319
Convenient for Edzell

**Golf Hotel**
Elie, Fife
Tel. (0333) 330209
Convenient for Elie

**Golf Links Hotel**
Golspie, East Sutherland

Tel. (04083) 3408
Convenient for Golspie, Brora
and Royal Dornoch

**Golf View Hotel**
Seabank Road, Nairn,
Highland
Tel. (0667) 52301
Convenient for Nairn

**Green Hotel**
Kinross, Tayside
Tel. (0577) 63467
Convenient for Kinross

**Kenmore Hotel**
Kenmore, Tayside
Tel. (08873) 205
Convenient for Taymouth
Castle Golf Club

**Kildonan Hotel**
Isle of Arran
Tel. (077082) 207
Convenient for Brodick and
all Isle of Arran courses

**Links Hotel**
Brora, Sutherland
Tel. (0408) 21225
Convenient for Brora, Golspie
and Royal Dornoch

**Lochanhully Lodges**
(self-catering)
Carrbridge, Inverness-shire
Tel. (0479) 84234
Convenient for Nairn and
Inverness

**Lockerbie House Hotel**
Lockerbie, Dumfriesshire
Tel. (05762) 2610
Convenient for Lockerbie and
Moffat

**Mabie House Hotel**
Mabie, Dumfriesshire
Tel. (0387) 63188
Convenient for Southerness
and Dumfries

**Machrie House Hotel**
Nr. Letham, By Ladybank,
Fife
Tel. (033) 781381
Convenient for Ladybank,

Machrie Hotel and Golf
Course
Portellen, Islay, Argyll
Tel. (0496) 2310
       (0496) 2085
Convenient for Machrie

**The Mallard**
East Links Road, Gullane,
East Lothian
Tel. (0620) 843288
Convenient for Gullane 1, 2
and 3

**Marine Hotel**
North Berwick
Tel. (0620) 2406
Convenient for North
Berwick

**Marine Hotel**
Troon, Ayrshire
Tel. (041–332) 6538
Convenient for Royal Troon

**Murrayshall Hotel**
Murrayshall, Perthshire
Tel. (0738) 51241
Convenient for Murrayshall

**Old Course Golf and**

Country Club
St Andrews, Fife
Tel. (0334) 74371
Convenient for St Andrews

**Park Hotel**
Montrose, Tayside
Tel. (0674) 72634
Convenient for Montrose

**Pitlochry Hydro Hotel**
Pitlochry, Tayside
Tel. (041–332) 6538
Convenient for Pitlochry,
Gleneagles and Blairgowrie

**Royal Golf Hotel**
Dornoch, Sutherland
Tel. (0862) 810283
Convenient for Royal
Dornoch

**St Andrews Golf Hotel**
St Andrews, Fife
Tel. (0334) 72611
Convenient for St Andrews

**Turnberry Hotel and Golf
Courses**
Turnberry, Ayrshire
Tel. (065–53) 202
Convenient for Turnberry

## Scottish tourist boards

**Aviemore and Spey Valley**
Grampian Road, Aviemore,
Inverness-shire
Tel. (0479) 810363

**Ayrshire and Burns Country**
39 Sandgate, Ayr
Tel. (0292) 284196

**Ayrshire and Clyde Coast**
Cunninghame House, Irvine,
Ayrshire
Tel. (0294) 74166

**Ayrshire Valleys**
PO Box 13, Civic Centre,
Kilmarnock, Ayrshire
Tel. (0563) 21140

**Banff and Buchan**
Collie Lodge, Banff
Tel. (026–12) 2789

**Caithness**
Whitechapel Road, Wick,
Caithness
Tel. (0955) 2596

**City of Aberdeen**
St Nicholas House, Broad
Street, Aberdeen
Tel. (0224) 632727

**City of Dundee**
City Chambers, Dundee
Tel. (0382) 23141

**City of Edinburgh District
Council**
9 Cockburn Street,
Edinburgh
Tel. (031–226) 6591

**Clyde Valley**
South Vennel, Lanark
Tel. (0555) 2544

**Dumfries and Galloway**
Douglas House, Newton

Stewart, Wigtownshire
Tel. (0671) 2549

**Dunoon and Cowal**
Pier Esplanade, Dunoon,
Argyll
Tel. (0369) 3755

**East Lothian**
Brunton Hall, Musselburgh
Tel. (031–665) 3711

**Fort William and Lochaber**
Travel Centre, Fort William,
Inverness-shire
Tel. (0397) 3781

**Forth Valley**
Burgh Hall, The Cross,
Linlithgow, West Lothian
Tel. (0506) 843306

**Gordon District**
St Nicholas House, Broad
Street, Aberdeen
Tel. (0224) 632727

**Greater Glasgow**
35–39 St Vincent Place,
Glasgow
Tel. (041–227) 4894

**Inverness, Loch Ness and
Nairn**
23 Church Street, Inverness
Tel. (0463) 234353

**Isle of Arran**
The Pier, Brodick, Isle of
Arran
Tel. (0770) 2140

**Isle of Skye and South-west
Ross**
Portree, Isle of Skye
Tel. (0478) 2137

**Kincardine and Deeside**
45 Station Road, Banchory,
Kincardineshire
Tel. (033–02) 2066

**Kirkcaldy District Council**
South Street, Leven, Fife
Tel. (0333) 29464

**Loch Lomond, Stirling and
Trossachs**
Beechwood House,
St Ninians Road, Stirling
Tel. (0786) 70945

**Mid Argyll, Kintyre and
Islay**
The Pier, Campbeltown,
Argyll
Tel. (0586) 52056

**Moray**
17 High Street, Elgin,
Morayshire
Tel. (0343) 2666

**Oban, Mull and District**
Boswell House, Argyll
Square, Oban, Argyll
Tel. (0631) 63122
       (0631) 63551

**Orkney**
Broad Street, Kirkwall,
Orkney
Tel. (0856) 2856

**Outer Hebrides**
4 South Beach Street,

Stornoway, Isle of Lewis
Tel. (0851) 3088

**Perthshire**
PO Box 33, George Inn Lane,
Perth
Tel. (0738) 27958

**Ross and Cromarty**
North Kessock, Inverness
Tel. (0463–73) 505

**Rothesay and Isle of Bute**
The Pier, Rothesay, Isle of
Bute
Tel. (0700) 2151

**St Andrews and North-east
Fife**
2 Queens Gardens,
St Andrews, Fife
Tel. (0334) 74609

**Scottish Borders**
Municipal Buildings, High
Street, Selkirk
Tel. (0750) 20555

**Shetland**
Market Cross, Lerwick,
Shetland
Tel. (0595) 3434

**Sutherland**
The Square, Dornoch,
Sutherland
Tel. (0862) 810400

## Irish golf clubs

### Northern Ireland

**Ardglass Golf Club**
Castle Place, Ardglass,
Co. Down
Tel. (0396) 841755

**Ballycastle Golf Club**
Cushendall Road, Ballycastle,
Co. Antrim
Tel. (026) 57 62536

**Ballyclare Golf Club**
Springvale Road, Ballyclare,
Co. Antrim
Tel. (096) 03 22857

**Ballymena Golf Club**
Raceview Road, Ballymena,
Co. Antrim
Tel. (0266) 861487

**Balmoral Golf Club**
Lisburn Road, Belfast
Tel. (0232) 668514

**Banbridge Golf Club**
Huntly Road, Banbridge, Co.
Down
Tel. (082) 06 22342

**Bangor Golf Club**
Broadway, Bangor,
Co. Down
Tel. (0247) 473922

**Belvoir Park Golf Club**
Newtownbreda, Belfast
Tel. (0232) 643693

**Bright Castle Golf Club**
Bright, Downpatrick,
Co. Down

Tel. (0396) 841319
**Bushfoot Golf Club**
Portballintrae, Co. Antrim
Tel. (026) 57 31317
**Cairndhu Golf Club**
Ballygally, Larne,
Co. Antrim
Tel. (0574) 83324
**Carnalea Golf Club**
Station Road, Bangor,
Co. Down
Tel. (0247) 461368
**Carrickfergus Golf Club**
North Road, Carrickfergus,
Co. Antrim
Tel. (096) 03 62203
**Castlerock Golf Club**
Castlerock,
Co. Londonderry
Tel. (0265) 848314
**City of Derry Golf Club**
Londonderry,
Co. Londonderry
Tel. (0504) 46369
**Clandeboye Golf Club**
Newtownards, Co. Down
Tel. (0247) 465767
**Cliftonville Golf Club**
Westland Road, Belfast
Tel. (0232) 744158
**County Armagh Golf Club**
Newry Rd, Armagh
Tel. (0861) 522501
**Craigavon Golf
(and Ski) Centre**
Lurgan, Co. Armagh
Tel. (0762) 6606
**Cushendall Golf Club**
Ballymena, Co. Antrim
Tel. (026) 67 71318
**Donaghadee Golf Club**
Warren Road, Donaghadee,
Co. Down
Tel. (0247) 883624
**Downpatrick Golf Club**
Saul Road, Downpatrick,
Co. Down
Tel. (0396) 2152
**Dungannon Golf Club**
Dungannon, Co. Tyrone
Tel. (086) 87 22098
**Dunmurry Golf Club**
Dunmurry Lane, Belfast
Tel. (0232) 610834
**Enniskillen Golf Club**
Enniskillen, Co. Fermanagh
Tel. (0365) 25250
**Fintona Golf Club**
Fintona, Omagh,
Co. Tyrone
Tel. (0662) 841140
**Fortwilliam Golf Club**
Downview Avenue, Belfast
Tel. (0232) 771770
**Greenisland Golf Club**
Greenisland, Carrickfergus,
Co. Antrim
Tel. (0231) 62236
**Helen's Bay Golf Club**
Helen's Bay, Bangor,
Co. Down
Tel. (0247) 852601
**Holywood Golf Club**
Demesne Road, Holywood,

Co. Down
Tel. (023) 17 3135
**Kilkeel Golf Club**
Ballyardle, Newry,
Co. Down
Tel. (069) 37 62296
**Killymoon Golf Club**
Cookstown, Co. Tyrone
Tel. (064) 87 63762
**Kilrea Golf Club**
Coleraine, Co. Londonderry
Tel. (026) 653 397
**Kirkistown Castle
Golf Club**
Cloughey, Newtownards, Co.
Down
Tel. (0247) 77 1233
**Knock Golf Club**
Dundonald, Belfast
Tel. (023) 18 3251
**Knockbracken
Golf Centre**
Newtownbreda, Belfast
Tel. (0232) 701648
**Larne Golf Club**
Islandmagee, Larne,
Co. Antrim
Tel. (096) 03 82228
**Lisburn Golf Club**
Eglantine Road, Lisburn,
Co. Antrim
Tel (084) 62 77216
**Lurgan Golf Club**
Windsor Avenue, Lurgan,
Co. Armagh
Tel. (076) 22 22087
**Mahee Island Golf Club**
Newtownards, Co. Down
Tel. (0238) 541234
**Massereene Golf Club**
Lough Road, Antrim,
Co. Antrim
Tel. (084) 94 62096
**Moyola Park Golf Club**
Magherafelt,
Co. Londonderry
Tel. (0648) 68468
**Newry Golf Club**
Forkhill Road, Newry,
Co. Down
Tel. (0693) 3871
**Newtownstewart
Golf Club**
Newtownstewart,
Co. Tyrone
Tel. (066) 26 61466
**Omagh Golf Club**
Dublin Road, Omagh,
Co. Tyrone
Tel. (0662) 3160
**Ormeau Golf Club**
Ravenhill Road, Belfast
Tel. (0232) 641069
**Portadown Golf Club**
Gilford Road, Portadown,
Co. Armagh
Tel. (0762) 335356
**Portstewart Golf Club**
Portstewart,
Co. Londonderry
Tel. (026) 583 2015
**Royal Belfast Golf Club**
Craigavad, Holywood,
Co. Down

Tel. (023) 17 2165
**Royal County Down
Golf Club**
Newcastle, Co. Down
Tel. (039) 67 23314
**Royal Portrush Golf Club**
Bushmills Road, Portrush,
Co. Antrim
Tel. (0265) 822311
**Scrabo Golf Club**
Newtownards, Co. Down
Tel. (0247) 812355
**Shandon Park Golf Club**
Shandon Park, Belfast
Tel. (0232) 794856
**Spa Golf Club**
Ballynahinch, Co. Down
Tel. (0238) 562365
**Strabane Golf Club**
Ballycolman Road, Strabane,
Co. Tyrone
Tel. (0504) 882271
**Tandragee Golf Club**
Craigavon, Co. Armagh
Tel. (0762) 840727
**Warrenpoint Golf Club**
Warrenpoint, Co. Down
Tel. (096) 37 73695
**Whitehead Golf Club**
Carrickfergus, Co. Antrim
Tel. (096) 03 78631


**Dublin and the East**

**Ardee Golf Club**
Ardee, Townparks,
Co. Louth
Tel. (041) 53227
**Arklow Golf Club**
Abbeylands, Arklow,
Co. Wicklow
Tel. (0402) 32492
**Athy Golf Club**
Geraldine, Athy,
Co. Kildare
Tel. (0507) 31729
**Balbriggan Golf Club**
Balbriggan, Co. Dublin
Tel. (01) 412173
**Ballinascorney Golf Club**
Ballinascorney, Tallaght, Co.
Dublin
Tel. (01) 512516
**Baltinglass Golf Club**
Baltinglass, Co. Wicklow
Tel. (0508) 81350
**Beaverstown Golf Club**
Beaverstown, Donabate, Co.
Dublin
Tel. (01) 452721
**Beech Park Golf Club**
Johnstown, Rathcoole,
Co. Dublin
Tel. (01) 580522
**Blainroe Golf Club**
Blainroe, Co. Wicklow
Tel. (0404) 3168
**Bodenstown Golf Club**
Bodenstown, Sallins,
Co. Kildare
Tel. (045) 97096
**Bray Golf Club**
Ravenswell Road, Bray,
Co. Wicklow

Tel. (01) 862484
**Carrickmines Golf Club**
Carrickmines, Dublin
Tel. (01) 895676
**Castle Golf Club**
Rathfarnham, Dublin 14,
Co. Dublin
Tel. (01) 904207
**Cill Dara Golf Club**
Little Curragh, Co. Kildare
Tel. (045) 21433
**Clontarf Golf Club**
Donnycarney House,
Malahide Road, Dublin 3,
Co. Dublin
Tel. (01) 311305
**Coolattin Golf Club**
Shillelagh, Co. Wicklow
Tel.(055) 29125
**Corballis Golf Club**
Donabate, Co. Dublin
Tel. (01) 350368
**County Louth Golf Club**
Baltray, Drogheda,
Co. Louth
Tel. (041) 22327
**Curragh Golf Club**
Curragh, Co. Kildare
Tel. (045) 41238
**Deerpark Courses**
Howth, Co. Dublin
Tel. (01) 322624
**Delgany Golf Club**
Delgany, Greystones,
Co. Wicklow
Tel. (01) 874536
**Donabate Golf Club**
Donabate, Co. Dublin
Tel. (01) 450346
**Dublin & County
Golf Club**
Corballis, Donabate,
Co. Dublin
Tel. (01) 452127
**Dublin Sport Golf Club**
Kilternan, Co. Dublin
Tel. (01) 893631
**Dundalk Golf Club**
Dundalk, Co. Louth
Tel. (042) 32731
**Dun Laoghaire Golf Club**
Eglinton Park, Tivoli Road,
Dun Laoghaire, Co. Dublin
Tel. (01) 801055
**Edmondstown Golf Club**
Rathfarnham, Dublin 16, Co.
Dublin
Tel. (01) 932461
**Elm Park Golf
& Sports Club**
Nutley House, Dublin 4,
Co. Dublin
Tel. (01) 693014
**Forrest Little Golf Club**
Cloghran, Co. Dublin
Tel. (01) 401183
**Four Lakes Golf
& Country Club**
Kill, Co. Kildare
Tel. (045) 66003
**Foxrock Golf Club**
Foxrock, Torquay Rd,
Dublin 18, Co. Dublin
Tel. (01) 893992

**Grange Golf Club**
Rathfarnham, Dublin 16, Co.
Dublin
Tel. (01) 932832
**Greystones Golf Club**
Greystones, Co. Wicklow
Tel. (01) 874614
**Greenore Golf Club**
Greenore, Dundalk.
Co. Louth
Tel. (042) 73212
**Headfort Golf Club**
Kells, County Meath
Tel.(046) 40146
**Hermitage Golf Club**
Lucan, Co. Dublin
Tel. (01) 264549
**Howth Golf Club**
Garrickbrack Road, Sutton,
Dublin 13, Co. Dublin
Tel. (01) 323055
**Kilcock Golf Club**
Co. Kildare
Tel.(01) 287283
**Killiney Golf Club**
Killiney, Co. Dublin
Tel. (01) 852823
**Knockanally Golf Club**
Donadea, Co. Kildare
Tel. (045) 69322
**Laytown & Bettystown Golf
Club**
Laytown, Co. Meath
Tel: (041) 27534
**Lucan Golf Club**
Celbridge Road, Lucan,
Co. Dublin
Tel. (01) 280246
**Malahide Golf Club**
Coast Road, Malahide,
Co. Dublin
Tel. (01) 451428
**Milltown Golf Club**
Lr. Churchtown Road,
Dublin 14, Co. Dublin
Tel. (01) 977060
**Naas Golf Club**
Kerdiffstown, Naas,
Co. Kildare
Tel.(045) 97509
**Newlands Golf Club**
Clondalkin, Co. Dublin
Tel. (01) 593157
**Portmarnock Golf Club**
Portmarnock, Co. Dublin
Tel. (01)323082
**Rathfarnham Golf Club**
Newtown, Dublin 16,
Co. Dublin
Tel. (01) 931201
**Royal Dublin Golf Club**
Bull Island, Dollymount,
Dublin 3, Co. Dublin
Tel. (01) 337153
**Royal Tara Golf Club**
Bellinter, Navan, Co. Meath
Tel. (046) 25244
**Rush Golf Club**
Co. Dublin
Tel. (01) 437548
**St Anne's Golf Club**
Bull Island, Raheney,
Dublin 5
Tel. (01) 336471

**Skerries Golf Club**
Skerries, Co. Dublin
Tel. (01) 491204
**Slade Valley Golf Club**
Lynch Park, Brittas,
Co. Dublin
Tel. (01) 582207
**Stackstown Golf Club**
Kellystown Road,
Rathfarnham, Dublin 16
Tel. (01) 942338
**Stepaside Golf Club**
Co. Dublin.
**Sutton Golf Club**
Cush Point, Burrow Rd,
Sutton, Dublin 13
Tel. (01) 323013
**The Island Golf Club**
Corballis, Donabate,
Co. Dublin
Tel.(01) 450595
**Trim Golf Club**
Newtownmoynagh, Trim,
Co. Meath
Tel. (046) 31463
**Wicklow Golf Club**
Dunbar Rd, Wicklow,
Co. Wicklow
Tel. (0404) 2379
**Woodbrook Golf Club**
Bray, Co. Wicklow
Tel. (01) 824799
**Woodenbridge Golf Club**
Arklow, Co. Wicklow
Tel. (0402) 5202

**The South-east**

**Abbey Leix Golf Club**
Abbey Leix, Portlaoise,
Co. Laois
**Athlone Golf Club**
Hodson Bay, Athlone,
Co. Westmeath
Tel. (0902) 2073
**Birr Golf Club**
Birr, Co. Offaly
Tel. (0509) 20082
**Borris Golf Club**
Borris, Co. Carlow
Tel. (0503) 23143
**Cahir Park Golf Club**
Kilcommon, Cahir,
Co. Tipperary
Tel. Cahir 41474
**Callan Golf Club**
Callan, Co. Kilkenny
Tel. (056) 25136
**Carlow Golf Club**
Deerpark, Carlow,
Co. Carlow
Tel. (0503) 31695
**Carrick-on-Suir Golf Club**
Garravóne, Carrick-on-Suir,
Co. Tipperary
Tel. Carrick-on-Suir 47
**Castlecomer Golf Club**
Castlecomer, Co. Kilkenny
Tel. (056) 41139

**Clonmel Golf Club**
Lyreanearla, Mountain Road,
Clonmel, Co. Tipperary
Tel. (052) 21183
**County Longford
Golf Club**
Longford
Tel. (043) 46310
**Courtown Golf Club**
Kiltennel, Gorey,
Co. Wexford
Tel. (055) 21533
**Dungarvan Golf Club**
Ballinacourty, Dungarvan,
Co. Waterford
Tel. (058) 41605
**Edenderry Golf Club**
Boherbree, Edenderry,
Co. Offaly
Tel. (0405) 31072
**Enniscorthy Golf Club**
Bloomfield, Enniscorthy, Co.
Wexford
Tel. Enniscorthy 33191
**Heath Golf Club**
Portlaoise, Co. Laois
Tel. (0502) 26533
**Kilkenny Golf Club**
Glendine, Co. Kilkenny
Tel. (056) 22125
**Lismore Golf Club**
Lismore, Co. Waterford
Tel. (058) 54026
**Moate Golf Club**
Moate, Co. Westmeath
Tel. (0902) 31271
**Mountrath Golf Club**
Mountrath, Co. Laois
**Mullingar Golf Club**
Mullingar, Co. Westmeath
Tel. (044) 48366
**Nenagh Golf Club**
Craigue, Nenagh,
Co. Tipperary
Tel.(067) 31476
**New Ross Golf Club**
Tinneranny, New Ross,
Co. Wexford
Tel. New Ross 21433
**Portarlington Golf Club**
Garryhinch, Portarlington,
Co. Laois
Tel. Portarlington 23115
**Rathdowney Golf Club**
Rathdowney, Co. Laois
**Roscrea Golf Club**
Roscrea, Co. Tipperary
Tel. Roscrea 21130
**Rosslare Golf Club**
Rosslare, Co. Wexford
Tel. (053) 32113
**Templemore Golf Club**
Templemore, Co. Tipperary
Tel. Templemore 53
**Thurles Golf Club**
Thurles, Co. Tipperary
Tel. (0504) 21983
**Tipperary Golf Club**
Rathanny, Co. Tipperary

Tel. (062) 51119
**Tramore Golf Club**
Newtown Hill, Tramore,
Co. Waterford
Tel. (051) 81247
**Tullamore Golf Club**
Tullamore, Co. Offaly
Tel. (0506) 21439
**Waterford Golf Club**
Newrath, Waterford
Tel. (051) 76748
**Wexford Golf Club**
Mulgannon, Wexford
Tel. (053) 42238

**The South-west**

**Adare Manor**
Adare, Co. Limerick
Tel. (061) 94204
**Ballybunion**
Ballybunion, Co. Kerry
Tel. (068) 27146
**Bandon**
Castlebernard, Bandon,
Co. Cork
Tel. (023) 41111
**Bantry**
Donemark, Bantry,
Co. Cork
Tel. (027) 50579
**Castletroy**
Castletroy, Limerick,
Co. Limerick
Tel. (061) 335753
**Ceann Sibeal**
Ballyferriter, Co. Kerry
Tel. (066) 56157
**Charleville**
Charleville, Co. Cork
Tel. (063) 257
**Clonlara**
(Landscape Leisure Centre)
Clonlara, Shannon,
Co. Cork
Tel. (061) 377477
**Cork**
Little Island, Cork, Co. Cork
Tel. (021) 353451
**Doneraile**
Doneraile, Co. Cork
Tel. (022) 24137
**Dooks**
Dooks, Nr. Glenbeigh,
Co. Kerry
Tel. (066) 68205
**Douglas**
Douglas, Co. Cork
Tel. (021) 295297
**Dromoland Castle**
Newmarket-on-Fergus,
Co. Clare
Tel. (061) 71144
**Dunmore**
Clonakilty, Dunmore,
Co. Cork
Tel. (023) 33352

**East Cork**
Gortacrue, Midleton,
Co. Cork
Tel. (021) 631687
**Ennis**
Ennis, Co. Clare
Tel. (065) 24074
**Fermoy**
Corin Cross, Fermoy,
Co. Cork
Tel. (025) 31642
**Glengarriff**
Glengarriff, Co. Cork
Tel. (027) 63150
**Kanturk**
Fairy Hill, Kanturk, Co.
Cork
Tel. (029) 50181
**Kenmare**
Kenmare, Co. Kerry
Tel. (064) 41291
**Kilkee**
East End, Kilkee, Co. Clare
Kilkee 150 (via operator)
**Killarney**
Mahony's Point, Killarney,
Co. Kerry
Tel. (064) 31034
**Kilrush**
Parknamoney, Kilrush,
Co. Clare
Tel. Kilrush 535
(via operator)
**Kinsale**
Ringnanean, Belgooly,
Kinsale, Co. Cork
Tel. (021) 72197
**Lahinch**
Lahinch, Co. Clare
Tel. (065) 81003
**Limerick**
Ballyclough, Limerick,
Co. Limerick
Tel. (061) 44083
**Macroom**
Lackaduve, Macroom,
Co. Cork
Tel. (026) 41072
**Mallow**
Balleyellis, Mallow,
Co. Cork
Tel. (022) 21145
**Mitchelstown**
Gurrane, Mitchelstown,
Co. Cork
Tel. (025) 24072
**Monkstown**
Parkgarriffe, Monkstown,
Co. Cork
Tel. (021) 841376
**Muskerry**
Carrigrohane, Co. Cork
Tel. (021) 85297
**Newcastle West**
Newcastle West,
Co. Limerick
Tel. (069) 62105
**Parknasilla**
Parknasilla, Co. Kerry

Tel. (064) 45122
**Shannon**
Shannon, Co. Clare
Tel. (061) 61849
**Skibbereen**
Skibbereen, Co. Cork
Tel. (028) 21088
**Spanish Point**
Miltown Malbay, Co. Clare
Tel. (065) 84198
**Tralee**
West Barrow, Ardfert,
Co. Kerry
Tel. (066) 51150
**Waterville**
Waterville, Co. Kerry
Tel. (0667) 4102
**Youghal**
Knockaverry, Youghal,
Co. Cork
Tel. (024) 2787

**The North-west**

**Achill Golf Club**
Achill, Co. Mayo
Tel. (098) 43202
**Athenry Golf Club**
Athenry, Co. Galway
Tel. (091) 84466
**Ballaghadeerreen
Golf Club**
Ballaghadeerreen,
Co. Roscommon
**Ballina Golf Club**
Ballina, Co. Mayo
Tel. (096) 21050
**Ballinamore Golf Club**
Ballinamore, Co. Leitrim
Tel. (078) 44346
**Ballinasloe Golf Club**
Rosgloss, Ballinasloe,
Co. Galway
Tel. (0905) 42126
**Ballinrobe Golf Club**
Ballinrobe, Co. Mayo
Tel. Ballinrobe 52
**Ballybofey & Stranorlar Golf
Club**
Ballybofey, Co. Donegal
Tel. (074) 31093
**Ballyhaunis Golf Club**
Ballyhaunis, Co. Mayo
Tel. Ballyhaunis 14
**Ballyliffen Golf Club**
Ballyliffen, Co. Donegal
Tel. Clonmany 19
**Ballymote Golf Club**
Ballymote, Co. Sligo
**Belmullet Golf Club**
Belmullet, Co. Mayo
**Belturbet Golf Club**
Belturbet, Co. Cavan
Tel. (049) 22287
**Blacklion Golf Club**
Blacklion, Co. Cavan
Tel. (072) 53024

**Boyle Golf Club**
Boyle, Co. Roscommon
Tel. (079) 62594
**Buncrana Golf Club**
Buncrana, Co. Donegal
**Bundoran Golf Club**
Bundoran, Co. Donegal
Tel.(072) 41302
**Cabra Castle Golf Club**
Kingscourt, Co. Cavan
Tel. (042) 67160
**Carrick-on-Shannon
Golf Club**
Carrick-on-Shannon,
Co. Leitrim
Tel. (078) 20157
**Castlebar Golf Club**
Rocklands, Castlebar,
Co. Mayo
Tel. (094) 21649
**Castlerea Golf Club**
Castlerea, Co. Roscommon
Tel. Castlerea 68
**Claremorris Golf Club**
Claremorris, Co. Mayo
Tel. (094) 71527
**Clones Golf Club**
Clones, Co. Monaghan
Tel. Scotshouse 17
**Co. Cavan Golf Club**
Cavan, Drumellis,
Co. Cavan
Tel. (049) 31283
**Co. Sligo Golf Club**
Rosses Point, Co. Sligo
Tel. (071) 77186
**Connemara Golf Club**
Ballyconneely, Co. Galway
Tel. (095) 21153
**Donegal Golf Club**
Murvagh, Ballintra,
Co. Donegal
Tel. (073) 34054
**Dunfanaghy Golf Club**
Dunfanaghy, Co. Donegal
Tel. (074) 36208
**Enniscrone Golf Club**
Inniscrone, Co. Sligo
Tel. (096) 36297
**Galway Golf Club**
Salthill, Galway,
Co. Galway
Tel. (091) 23038
**Gort Golf Club**
Gort. Co. Galway
Tel. (091) 31336
**Greencastle Golf Club**
Greencastle, Co. Donegal
Tel. Greencastle 13
**Gweedore Golf Club**
Gweedore, Co. Donegal
Tel. (075) 31140
**Letterkenny Golf Club**
Barnhill, Letterkenny,
Co. Donegal
Tel. (074) 21150

**Loughrea Golf Club**
Loughrea, Co. Galway
Tel. (091) 41049
**Mountbellew Golf Club**
Mountbellew, Co. Galway
Tel. (0905) 79259
**Mulrany Golf Club**
Mulrany, Co. Mayo
**Narin & Portnoo Golf Club**
Narin-Portnoo, Co. Donegal
Tel. Clooney 7
**North West Golf Club**
Fahan, Lifford, Co. Donegal
Tel. (074) 61027
**Nuremore Golf Club**
Carrickmacross,
Co. Monaghan
Tel. (042) 61438
**Otway Golf Club**
Rathmullen, Co. Donegal
Tel. (074) 58319
**Oughterard Golf Club**
Oughterard, Co. Galway
Tel. (091) 82131
**Portsalon Golf Club**
Portsalon, Co. Donegal
Tel. Portsalon 11
**Portumna Golf Club**
Portumna, Co. Galway
Tel. (0509) 41059
**Redcastle Golf Club**
Molville, Co. Donegal
**Rosapenna Golf Club**
Rosapenna, Co. Donegal
Tel. (074) 55301
**Roscommon Golf Club**
Roscommon,
Co. Roscommon
Tel. (0903) 6382
**Rossmore Golf Club**
Monaghan, Co. Monaghan
Tel. (047) 81316
**Strandhill Golf Club**
Strandhill, Co. Sligo
Tel. (071) 68188
**Swinford Golf Club**
Swinford, Co. Mayo
Tel. Swinford 278
**Tuam Golf Club**
Barnacurragh, Tuam,
Co. Galway
Tel. (093) 24354
**Virginia Golf Club**
Virginia, Co. Cavan
Tel. Virginia 35
**Westport Golf Club**
Westport, Co. Mayo
Tel. (098) 25113

## Irish travel

**Aer Lingus**
Tel. (01-734) 1212
**Belfast Car Ferries**
47 Donegall Quay, Belfast,
Northern Ireland

**British Airways**
Passenger reservations:
Tel. (01-897) 4000
**Ryanair**
Tel. (01-372) 5341
    (01-777) 4422
**Irish Tourist Board**
13/14 Upper O'Connell's
Street, Dublin
Tel. (01) 747733
London Office:
150/151 New Bond Street,
London W1
Tel. (01-493) 3201
**Northern Ireland Tourist
Board**
River House, High Street,
Belfast, Northern Ireland
Tel. (0232) 231221
**Sealink UK Ltd** (car ferries)
Tel. (01-834) 8122
**South West Ireland Golf Ltd**
7 Day Place, Tralee,
Co. Kerry
Tel. (066) 25733

## Irish hotel guide

It would be impossible to feature all the hotels in Northern Ireland and the Republic of Ireland here, as there are several thousand. The ones listed below are known to be convenient for some of the most famous golf courses. However, if you require further information regarding accommodation, contact the Tourist Boards at the addresses and telephone numbers given.

**Aberdeen Arms Hotel**
Lahinch, Co. Clare
Tel. (065) 81100
Convenient for Lahinch
**Aghadoe Heights Hotel**
Killarney, Co. Kerry
Tel. (064) 31766
Convenient for Killarney
**Ambassador Hotel**
Ballybunion, Co. Kerry
Tel. (068) 27111
Convenient for Ballybunion
**Ardnavaha House Hotel**
Ballinascarthy, Co. Cork
Tel. (023) 49135
Convenient for Bandon
**Ashford Castle**
Cong, Co. Mayo
Tel. (092) 46003
Convenient for Ashford
Castle, Rosses Point,
Westport and Ballyconneely

**Barberstown Castle**
Nr. Celbridge, Co. Kildare
Tel. (01) 288206
    (01) 288157
    (01) 288020
Convenient for Newlands,
Bodenstown, Naas, Curragh
and Cill Dara
**Bayview Hotel**
Ballycotton, Co. Cork
Tel. (021) 646746
Convenient for East Cork
**Butler Arms Hotel**
Waterville, Co. Kerry
Tel. (0667) 6144
Convenient for Waterville
**Cathernane Hotel**
Killarney, Co. Kerry
Tel. (064) 31895
Convenient for Killarney
**Coakley's Atlantic Hotel**
Garrettstown, Ballinspittle,
Co. Cork
Tel. (021) 778215
    (021) 778258
Convenient for Bandon, Cork
City and West Cork
**County Louth Golf Club**
(accommodation)
Baltray, Drogheda,
Co. Louth
Tel. (041) 22327
Convenient for County Louth
**Culloden Hotel**
Craigavad, Co. Down,
Northern Ireland
Tel. (023–17) 5223
Convenient for all Belfast
courses and Royal Belfast
**Deer Park Hotel**
Howth, Co. Dublin
Tel. (01) 322624
Convenient for Deer Park
**Dromoland Castle**
Newmarket-on-Fergus,
Co. Clare
Tel. (061) 71144
Convenient for Dromoland
Castle and Lahinch
**Dublin Sport Hotel**
Kilternan, Co. Dublin
Tel. (01) 955559
Convenient for Dublin Sport
**Ernan Park Hotel**
Donegal
Tel. (073) 21065
Convenient for Murvagh
**Garryvoe Hotel**
Garryvoe, Co. Cork
Tel. (021) 646718
Convenient for East Cork
**Gleneagle Hotel**
Killarney, Co. Kerry
Tel. (064) 31870
Convenient for Killarney and
Ballybunion

**Hotel Dunloe Castle**
Beaufort, Killarney,
Co. Kerry
Tel. (064) 44111
Convenient for Killarney
**Hotel Europe**
Killarney, Co. Kerry
Tel. (064) 31900
Convenient for Killarney
**International Hotel**
Killarney, Co. Kerry
Tel. (064) 31816
Convenient for Killarney
**Irish Farm Holidays**
Lahardan, Crusheen,
Co. Clare
Tel. (065) 27128
**Marine Hotel**
Ballybunion, Co. Kerry
Tel. (068) 27139
Convenient for Ballybunion
**Mount Brandon Hotel**
Tralee, Co. Kerry
Tel. (066) 23333
Convenient for Tralee,
Ballybunion, Killarney,
Waterville and Dooks
**Rathmullen House Hotel**
Rathmullen, Co. Donegal
Tel. (074) 58117
Convenient for Ottway,
Portsalon, Rosapenna and
Letterkenny
**Rock Glen Country House
Hotel**
Clifden, Connemara,
Co. Galway
Tel. (095) 21035
Convenient for Connemara
**Rosapenna Golf Hotel**
Downings, Co. Donegal
Tel. (074) 55301
Convenient for Rosapenna
**Slieve Donard Hotel**
Newcastle, Northern Ireland
Tel. (03967) 23681
Convenient for Royal County
Down
**Sligo Park Hotel**
Pearse Road, Sligo
Tel. (071) 60291
Convenient for Rosses Point
and Strandhill
**Tramore Golf Club**
(accommodation)
Newtown Hill, Tramore,
Co. Waterford
Tel. (051) 86583
Convenient for Tramore
**White Sands Hotel**
Ballyheigue, Tralee,
Co. Kerry
Tel. (066) 33102
Convenient for Tralee,
Ballybunion and Killarney

# Index